Walking Methodologies in a More-than-Human World WalkingLab

D1260512

As a research methodology, walking has a diverse and extensive history in the social sciences and humanities, underscoring its value for conducting research that is situated, relational, and material. Building on the importance of place, sensory inquiry, embodiment, and rhythm within walking research, this book offers four new concepts for walking methodologies that are accountable to an ethics and politics of the more-than-human: *Land and geos*, *affect*, *transmaterial* and *movement*. The book carefully considers the more-than-human dimensions of walking methodologies by engaging with feminist new materialisms, posthumanisms, affect theory, trans and queer theory, Indigenous theories, and critical race and disability scholarship. These more-than-human theories rub frictionally against the history of walking scholarship and offer crucial insights into the potential of walking as a qualitative research methodology in a more-than-human world. Theoretically innovative, the book is grounded in examples of walking research by *WalkingLab*, an international research network on walking (www.walkinglab.org).

The book is rich in scope, engaging with a wide range of walking methods and forms including: long walks on hiking trails, geological walks, sensory walks, sonic art walks, processions, orienteering races, protest and activist walks, walking tours, dérives, peripatetic mapping, school-based walking projects, and propositional walks. The chapters draw on *WalkingLab*'s research-creation events to examine walking in relation to settler colonialism, affective labour, transspecies, participation, racial geographies and counter-cartographies, youth literacy, environmental education, and collaborative writing. The book outlines how more-than-human theories can influence and shape walking methodologies and provokes a critical mode of walking-with that engenders solidarity, accountability, and response-ability.

This volume will appeal to graduate students, artists, and academics and researchers who are interested in Education, Cultural Studies, Queer Studies, Affect Studies, Geography, Anthropology, and (Post)Qualitative Research Methods.

Stephanie Springgay is an Associate Professor in the Department of Curriculum, Teaching, and Learning at the Ontario Institute for Studies in Education, University of Toronto. She is a leader in research-creation methodologies, with a particular interest in theories of matter, movement, and affect. With Sarah E. Truman she co-directs *WalkingLab*. Her research-creation projects are documented at: www.thepedagogicalimpulse.com, www.walkinglab.org, and www.artistsoupkitchen.com. Stephanie has published widely in academic journals and is the co-editor of *Mothering a Bodied Curriculum: Emplacement, Desire, Affect*; co-editor of *Curriculum and the Cultural Body*; and author of *Body Knowledge and Curriculum: Pedagogies of Touch in Youth and Visual Culture*.

Sarah E. Truman is Postdoctoral Research Fellow at Melbourne Graduate School of Education, University of Melbourne, Australia. Her research focuses on reading and writing speculative fiction in high schools. She also conducts ongoing research on walking methodologies and public pedagogy, and co-directs *WalkingLab* with Stephanie Springgay. Sarah's research is informed by the feminist new materialisms with a particular interest in theories of affect, queer theory, and speculative pragmatism. Sarah is co-editor of *Pedagogical Matters: New Materialism and Curriculum Studies*; and author of *Searching for Guan Yin*. Her research is detailed at www.sarahetruman.com and www.walkinglab.org.

Routledge Advances in Research Methods

www.routledge.com/Routledge-Advances-in-Research-Methods/book-series/RARM

Walking Methodologies in a More-than-Human World: WalkingLab

Stephanie Springgay and
Sarah E. Truman

Routledge
Taylor & Francis Group

LONDON AND NEW YORK

First published in paperback 2019

First published 2018
by Routledge
2 Park Square, Milton Park, Abingdon, Oxon OX14 4RN

and by Routledge
52 Vanderbilt Avenue, New York, NY 10017

Routledge is an imprint of the Taylor & Francis Group, an informa business

British Library Cataloguing-in-Publication Data
A catalogue record for this book is available from the British Library

Library of Congress Cataloging-in-Publication Data
Names: Springgay, Stephanie, author. | Truman, Sarah E., author.
Title: Walking methodologies in a more-than-human world : WalkingLab /
    Stephanie Springgay and Sarah E. Truman.
Description: Milton Park, Abingdon, Oxon ; New York, NY : Routledge, 2018. |
    Series: Routledge advances in research methods | Includes bibliographical
    references and index.
Identifiers: LCCN 2017047045 | ISBN 9781138293762 (hbk) |
    ISBN 9781315231914 (ebk)
Subjects: LCSH: Walking—Research. | Walking—Social aspects. | Sociology—
    Methodology.
Classification: LCC QP310.W3 S67 2018 | DDC 613.7/176072—dc23
LC record available at https://lccn.loc.gov/2017047045

ISBN: 978-1-138-29376-2 (hbk)
ISBN: 978-0-367-26495-6 (pbk)
ISBN: 978-1-315-23191-4 (ebk)

Typeset in Times New Roman
by Apex Co Vantage, LLC

For our friends, colleagues, and family that have walked-with us at *WalkingLab*.

Contents

Permissions

Chapter 5 has been reprinted with permission from SAGE Publications. It originally appeared as: Springgay, S. & Truman, S. E. (2017). On the Need for Methods Beyond Proceduralism: Speculative Middles, (In)Tensions, and Response-Ability in Research. *Qualitative Inquiry*. Online First DOI: 10.1177/1077800417704464

Portions of Chapter 3 appeared in a different version as Springgay, S. & Truman, S. E. (2017). A transmaterial approach to walking methodologies: Embodiment, affect, and a sonic art performance. *Body & Society*. Reprinted with permission from SAGE Publications.

Acknowledgements

We are indebted to the many friends, colleagues, and family members who have supported our writing and research. The book emerged from a *Social Sciences and Humanities Research Council of Canada* grant, and we appreciate the wonderful collaborations and conversations we shared with co-investigator Kimberly Powell over the past number of years; we look forward to ongoing and future projects with you. We also thank Andrew Hickey and Louise Phillips, grant co-investigators, for their involvement in the grant projects and the events they planned in Brisbane, Australia. We thank the many graduate research assistants, particularly Zofia Zaliwska, Aubyn O'Grady, and Lee Cameron for their support.

Many colleagues and friends workshopped early drafts, joined us on *Itinerant Reading Salons*, and pushed our theoretical understandings. We walked-with Mindy Blaise, Linda Knight, Affrica Taylor, Lesley Instone, Astrida Neimanis, Margaret Somerville, Eve Mayes, and Liz de Freitas and we are immensely grateful for your generosity, walking companionship, laughter, vegan meals, go-go dancing, and journeys to freshwater swimming holes.

This book would not be conceivable without the many artists, researchers, and bloggers who have contributed to *WalkingLab* over the past four years. It's not possible to mention every one of our walking-with collaborators, but we want to note those artists who created commissioned projects for us: Rebecca Conroy, Lenine Bourke, Matt Prest, TH&B, Mary Tremonte, Carmen Papalia, Camille Turner, Walis Johnson, Dylan Miner, and Public Studio. We also thank the scholars, artists, and activists who contributed to our public walking events and walking and sensory seminars: Bonnie Freeman, Kaitlin Debiki, Katherine Wallace, Randy Kay, Leuli Eshragi, Latai Taumoepeau, Rosie Dennis, Cigdem Aydemir, Jennifer Hamilton, Keg de Souza, Astrid Lorange, Lucas Ilhein, Francis Maravillas, Elaine Swan, and Ilaria Vanni.

As with all writing projects, this book was a labour that included many re-writes and edits. Phillip Vannini deserves appreciation for encouraging us to pursue a contract with Routledge and for early feedback on our proposal. To Erin Manning, whose friendship and inspiration guides our ethical understanding of research-creation. Early drafts of chapters were read by colleagues and we're thankful for the attention you gave to our work, when the demands of your own academic semesters weighed on you. Of note, we thank: Nathan Snaza, Jenny Sandlin, Lone Bertelsen, and Andrew Murphie. We are especially grateful to David Ben Shannon (Shanny) who copy-edited, sometimes more than once, each of the final chapters. Anise Truman joined us on many of our *WalkingLab* projects and we appreciate her role in documenting public walking events and vegan cooking.

Our families have made considerable contributions to our lives as artists and scholars. Sarah would like to thank her parents Maureen and Wayne, her brother Jamie, and nieces and nephew Anise, Astara, and Theo for their generous use of the family cottage as a writing space. And David H. Forsee, who died before he got a chance to read the final draft, for his inspiration and forever-support of her writing and research. Sarah would like to thank her colleagues at *Hamilton Perambulatory Unit*, Taien Ng-Chan, and Donna Akrey, and many fierce friends who supported her during the dark winter months of writing this past year, particularly Shara Claire, Marcelle McCauley, Julian McCauley, Joe Ollmann, and Dawn Dawson. Singularly, Sarah would like to thank Stephanie, the most splendid collaborator and friend, for walking-thinking-writing with her through the past few years.

Stephanie is immensely grateful to her mother for her unwavering support of her feminist academic life. Barbara Springgay provides many hours of childcare, driving to weekly afterschool programs, and meal preparation, enabling Stephanie to write for long periods of time. Barbara also introduced Stephanie to the love of reading and art. To Maurya and Liam Shah, Stephanie is so fortunate to have such loving and intelligent children who challenge her thinking on a daily basis. Stephanie would also like to thank her many friends, students, and colleagues who have sustained her during this writing project. Most importantly, she thanks her writing partner, Sarah. It's not easy to write collaboratively, but Sarah's theoretical insights, creativity, and generally ridiculous humour kept us going even in challenging times.

Paras Shah supported the writing of this book and we're particularly grateful for pizza parties and long talks over scotch on the deck.

We thank Patricia Clough and Bibi Calderaro for the generous and insightful forward to the book. We would also like to thank Neil Jordan, our editor at Routledge, for his support in seeing the manuscript through to publication. To Cheryl Clarke and Christine Lowe at the Ontario Institute for Studies in Education, University of Toronto for their meticulous financial accounting of our grant funds. And to Loredana Polidoro, who assisted in preparing the grant proposal, we appreciate your help.

There are many other humans and nonhumans who have influenced our walking-writing and we acknowledge the places and land where we walked and wrote. We are thankful for the creative co-authorship and the intellectual friendship we have built and sustained, and we are grateful for the generosity of feminist collaboration and an ethics of solidarity and care, that the *WalkingLab* research-creation events and this book encapsulate. This has become a model for how we will continue to work in the future.

Endorsements

Walking typifies the dual experience of colonialism: the lone white subject of Western Modernity surveying His landscape as possession and diasporic subjects walking their displacement and dispossession. In *Walking Methodologies in a More-than-Human World,* Stephanie Springgay and Sarah E. Truman "queer the trail" providing an interrogating praxis for walking within the colour lines of race, the patriarchies of gender, the possession of settler colonialism, the ableism of the ideal body, and the anthropocism of human exceptionalism. Staying with the friction of queer walks, Springgay and Truman invite the reader to "walk-with" these politics on the move, hard grit 'n all.

Dr Kathryn Yusoff,
Reader in Human Geography
School of Geography
Queen Mary, University of London, UK

This extraordinary and generous book shares decades of scholarship and research undertaken through 'deep walking.' Deep walking uniquely invites thinking with productive critiques that Indigenous, critical race, queer, and trans scholars have brought to the more-than-human turn. Walking becomes thinking-in-movement, understood as a practice of concept formation, experimental and speculative, viscous, intense and collaborative. Methods of inquiry are engaged propositionally, speculatively, and experimentally through speculative middles that continually emerge and incite further action. Thinking always through transcorporeality, new ontologies are both offered and questioned. Through rhythms of walking, concepts of the senses are interrogated as producing gendered, racialized, and classed bodies. Inclusion is reconceptualised to keep things unsettled, ungrounded, and unmoored. Intimacy is challenged as a frictional concept always entangled with politics. In its refusal to settle for any easy resolution this book is essential reading for anyone seeking to engage with the complex problems planet earth is posing for humanity in these precarious times.

Margaret Somerville
Professor of Education
Western Sydney University
Australia

Foreword

Patricia Ticineto Clough and Bibi Calderaro

Stephanie Springgay and Sarah E. Truman have a curiosity typical of walkers on a walk. But they do not rest where others might. Where others stop, curiosity moves them on; at every turn they refuse taken-for-granted understandings of land, people, movement and memory. The privileges of race, class, gender, sexuality, region and ableism are interrogated as Springgay and Truman turn their attention, and ours, to what is often beneath what has become normalized. Definitions, frameworks, and the use of categories become objects of critical reflection as their walking becomes a performative writing of fresh conceptualization. Or as Springgay and Truman put it: "Walking activates the creation of concepts. To walk is to move-with thought." And: "We write as we walk." "We walk a concept."

On their walks, in their mode of 'walking-with,' Springgay and Truman seek the collaboration of Indigenous, queer, trans, women, people of color and differently abled walkers. In *Walking Methodologies in a More-than-Human World*, they share these collaborations of walking/writing/conceptualizing and draw on exemplifications from *WalkingLab*'s many research-creation events. Taking up embodiment, place, sensory inquiry, and rhythm, four major concepts that shape what has already been dubbed 'the new walking studies,' Springgay and Truman offer a timely and important contribution through the expanded concepts of Land and geos, affect, transmateriality, and movement. In their reflections on method, they provide strategies for turning processes of collecting data to experimentation and invention that will greatly enrich qualitative research including walking methodologies.

In *Walking Methodologies in a More-than-Human World*, Springgay and Truman offer a critical account of the way the new materialisms, posthumanisms and speculative realisms can inform methods of walking, having instigated a lively debate in the social sciences about knowledge production, about the subject and object of knowledge. While traditionally, method has been regimented through the opposition of subject and object, Springgay and Truman follow the current ontological turn deconstructing human privilege, not only inviting a reconsideration of the relationship of subject and object, but the organic and the nonorganic as well. In walking-with, foot touches matter but matter touches foot as breeze touches skin; the world displays sensibilities other than our own, prior to consciousness, even to bodily-based perception. There is a sense, if not recognition, of the vibrancy of matter, of a worldly sensibility, of the force of the world's causal efficacy.

The more-than-human, in Springgay's and Truman's usage, points to the ethical and political relevancy of walking-with to feel/think or surface the intensities of the entanglements of knower and world. Becoming accountable to the more-than human also involves taking account of the erasures of other knowledges and methods, erasures which, in part, have enabled thinking about the more-than-human as only a recent turn in thought. Walking-with becomes a movement of thought not only with others, but a process of engaging with erased or disavowed histories. It is also a moving re-engagement with the ways that the earth and the elements have been understood, protected, feared and treasured.

In this sense, walking-with is not to be understood simply as a matter of conviviality or therapy, or a neoliberal inspired self-investment in well-being. Rather, walking-with must carry with it a sensitivity to a politics of knowledge production that has become central to the capitalist economy more recently described as an 'affect economy' or an 'experience economy.' Walking-with encourages walkers to make what Bibi Calderaro[1] describes as an 'ontological shift,' to think about experience differently, to experience differently, and to experience difference in experiencing.

Springgay and Truman trouble experience in a way that is resonant with queer/trans ontologies of the human. Beyond a simple move from identity to difference, the ontological shift encouraged in walking-with requires a recognition of an alterity within the self, an indeterminacy prior to consciousness and even bodily based perception – that is, the nonexperienced or inhuman condition of all experience. This is not simply a matter of inclusion or exclusion of the 'other.' Rather as Springgay and Truman propose, recognizing the inhuman within the self is at the same time an opening to all that has been defined as other than human, nonhuman, or inhuman. Walking-with invites a sense of multiplicities in a queering of being and time, a nonexperienced time at all scales of being that affords infinite variation and multiplicities of space. The falling of the foot, and the catching-up of the body moving along with the world, allows for the rhythmicity of a multitude of indeterminate beings diffracted through different spacetimes. But because every moment conceals the bifurcation by which anything can take a conflictive turn, utmost care must be taken to move in an affirmative register.

Walking Methodologies in a More-than-Human World demonstrates that walking-with is an important methodology for thinking ethically and politically. Yet, Springgay and Truman assure us that 'walking-with' is best practiced with a method that betrays any strict adherence to method. While there is no stone left unturned (and if there is, it is because they have chosen to leave it there for the reader to engage with), their thinking is certainly not one that aims for an anchor. On the contrary, it is thought as provocation, as 'research-creation' of frictions, entanglements (in)tension with the world. What a courageous intent given the spacetime in which they practice this endeavor, when global affect has reached a point of hatred with horrifying implications.

With some urgency, Springgay and Truman ask their readers to take up their own methodological reflection, asking: What is knowledge? What are the occasions in which it emerges? How is it called forth and by what means? How is it that once provoked, knowledges become settled, sedimented into racial, gendered, classed particulars, the stuff regularly called the social, the political, the economic? Readers are asked to reflect on the way method is a matter of social, political, and economic interests, so that they can instead be open, aware of consequences now and in the future, always with a regard for multiple pasts.

Reading *Walking Methodologies in a More-than-Human World*, we often had to pause and think and then walk and then think and walk again, always writing together. We were surprised finally at the near end of our reading to discover how our own way of working together is just like Springgay's and Truman's is: walking, thinking, and writing together. We hope the readers of *Walking Methodologies in a More-than-Human World* will find their own way through, but we recommend attending to Springgay's and Truman's voices inviting you to: *Go on a walk. Feel your feet on the earth. Touch the breeze. Attend to impressions. Caress the thoughts that weigh on you as you amble. Feel the haptic; the corporeal. Walk in a graveyard if you can find one.*

Note

1 See: Calderaro, B. (forthcoming). Walking as Ontological Shifter. In C. Qualmann and M. Myers (Eds.), *Where to? Steps Towards the Future of Walking Arts*. Dorset, UK: Triarchy Press.

Introduction
Walking methodologies in a more-than-human world

The impetus for this book sprang from a walk-with Micalong Creek, in Wee Jasper, New South Wales, Australia. We had gathered in Wee Jasper with a group of women at the creek, for a queer feminist *Bush Salon*, to think and walk-with water, and to open up questions about human and nonhuman entanglements.[1] Walking the rocky crevices of the Micalong Creek, we paused to swim and sit on the grassy shore. Stephanie engaged the group in felting red wool around small rocks, and Affrica Taylor and Lesley Instone, the *Bush Salon* organizers, read aloud from a series of texts. Astrida Neimanis invited us to float in the creek as she read from a poem, and Mindy Blaise captured some of our fleeting gestures with her Artographer, a body-mounted camera. The group experimented with perambulatory writing techniques, proposed by Sarah. Insects buzzed and dogs chased each other through the shallows of the water. The air screamed with Australian heat. A bag of cherries was passed around the group of women wearing 'trucker' style hats with the word 'quivering' emblazoned on them.

Informed by Isabelle Stengers' (2005) 'politics of slowness,' and Rosi Braidotti's (2013) 'becoming-earth,' we sat on the banks of the creek and raised questions about research methodologies. We attuned ourselves to what Stengers (2005) calls a collective thinking "in the presence of others" (p. 996).[2] For Stengers, to think 'in the presence of others' creates a space for hesitation and resistance that produces new modes of relating. Collective thinking demands "that we don't consider ourselves authorized to believe we possess the meaning of what we know" (Stengers, 2005, p. 995). Rather, thinking 'in the presence of others' is about the "unpredictability of opening ourselves to possibility" (Instone & Taylor, 2015, p. 146). Braidotti (2013) contends that this presentness must include a "geo-centred dimension," which requires we consider different scales than those that are human centered. The *how* of the slow demands that we respond to the question of inheritance where 'in the presence' does not mean we know beforehand how to respond, but rather in the event of relation, ethics and politics become situated, indeterminate, and artful. For Donna Haraway (2008a), inheritance begs the question of accountability.

We walked-with many other freshwater creeks in Australia, ambled through lush valleys, clambered along the rocky sea coast, and facilitated a series of walking events and research-creation projects in urban spaces. Research-creation draws attention to the conjunctive at work in its process. Instead of perpetuating an idea of art as separate from thinking, the hyphenation of research-creation engenders "concepts in-the-making" which is a process of "thinking-with and across techniques of creative practice" (Manning and Massumi, 2014, p. 88–89). Research-creation can be thought of as "the complex intersection of art, theory, and research" (Truman and Springgay, 2015, p. 152).

In Canada, we continue to walk and organize walking research-creation events. Our walking research has evolved over a number of years through a diverse range of practices and theories. *WalkingLab*, which is the collective research-creation practice of Stephanie Springgay and Sarah E. Truman, emerged from a Social Sciences and Humanities Research Council Partnership Development Grant, *Performing Lines: Innovations in Walking and Sensory Methodologies*. The Partnership Grant was between Principal Investigator Stephanie Springgay and co-applicants Kimberly Powell, Andrew Hickey, and Louise Phillips. Sarah E. Truman was Lead Research Officer for the grant.

WalkingLab often works in collaboration with other artists and scholars, and the online hub [www.walkinglab.org] archives these networked activities. We gratefully acknowledge the many collaborators and artists who have worked with us over the years. *WalkingLab* also hosts an online residency and supports a blog that investigates what it means to move. Provoked by the encounter on the banks of Micalong Creek, and ongoing conversations about walking research and qualitative methodologies, we began to respond to the question of inheritance.

This introductory chapter situates the book in two methodological areas in qualitative research: i) walking methodologies in the humanities and social science; ii) qualitative methodologies that are informed by new materialisms and posthumanisms, and which are called by different names including non-representational methodologies and post-qualitative methodologies. We refer to these as more-than-human methodologies. The research-creation events that compose the empirical research in each of the chapters bring more-than-human methodologies to bear on walking research. The introductory chapter unfolds as a preliminary map for the book, acquainting readers with the theoretical frameworks and questions that inform our research-creation walking practices.

In the first section of the chapter, we summarize the impact of walking methodologies on qualitative research. In our extensive review of the field of walking methodologies, four major concepts appeared repeatedly within walking research: *place*, *sensory inquiry*, *embodiment*, and *rhythm*. These concepts, we maintain, mark significant contributions to social science and humanities research in that they foreground the importance of the material body in disciplines that have traditionally privileged discursive analysis. Building on the important work that has been in walking research, we offer four expanded concepts that are accountable to an ethics and politics of the more-than-human: **Land and geos**, **affect**, **transmaterial**, and **movement**. These concepts inform our theoretical orientations to the research-creation walking events that we activate in each of the remaining chapters.

Following our discussion on walking methodologies, we return to the problems of inheritance, accountability, and more-than-human ethics introduced in our opening narrative. *Walking Methodologies in a More-than-Human World* interrogates the more-than-human turn in qualitative methodologies. Each chapter engages theoretically and conceptually with ongoing debates in qualitative research on *matter*. Specifically, we make new materialist methodologies and walking research accountable to critical race, feminist, Indigenous, trans, queer, critical disability, and environmental humanities scholarship. Indigenous scholars have interrogated the more-than-human turn, arguing that it continues to erase Indigenous knowledges that have always attended to nonhuman animacy (Todd, 2016). Queer, trans, disability, and critical race scholars argue that while a decentering of the human is necessary, we need to question whose conception of humanity more-than-human theories are trying to move beyond. As Zakiyyah Jackson (2015) argues, "appeals to move 'beyond the human' may actually reintroduce the Eurocentric transcendentalism this movement purports to disrupt, particularly with regard to the historical and ongoing distributive ordering of race" (p. 215).

The final section in this introductory chapter provides an overview of the chapters. Each chapter thinks-with exemplifications from *WalkingLab's* many research-creation events. Exemplification, according to Brian Massumi (2002), is not concerned with illustration or explanation, where an example becomes a model for research. Rather exemplification is concerned with improvisation and a degree of conceptual openness. In thinking-with walking we shift from an individual account of a human walker to consider an ethics and politics of 'walking-with.'

Walking methodologies

Walking as a method and methodology in qualitative research is practiced and theorized through different and varied approaches (Lorimer, 2010; Springgay & Truman, 2017a). Examples include Wylie (2005) and Solnit's (2001) discussion of walking's relationship to leisure and landscape; and Lorimer and Lund's (2008) exploration of human experience and knowledge of the natural environment. There are walking accounts of mundane urban practices (Vergunst, 2010), of pedestrianism (Middleton, 2010), mapping (O'Rourke, 2013), and writing and thinking (Gros, 2014). Walking features in mobilities research (Bissell, 2016; Vannini, 2012) with an emphasis on technologies, movement, and stillness, and in research on place-making and space (Ingold, 2007; McCormack, 2014; Pink, 2009/2015). In ethnographic methods, walking has been utilized through the 'go-along' (Kusenbach, 2003) or the walking interview (Jones & Evans, 2012), which recognize the ways in which lived experiences, perception, and meaning-making are constructed through place and spatial practices of sociality and positionality. In the arts, walking proliferates as both an individual aesthetic and as a relational and socially engaged practice (Evans, 2013). Walking has also been addressed by sensory ethnographers (Gallagher, 2015; Pink, 2009/2015) and by

feminist scholars examining the politics of location and the ideologies and practices that govern and limit bodies in movement (Heddon & Turner, 2012). Educational scholars incorporate walking methods in qualitative research, particularly
in relation to somatic and sensory place-making (Banerjee & Blaise, 2013; Powell, 2017; Springgay & Truman, 2017b), as critical place inquiry (McKenzie &
Bieler, 2016) and as defamiliarization (Truman & Springgay, 2016). Margaret
Somerville's (2013) contribution to walking, water, and Indigenous knowledges
offers cogent ways to think critically about place and movement. Recent articulations of walking as a social science methodology are found in Charlotte Bates and
Alex Rhys-Taylor's (2017) edited collection *Walking through Social Research*.
Maggie O'Neill's (2017) work on walking, mapping, borders, and resistance is
another important contribution to critical walking methodologies.

We identify four major themes in walking research: *place*, *sensory inquiry*,
embodiment, and *rhythm*. Here we offer a brief summary of each of these themes
as they appear in walking research. Each of these concepts are critically investi-
gated in more detail in the first four chapters of the book.

Place

Place features as a significant concept in walking research. Place is understood as
a specific location and as a process or an event. Walking scholars discuss the ways
that walking is attuned to place, how place-making is produced by walking, and
the ways that walking connects bodies, environment, and the sensory surrounds of
place. Walking becomes a way of inhabiting place through the lived experience of
movement. Walking is a way of becoming responsive to place; it activates modes
of participation that are situated and relational.

Sensory inquiry

With the turn to alternative ethnographic methods that would enable researchers
to investigate non-visual senses, walking became an important means by which to
conduct sensory inquiry. If, as walking researchers contend, walking is a way of
being in place, then walking enables researchers and research participants to tune
into their sensory experiences. Walking researchers interested in sensory inquiry
sometimes isolate a sense on a walk – for example, a soundwalk – or they consider the ways that the walking body is immersed in a sensory experience of place,
such as the texture of feet touching the ground, air brushing against cheeks, or the
smells of city streets.

Embodiment

Walking methodologies privilege an embodied way of knowing where movement connects mind, body, and environment. Walking scholars typically describe
embodiment as relational, social, and convivial. Embodiment is conventionally
understood through phenomenology, where researchers and participants examine

the lived experiences of what it means to move in a particular place. This experiential understanding either focuses on an individual account of a walker, or is conceptualized through community-based or group walking practices that highlight the social aspects of walking.

Rhythm

The pace and tempo of walking is another theme that emerges in walking research. Here, researchers are interested in the flows of everyday life, pedestrian movements in a city, or the topological features of walking in a landscape. Rhythm is described through embodied accounts of moving and sensory expressions of feet, limbs, and breath. In other instances, rhythm pertains to the pulse of the city, such as traffic, crowds, music, and other environmental phenomena that press on a walker.

The chapters in this book extend these four themes through more-than-human theories that are accountable to critical race, feminist, Indigenous, trans, queer, and critical disability theories. We propose four additional concepts: **Land and geos**, **affect**, **transmaterial**, and **movement**. We use these concepts to think frictionally with *WalkingLab* research-creation events. Friction is a force that acts in the opposite direction to movement. It slows movement, "resist[s] the consensual way in which the situation is presented" (Stengers, 2005, p. 994). Friction exists every time bodies come into contact with each other, like different strata grinding against one another. Writing about the intersection between assemblage theory and intersectionality, Jasbir Puar (2012) argues that the convergence of the two theoretical frameworks is neither reconcilable nor oppositional, but *frictional*. Puar (2007) argues that theoretical concepts need not be united or synthesized, but that it can be productive to hold concepts together in tension.

Land and geos

More-than-human walking methodologies must take account of the ways that place-based research is entrenched in ongoing settler colonization. As such, place in walking research needs to attend to Indigenous theories that centre Land, and posthuman understandings of the geologic that insist on a different ethical relationship to geology, where human and nonhuman are imbricated and entwined. Land and geos are important concepts for walking methodologies because they are attentive to situated knowledges that disrupt humancentrism.

Affect

In tandem with more-than-human methodologies is a turn to affect theory. Affect, informed by vital and materialist theories, attends to the intensities and forces of an affecting and affected body. However, because there is a tendency to ascribe affect to pre-personal sensations, some uses and theorizing of affect can consequently erase identity. In contrast, 'affecting subjectivities' brings intersectional theories to bear on affect theories, emphasizing the ways that subjectivity is produced as intensive flows and assemblages between bodies (Lara, Lui, Ashley, Nishida, Liebert, Billies, 2017).

Transmateriality

If embodiment conventionally focuses on a phenomenological and lived account of human movement, then trans theories, which rupture heteronormative teleological understandings of movement and reproduction, disrupt the notion of an embodied, coherent self. Trans theories emphasize viral, tentacular, and transversal conceptualizations of difference.

Movement

Movement, as it is conventionally understood in relation to walking, suggests directionality. One walks to move from one place to another. The movement theories we draw on in this book understand movement as inherent in all matter, endlessly differentiating. Movement as force and vibration resist capture. This understanding of movement is indeterminate, dynamic, and immanent and intimately entangled with transmaterial theories and practices.

In addition, there are particular inheritances that proliferate in walking research. For example, walking is often positioned as inherently radical, and a tactic to subvert urban space, yet often ignores race, gender, and disability. Figures like the flâneur and the practices of the dérive become common tropes, often assuming that all bodies move through space equally. In Chapter 3 we analyze these methods in detail and offer crucial insights from critical disability scholars and critical race scholars, arguing that the unequal labour of walking needs to be more fully interrogated.

In the next two sections of the introductory chapter, we situate *Walking Methodologies in a More-than-Human World* within the new materialist and posthumanist methodological approaches to qualitative research. It is these theoretical frameworks that we use to conceptualize and enact our four concepts of *Land and geos*, *affect*, *transmaterial*, and *movement*.

Accountability and more-than-human ethics: walking queerly

A key concept that has gained momentum in qualitative methodologies is Karen Barad's 'intra-action.' For Barad (2003), matter and meaning do not pre-exist as individual entities. Rather the world is composed of intra-acting phenomena which "are the ontological inseparability of agentially intra-acting components," meaning that they become determinate, material, and meaningful through relations (p. 815). Objects do not exist as discrete entities that come together through interactions but are produced through entanglement. Katrin Thiele (2014) notes that such an ontological view privileges relations. Relations, she writes are "*all there is*" (p. 206, italics in original). Thus, a materialist ontology recognizes the interconnections of all phenomena where matter is indeterminate, constantly forming and reforming. As Barad (2007) makes clear, ethics then is not concerned with how we interact with the world as separate entities. "Ethics is about mattering, about taking account of the entangled materializations of which we are a part, including new configurations, new subjectivities, new possibilities" (p. 384). The consequences of this ethico-onto-epistemology for qualitative methodologies and walking research are significant, as it challenges individualism and humanist notions of intentionality, destabilizes conventional notions of space as a void, and directs our attention to the highly distributed nature of collectivity and relationality. It also, as Thiele (2014) argues, requires that we reconfigure how we think about accountability.

If ontology and ethics, or being and acting, are always already relational, then ethics shifts from a responsibility to act on the world in a particular moral way "to on-going precariously located practices, in which 'we' are never categorically separate entities, but differentially implicated in the matters 'we' engage with" (Thiele, 2014, p. 207, italics in original). Furthermore, if 'we' are intra-actively entangled in worlding, then there will never be a final solution or outcome, rather new matterings will emerge for our entangled intra-actions. To be accountable is about "making commitments and connections" (Barad, 2007, p. 392). Accountability shifts from being responsible for, to a response-ability-with (Manning, 2012; Thiele, 2014), or what we have described earlier as a being 'in the presence' of others. This is an ethics, Barad (2011) contends, of entanglements, "enfolded traces" and an indebtedness to an irreducible other, where "'Otherness' is an entangled relation of difference" (p. 150).

Part of this accountability is in the use of queer theory to rupture the normalizing inheritances of walking research. Queer has been used to denote practices and theories that unsettle norms, and to call attention to how sexuality, gender, and race are constituted and regulated by hierarchies of humanness (Giffney & Hird, 2008). Eli Clare (2001) uses the term queer in its "general sense, as odd, quirky, not belonging; and in its specific sense, as referring to lesbian, gay, bisexual, and transgender identity" (p. 361). According to Kath Browne and Catherine Nash (2010), queer research can be "any form of research positioned within conceptual frameworks that highlight the instability of taken-for-granted meanings and resulting power relations" (Browne and Nash, 2010, p. 4). For Jack Halberstam (2005), self-identification as 'queer' has a place in queer theory, but thinking beyond subject identification and with a queer relationality opens up new possibilities for understanding space and time. Understanding queer as non-normative logic of space-time, Halberstam outlines 'queer time' as time outside normative temporal frames of inheritance and reproduction, and 'queer space' as new understandings of space enabled by the "production of queer counter-publics" (p. 6). Deborah Britzman (1995) discusses how queer theory can signify both "improper subjects *and* improper theories, even as it questions the very grounds of identity and theory" (p. 153). As such, queer can tend in a multitude of directions. For example, Eve Sedgwick (2003) uses the idea of 'queer performativity' as a production of meaning making, specifically related to shame, while Donna Haraway (2008b) states, "Queering has the job of undoing 'normal' categories, and none is more critical than the human/nonhuman sorting operation" (p. xxiv). Dana Luciano and Mel Chen (2015) maintain that "the figure of the queer/trans body does not merely unsettle the human as norm; it generates other possibilities – multiple, cyborgian, spectral, transcorporeal, transmaterial – for living" (p. 187). However, Luciano and Chen (2015) also warn against reducing queerness to solely a "movement of thought, or of affirmation or negation" in that it can slide into a kind of queer exceptionalism that resonates too easily with Western notions of progress or modernity (p. 95). As such, queer theory must remain accountable to "located histories of precarity" (p. 94). Furthermore, Lorena Muñoz (2010) calls attention to 'whiteness' in queer research where " '[q]ueer' sensibilities are theorized and understood through lenses that are largely academic, western, white, and privileged" (p. 57). Puar (2007) similarly argues that when queer is linked with transgression and resistance, it relies "on a normative notion of deviance, always defined in relation to normativity, often universalizing" (p. 23). When viewed through this framework the queer identity and the *ability* to queer is tied to Western rational individualism and the liberal humanist subject who can afford to be queer and to queer. It is also consequently tied to the liberal humanist subject who asserts their agency to *queer* or *be* queer. So, while many qualitative researchers in the social sciences and humanities often take up the word queer to describe letting go of traditional research boundaries such as data and theory, or researcher/researched, and utilize 'queer' as methodology, we need to account for the subjectivities that don't enjoy the benefit of sliding in and out of being conveniently queer.

Unsettling the 'ontological turn'

The concept of the more-than-human emerges at time in scholarly debates that seek to challenge and de-centre human exceptionalism, taxonomies of intelligence and animacy, and the distinctions made between humans and nonhumans, nature and culture (Springgay & Truman, 2017c). Animacy, according to Chen (2012), has been historically aligned to the category of the human. Linguistically, animacy refers to the "quality of liveness, sentience, or humanness of a noun or a noun phrase" (p. 24). At the top of the animacy taxonomy are masculine, heteronormative, able bodies, with intact capacities. As you move down the schema, as bodies and things are perceived as less agentic, they become less animate. Race, disability, and gender, for example, fall at the lower end of the animacy taxonomy. This taxonomy, Chen (2012) argues, is a contributing factor in dehumanization, where qualities valued as 'human' are removed, and those who do not fit into the category of the human are considered 'inhuman.' Luciano and Chen (2015) argue that the problem with liberal-humanism and its "politics of rehabilitation and inclusion" is that any conceptualization of human is always marked with an outside (p. 188). The dehumanization of particular subjects – Indigenous, Black, trans – posits a particular human body and human sexuality as a norm. Rather than view the inhuman as the opposite of the human, the inhuman becomes a process by which human and nonhuman frictionally come together. In fact, Luciano and Chen (2015) question the ways that posthumanism melts the boundaries between human and nonhuman as an easy flow. They posit the inhuman as a method of thinking otherwise. Jeffrey Cohen (2015) notes that the inhuman, as a concept, emphasizes both difference and intimacy. 'In' as a negative prefix presumes difference from something. It assumes a negative, or inept capacity. Likewise, 'in,' he argues, describes being within something, a touching intimacy, or an "estranged interiority" (p. 10).

Lee Edelman (2004) argues that enlivening the inhuman with animacy isn't about demanding recognition into the category of human. Therefore, the more-than-human should not become an inclusive concept that folds bodies and subjects that have typically been positioned on the outside into the fabric of the human. Likewise, the more-than-human must not merely blur the boundaries between human and nonhuman, but operate as a *strategy* that asks, "how those categories rub on, and against, each other, generating friction and leakage" (Luciano & Chen, 2015, p. 186). A similar argument is developed by Barad (2011). She argues that terms like human and nonhuman can't be established as polar ends and as givens, where particular actions aim to bring them into moral equivalence. Rather, she writes, "the 'posthumanist' point is not to . . . cross out the distinctions and differences, and not to simply invert humanism, but rather to understand the materializing effects of particular ways of drawing boundaries between 'humans' and 'non humans'" (p. 123–124). Queer Crip scholar Alison Kafer (2013) writes that the human/nonhuman distinction assumes an able-bodiedness of the human. Disability, she claims, has always been marked as unnatural, or as limited, and as such is something to be overcome in order to become fully 'human.' Writing from a political/relational framework of disability studies, Kafer wonders how we might think disability through intra-active concepts such as interdependence, collectivity, and responsibility.

For Jin Haritaworn (2015), the question of the inhuman is risky and requires anti-colonial methodologies that would in turn be aligned with Indigenous sovereignty. This brings us to Zoe Todd's (2016) arguments that the 'ontological turn' is itself a form of colonization. She writes that non-Indigenous scholars' realization that nonhumans entities "are *sentient* and *possess agency*, that 'nature' and 'culture,' 'human' and 'animal' may not be so separate after all – is itself perpetuating the exploitation of Indigenous peoples" (p. 16, italics in original). From an Indigenous perspective, it isn't simply about the idea that all things have vitality but that such epistemological and ontological orientations in Indigenous thought are about "legal orders through which Indigenous peoples throughout the world are fighting for self-determination, sovereignty" (Todd, 2016, p. 18). Here we think of the examples given by Elizabeth Povinelli (2016). If rock/minerals are inanimate and non-Life they can be mined for human use. If they are sacred from an animist position then they can be protected, but therefore excised and rendered of no-use. Both of these examples are grounded in legal struggles over land, access, and sovereignty. Todd (2016), like other Indigenous scholars, insist that ontological discussions of matter must take into consideration not only Indigenous worldviews but material legal struggles over matter and sovereignty.

Furthermore, while Todd demands that non-Indigenous scholars engage in a politics of citation, her calls to action come with a cautionary note, one that is similarly articulated by Indigenous scholar Vanessa Watts. Watts (2013) writes:

> When an Indigenous cosmology is translated through a Euro-Western process, it necessitates a distinction between place and thought. The result of this distinction is a colonized interpretation of both place and thought, where land is simply dirt and thought is only possessed by humans.
>
> (p. 32)

Indigenous scholar Sarah Hunt (2014) also critiques the position that in order to be "legible" Indigenous knowledges "must adhere to recognized forms of representation" (p. 29). These 'recognized' forms of representation become institutionalized through academic and Euro-Western cultural discourses. We attend to the challenges of recognition in Chapter 6, proposing a re-mapping practice that is speculative and future oriented.

Similarly, Jackson (2015) cautions the use of terms like 'post' and 'beyond' in posthuman scholarship as such terms might actually re-inscribe Eurocentric values, time, and knowledge systems. Furthermore, she argues that the turn to the more-than-human signals the continued erasure of race from materialist accounts of vitality. Jackson (2013) states that although posthuman scholarship is important for its attention to vitality, it has often ignored race, colonialism, and slavery. While recognizing the contributions by feminist and queer scholars, Jackson (2013) contends that too often posthuman theories remain committed to a particular Euro-Western rationality and humanism, or what Sylvia Wynter (2003) calls 'Man.' For Jackson, and other critical races scholars who engage with posthumanism, the aim is not that people of colour will somehow "gain admittance into the fraternity of Man" that they have always been outside of, the aim is to "displace the order of Man altogether" (p. 672). This means re-thinking posthumanism, not as a politics of inclusion for those enslaved or colonized under liberal humanist ideals, but as a strategy of transforming *humanism*.

As more-than-human theories gain momentum in re-conceptualizing qualitative methodologies in the social sciences and humanities its fault lies in broad definitions. While consideration is given to all forms of matter and the intra-relatedness of entangled ethics, its politics is often consumed in a rhetoric of undoing dualisms where 'everything matters' and thus becomes flattened. Questions about the politics of new materialism are typically elided. They are absent, Peta Hinton and Iris van der Tuin (2015) reason, because there is a tendency to think that arguments about matter as dynamic, self-organizing, and intensive *are political in and of themselves*. They maintain that new materialism's general insights into matter assume that politics is everywhere – but to the extent that it disappears. Celia Åsberg, Katrin Thiele, and Iris van der Tuin (2015) argue that not only has the question of the political been eclipsed in a lot of new materialist scholarship, queries regarding its contributions to queer feminist political agency have been lost.

Feminist geographer Juanita Sundberg (2014) takes up a further concern, stating that posthumanist scholarship in its attempt to critique dualisms actually works to "uphold Eurocentric knowledge" (p. 33). Despite the usefulness of posthumanism, Sundburg contends that it is deeply entrenched in Western European dualistic ontologies and as such does not entertain complex knowledge systems of the Indigenous Americas. Sundburg shares similar critiques of the 'ontological turn' to that of Todd (2016). She argues that dominant posthuman scholars operate universally and often neglect the fact that the humanist traditions they write against "originated in European societies involved in colonization, were globalized in and through colonial practices, and are currently given life in white supremacist settler societies" (Sundberg, 2014, p. 36). The "silence of location" coupled with "circumscribed references to Indigeneity" continues the legacy of colonial violence (Sundberg, 2014, p. 36). Sundburg argues that universalisms suppress other worlds, where "radical alterity is contained and reduced to sameness" (p. 38). Sundburg finds more-than-human theories productive, but articulates a need to ensure that while attending to the 'more,' colonization, racial violence, and legal oppressions are not ignored in the name of animacy.

In attending to multiple and other world views of animacy, Sundberg (2014) offers walking as a strategy for decolonizing research. In thinking how to move collectively, of being accountable in the presence of others, she reasons that walking enacts situated and contingent ontologies between land, peoples, and nonhuman others. She draws on examples such as Idle No More, a Canada-wide Indigenous movement, and Mexican activists, the Zapatistas movement, who articulate their practice as 'walking-with.' Walking-with, she states, entails "serious engagement with Indigenous epistemologies, ontologies, and methodologies" (p. 40). Walking-with should not be misconstrued with conviviality and sociality, or the idea that one needs to walk with a group of people. You could walk-with alone. We situate our conceptualization and practice of walking-with alongside Sundberg and the walkers she works with. We are also indebted to the rich feminist work on citational practices (see Chapter 8) and Alecia Jackson and Lisa Mazzei's (2013) on thinking-with theory. Walking-with is explicit about political positions and situated knowledges, which reveal our entanglements with settler colonization and neoliberalism. Walking-with is accountable. Walking-with is a form of solidarity, unlearning, and critical engagement with situated knowledges. Walking-with demands that we forgo universal claims about how humans and nonhumans experience walking, and consider more-than-human ethics and politics of the material intra-actions of walking research.

Walking-with: chapter overviews

Place is a central concept in walking research – from considerations of the textures of gravel and pavement that shape how one walks (Vergunst, 2008; Edensor, 2008) – to the ways that everyday pedestrianism structure and produce place (Middleton, 2010). But place, Eve Tuck and Marcia McKenzie (2015) argue, is entrenched in settler colonial histories and ongoing practices that have not sufficiently attended to Indigenous understandings of Land. In Chapter 1 we walk-with Indigenous theories of Land and critical place inquiry (Tuck & McKenzie, 2015; Watts, 2013); posthuman theories of the geologic that disrupt taxonomies of what is lively and what is inert (Ellsworth & Kruse, 2012; Povinelli, 2016; Yusoff, 2013); and a posthuman critique of landscape urbanism (Foster, 2010). The chapter is activated by a *WalkingLab* research-creation event *Stone Walks on the Bruce Trail: Queering the Trail* that convened on the Bruce Trail in Ontario, Canada. Seventy people participated in the four-hour group walk, which was stimulated by 'pop-up' lectures by geologists, community activists, Indigenous scholars, and artistic interventions.

Walking methodologies invariably invoke sensory, haptic, and affective investigations (MacPherson, 2009; Gallagher, 2015). While sensory studies (Howes, 2013; Pink, 2009/2015) and affect theories (Seigworth & Gregg, 2010; Ahmed, 2004) have evolved separately, they are both concerned with non-conscious, non-cognitive, transmaterial, and more-than representational processes. Chapter 2 examines a number of *WalkingLab* walking projects through sensory, haptic, or affect theories. Crucial to our examinations of walking research is a focus on critical sensory studies that interrogate the ways that walking and the senses produce gendered, racialized, and classed bodies. Similarly, we turn to Stefano Harney and Fred Moten's (2013) use of hapticality to think about how walking constitutes a politics-in-movement. This turn to politics is extended through our discussion of different affect theories, in particular we address recent scholarship on 'affecting subjectivities,' which attend to the affective messiness of race, sexuality, gender, disability and additional forms of difference (Lara, Lui, Ashley, Nishida, Liebert, & Billies, 2017). In the final section of the chapter, we argue that 'feelings futurity' in walking methodologies requires that sensory inquiry, haptic modulations, and affective tonalities ask questions about 'what matters.'

Chapter 3 examines a sonic walk called *Walking to the Laundromat* by Bek Conroy, in order to develop a theory of transmateriality. Sonic or audio walks can be described as walks that use pre-recorded and choreographed audio tracks downloaded to phones or other electronic devices. *Walking to the Laundromat* probes bodily, affective, and gendered labour including domestic labour, money laundering, and the proliferation of new age self-help audio books to question how some bodies are perceived as disposable in order for other bodies to thrive (Mbembe, 2003; Puar 2007). We critique normalized and universal references to the flâneur, a man of leisure, who is able to walk, detached and privileged in a city. The flâneur, we argue, is a problematic emblem for walking methodologies. We introduce Stacy Alaimo's (2010, 2016) important concept 'transcorporeality,' which takes into consideration the material and discursive entanglements between human and nonhuman entities. We extend this discussion by thinking-with a number of trans theories (Barad, 2015; Colebrook, 2015; Hird, 2006; Stryker, Currah, & Moore, 2008). Trans theories, we contend, complicate walking as embodied and emplaced in order to disassemble and disturb taxonomies, and confound the notion of an embodied, coherent self.

Walking methodologies are often framed as participatory, inclusionary, and thereby convivial. The problem with participation as inclusion is that while it promotes diversity and equity, inclusion also operates as a symbolic gesture that fails to undo the structural logics of racism, ableism, homophobia, and settler colonialism. Participation as inclusion is a universalizing and normalizing practice. In Chapter 4 we critique how participation has been framed through inclusionary logics (Sykes, 2016, 2017) and as rehabilitation (Kafer, 2013; Puar, 2017; Shildrick, 2015; Titchkosky, 2011). To do so we lean on two walking projects: *Ring of Fire*, which was a mass procession for the opening of the Parapan Am games by Trinidadian artist Marlon Griffin and the Art Gallery of York University, and *The Warren Run*, a group orienteering event by Matt Prest commissioned by *WalkingLab*. Following these crucial critiques of participation as inclusion, we ask questions about how we might think differently about participation drawing on theories of movement. While numerous walking scholars have used Henri Lefebvre's (2004) rhythmanalysis, we turn to Erin Manning's (2012, 2016) theories of movement to argue that participation begins before the invitation of inclusion commences. Here we frame movement through a different discussion of *Ring of Fire* and *The Warren Run*, and also the project *White Cane Amplified*, by Carmen Papalia.

Chapter 5 responds to agitations that are occurring in qualitative research, particularly issues related to: the incompatibility between new empiricist methodologies and phenomenological uses of methods (St. Pierre, 2016a); the preponderance of methodocentrism (Weaver & Snaza, 2016); the pre-supposition of methods (Manning, 2016); a reliance on data modeled on knowability and visibility (Lather & St. Pierre, 2013; Maclure, 2013); the ongoing emplacement of settler futurity (Tuck & Mckenzie, 2015); and the dilemma of representation (Lorimer, 2005; Thrift, 2007; Vannini, 2015). These agitations have provoked some scholars to suggest that we can do away with method. Rather than a refusal of methods, we propose that methods need to be generated speculatively and in the middle of research, and further that particular (in)tensions need to be immanent to whatever method is used. We draw on numerous *WalkingLab* exemplifications to ask how we might go about doing research differently.

Walking and mapping have been experimented with by artists and scholars for decades (O'Rourke, 2013). Walking cartographers incorporate hand-drawn maps, Global Positioning Systems (GPS), sensory maps, psychogeography, narrative, photography, scores, and networked databases to name just a few. Despite the many creative and inventive techniques used to walk and map place, the prevailing history of mapping is entrenched in imperial and colonial powers who use and create maps to exploit natural resources, claim land, and to legitimize borders. Cree scholar Dallas Hunt and Shaun Stevenson (2017) argue that conventional mapping practices continue to reaffirm dominant conceptualizations of Canada. Kathrine McKittrick and Clyde Woods (2007) assert that mapping and normalized geographic understandings continue the erasure and segregation of Black subjects. The racialization of space, they argue, is often theorized as essentialized or detached from actual geographic places. Chapter 6 examines three *WalkingLab* projects that re-map – as a form of counter-cartography – erased and neglected histories. Taking up the ways that maps produce and reinforce geopolitical borders, and the geographies of race, we consider the ways that re-mapping offers possibilities for conceptualizing space that is regional and relational, as opposed to state sanctioned and static. We consider how walking can re-map archives and disrupt linear conceptualizations of time. Walking as 'anarchiving' attends to the undocumented, affective, and fragmented compositions that tell stories about a past that is not past but is the present and an imagined future. As counter cartographies and anarchiving practices the walking projects disrupt dominant narratives of place and futurity, re-mapping Land 'returning it to the landless.'

In educational contexts, walking is valued because it increases creativity, focuses student attention, promotes healthy lifestyles, and supports environmental sustainability. While these claims might be important reasons to advocate for movement in schools, the tenuous link between walking and creativity can easily be commodified and normalized by neoliberalism. Furthermore, when the rhetoric of benefits or value is ascribed to walking, educational research becomes trapped in an outcomes-based model. Chapter 7 deviates from these conceptualizations of walking and focuses on two examples of walking-with research in school contexts. In contrast to an outcomes-based model that continues to uphold a particular notion of humanism, our two examples offer the potential for students to critically interrogate humanist assumptions regarding landscape and literacy. We examine the complex ways that students can engage in walking-with as a method of inquiry into their world-making. This is the *how* of walking-with as learning.

Chapter 8, which functions as a speculative conclusion or summary, is enacted as a series of walking-writing propositions that respond to questions concerning the relationship between walking and writing, and our collaborative process. Propositions are different from methods in that they are speculative and event oriented (Truman & Springgay, 2016). Propositions are not intended as a set of directions, or rules that contain and control movement, but as prompts for further experimentation and thought. Over the past number of years, as we presented early drafts of our walking research at international conferences, we were frequently asked about our collaborative walking-writing practice: how we understand the relationship between walking and writing, and how we collaborate. The chapter unfolds through a series of walks that we invite the reader to take: differentiation walks, surface walks, activation devices, 'with,' touch, and contours. Walking-writing we contend is an ethics that is "about responsibility and accountability for the lively relationalities of becoming of which we are a part" (Barad, 2007, p. 303).

As a research methodology walking has a diverse and extensive history in the social sciences and humanities, underscoring its value for conducting research that is situated, relational, and material. Yet, as we argue throughout the book, walking is never neutral. In a time of global crisis – emboldened White supremacy – it is crucial that we cease celebrating the White male flâneur, who strolls leisurely through the city, as the quintessence of what it means to walk. Instead, we must *queer* walking, destabilizing humanism's structuring of human and nonhuman, nature and culture.

Walking Methodologies in a More-than-Human World provokes a critical mode of walking-with that engenders solidarity, accountability, and response-ability 'in the presence of others.' We opened the introduction, by invoking Stengers' (2005) 'politics of slowness.' However, such a concept is risky because of dominant understandings of walking as slow, antiquated, and in opposition to more efficient forms of transportation. Rather, as Stengers so carefully articulates, slow is not necessarily about variations in speed (although it can be), rather it is intended to ask critical questions, and to create openings where different kinds of awareness and practices can unfold. Slowness is a process of unlearning and unsettling what has come before. In approaching walking methodologies from the perspective of slow, we intend to critically interrogate the many inheritances of walking, to agitate, and to arouse different ethical and political concerns.

Notes

1 The Bush Salons are the collective efforts of Affrica Taylor and Lesley Instone and typically take place in Wee Jasper, New South Wales, Australia. See here for more information: https://collectivewalkingmethods.wordpress.com/category/wee-jasper-bush-salons/; http://commonworlds.net/bush-salon-wee-jasper-july-2015/
2 See Haraway (2008a, p. 83) for a discussion of Stengers' 'slow' based on Deleuze and Guattari's idiot.

1 Walking-with place through geological forces and Land-centred knowledges

Walking where the Chedoke Radial Trail and Bruce Trail merge in Hamilton, Ontario, is a journey along a geological formation that took 30 million years to shape, approximately 450 million years ago. During the Ordovician period, the area now known as the Niagara Escarpment was covered by a tropical sea teaming with coral and invertebrates, including molluscs and arthropods. The escarpment was produced by sediments deposited on top of the sea floor that over millions of years became the sedimentary rock, shale, sandstone, and dolostone we see today. During the last ice age, layers of shale continued to erode and cut into the harder dolostone layers on top, which caused them to break off and create the long, steep slope of the escarpment. Many of the layers are comprised of visible fossils of coral, sea sponges, and brachiopods. Queenston shale – the softer bottom layer – was quarried for brick making in the Hamilton area. And the caprock Dolestone is still extracted for building-stone, crushed-stone, and lime products. In the section of the escarpment where the Bruce Trail and Radial Trail merge, layers of rock are exposed due to the former Brantford and Hamilton electric railway that cut through the rocks. This is the traditional territory shared between the Haudeno-saunee confederacy and the Anishinaabe nations.

This chapter is activated by a *WalkingLab* research-creation event *Stone Walks on the Bruce Trail: Queering the Trail* that convened on the Chedoke to Iroquoia Heights loop trail, a 9-kilometer section of the Radial Trail and Bruce Trails in Ontario, Canada. Seventy people participated in the four-hour group walk, which was stimulated by 'pop-up' lectures by geologists, community activists, Indigenous scholars, and artistic interventions by queer artist and activist Mary Tremonte, and a Hamilton arts collective TH&B.[1]

The sections of the trails where we walked, because of their proximity to the city of Hamilton, are predominantly used for fitness, dog-walking, and leisure. The *WalkingLab* research-creation event sought ways to disrupt the typical uses of the trails in order to think about *walking-with place* through geologic forces and animacies, and in relation to Indigenous Land-centred knowledges. As White settlers, we write about place informed by our conversations and readings-with Indigenous scholars and artists.

Place is a central concept in walking research – from considerations of the textures of gravel and pavement that shape how one walks (Vergunst, 2008;

Edensor, 2008) – to the ways that everyday pedestrianism structure and produce place (Middleton, 2010). Walking research has also significantly contributed to theories of place, shifting the logic of place as something fixed and known, to understandings of place as an event, in process, and relationally produced (Massey, 2005). However, Eve Tuck and Marcia McKenzie (2015) argue that place-based learning and research is entrenched in settler colonial histories and ongoing practices and have not sufficiently attended to Indigenous understand-ings of Land.

Likewise, place in walking studies has rarely taken into account how human bodies and geologic bodies are co-composed. Interrogating a geosocial under-standing of human and nonhuman world-making, Kathryn Yusoff (2013) argues that we are all geologically composed and that the geologic is a "defining strata of contemporary subjectivity" (p. 780). The Anthropocene thesis, Yusoff (2013) asserts, marks the human as "a being that not just affects geology, but is an intem-perate force within it" (p. 779). Geosociality, the enmeshment of bios and geos expands notions of agency, vitality, politics, and ethics.

This chapter takes *place* as a starting point and extends investigations into walking-with place through more-than-human theories of the geologic that dis-rupt taxonomies of what is lively and what is inert (Ellsworth & Kruse, 2012; Povinelli, 2016; Yusoff, 2013), Indigenous knowledges that centre Land (Styres, Haig-Brown, & Blimkie, 2013; Tuck & McKenzie, 2015; Watts, 2013), and a posthuman critique of landscape urbanism (Foster, 2010).

The chapter unfolds via a brief look at theories of place and how place appears in walking research. Following this overview, the chapter describes in more detail the *WalkingLab* research-creation event *Stone Walks on the Bruce Trail: Queering the Trail*. This event sought to unsettle settler logics of place by thinking-with i) geo-theories; ii) Indigenous theories of Land; and iii) posthuman critiques of land-scape urbanism. This is not to suggest that such theoretical orientations are analo-gous, rather we frictionally rub them together to think a different ethics-of-place.

When walking does attend to landscape, it is typically connected to issues of environmentalism, sustainability, and conservation. Dominant sustainability dis-courses assume that knowledge of, and preservation through, technological fixes will control the ecological crises. Nature hikes, long walks, and ecotourism rely on human impact, control, and subsequent care. Public parklands that foster trail systems, including those created as a form of landscape urbanism that restore de-industrialized places, are embedded within dominant sustainability discourses and practices where landscape is enjoyed and consumed while maintaining the separation between nature and culture. Nature is something we visit for a period of time. Yet, as Alaimo (2016) contends, "the epistemological stance of sustain-ability, as it is linked to systems management and technological fixes, presents rather a comforting, conventional sense that the problem is out there, distinct from oneself" (p. 173). In this regard, walkers become spectators and are external to wider transcorporeal relations including an entanglement with the geosocial and Indigenous Land. Our research-creation event, *Stone Walks on the Bruce Trail: Queering the Trail* aimed to queer and rupture walking-with place.

Theories of place

Conventional usages of the term place mean a specific location, such as the city of Mumbai, Tiananmen Square, Yorkdale Shopping Mall, or the corner of Haight and Ashbury. In these instances, place refers to a specific, fixed, and concrete location, while the term space refers to something that is abstract and a void. For example, Phil Jones and James Evans (2012) write that "humans layer their own understandings onto abstract space in order to create subjective places" (p. 2319). Place scholar Tim Cresswell (2004) counters this understanding, suggesting that "most places are the products of everyday practices. Places are never finished but produced through the reiteration of practices – the repetition of seemingly mundane practices on a daily basis" (p. 82). Place, as such, is conceived of as a process. The idea of place and space as separate distinctions for Tim Ingold (2000) is fraught with problems. People, he argues, do not live in a place, but move through, around, and between them, such that places are more akin to knots "and the threads from which they are tied are lines of wayfaring" (p. 33). Wayfaring is less a path from point A to B, and more of a meshwork of lines and movement, "a trail along which life is lived" (Ingold, 2011, p. 69). Feminist geographer Doreen Massey (2005) has been a highly influential scholar in re-conceptualizing space and place as socially constructed, relational processes. Space, writes Massey (2005), is contingent and in flux, "the product of interrelations," and is "always under construction" (p. 9). If space is open and place cannot be assigned a prior location, then we need different ways to articulate place-making. Massey (2005) calls this the "event of place," where it is movement that constructs place. In the event of place there is "the coming together of the previously unrelated, a constellation of processes rather than a thing. This place as open as internally multiple" (p. 141). For Massey, re-conceptualising place as event demands different political questions. In the event of place there can be no assumption about location or identity, rather the constellation processes require negotiation. She writes: "In sharp contrast to the view of place as settled and pre-given, with a coherence to be disturbed by 'external' forces, places . . . necessitate intervention" (p. 141). Walking researchers from different disciplines draw on these varied theories of place and space.

Walking research and place

Place, much like embodiment, figures in almost all walking research regardless of the discipline and is a fundamental part of walking research. In this section, we discuss how place is understood through five threads. This by no means suggests that place is limited to these five threads. However, in our review of the field these threads occurred frequently. In each thread we offer a few examples, recognizing that there are far more cases than it is possible to capture. The intent of this section is not to perform an exhaustive literature review of walking and place, but to articulate how place is conceptualized, theorized, materialized, and enacted in walking research. The five threads that we have identified are: 1) the go-along or walking interview; 2) pedestrianism; 3) walking tours and ethnographic research; 4) mapping practices; and 5) landscape and nature.

Go-along interviews

Walking interviews, Evans and Jones (2011) argue, "produce more spontaneous data as elements of the surrounding environment prompt discussion of place" (p. 856). Evans and Jones (2011) differentiate between mobile methods and sedentary methods in motion, stating that although a person on a train is technically moving, the participant's "movement is experienced as a visual flow through windows and the primary haptic sensation is merely that of background vibration" (p. 850). Whereas walking through a crowded street or cycling up a mountain would expose both interviewee and interviewer to more "multi-sensory stimulation of the surrounding environment" (p. 850). Walking interviews offer evidence about how people specifically relate to place as a process rather than a "biographical account of their history 'in place'" (p. 856). Jones and Evans (2012) suggest in walking interviews that "rather than place being bounded, inward-looking and resistant to change, place becomes a dynamic concept, interpenetrated by connections to other social and economic worlds" (p. 2320). As opposed to a point on a map that is circumscribed, place becomes porous and emergent.

Jon Anderson (2004) similarly uses walking interviews to examine the social construction of knowledge and place with environmental activists. The walking interview, he notes, enables him to have a different access to his participants' knowledge because walking helps overcome the typical power arrangements between researcher and participant. The go-along interview shapes a co-constitutive understanding of people and place. Anderson (2004) writes: "Through talking whilst walking, by conversing and traversing pathways through an environment, we are able to create a world of knowledge (or pathways of knowledge through the world) by taking meanings and understandings into existence" (p. 260). Walking interviews allow a researcher to physically go to a specific place with a participant, in order to re-create that place, rather than recall place via memory out of context.

Sarah Pink (2009/2015) argues that walking interviews are not only an aural account but a "social encounter – an event – that is inevitably both emplaced and productive of place" (p. 82). The ensuing narrative of the interview is affected by the spaces the participants move through and the spaces materialized during the walk. Walking interviews emphasize the dynamic relations of place-making, or as John Wylie (2005) reminds us, "the body and its surroundings should not be considered as one, but rather that the self and the world continually enfold and unfold" (p. 24).

Phillip Vannini and April Vannini (2017) offer an insightful critique of the go-along or walking interview. They argue that conventional forms of the go-along rely on representationalism and are "too methodical, systematic, and pre-determined by a priori research agendas" (p. 179). In conventional uses of the go-along, walking becomes instrumentalized and detached from the relational and embodied process of moving together. Phillip Vannini urges walk-along methods that foreground sensuous and rhythmic interrelations. For him, the use of a wearable camera, which captures not only the interview data, but the sounds and movement of walking, is a key technique for the walk-along method. He writes that cinema offers "sonic impression of places and voices, with their unique texture, pitch, volume, intonation, cadence, grain, and rhythm" (p. 183). We have experimented with camera movements using a digital camera and a pinhole mount (Chapter 5), where the movement of walker and the camera movement of shutter speed intra-act with each other producing a kind of quivering image.

Pedestrianism

Studies of pedestrianism include walking as a means of questioning and examining everyday practices and places (Fuller, Askins, Mowl, Jeffries, Lambert, 2008; Middleton, 2011). 'Walking the everyday' is a process by which participants use walking to consider their local environment, particularly in relation to values and attitudes related to place, how walkers use place or identify themselves in relation to place, create stories of place, and navigate changes to place. Cheng Yi'Eng (2014) contends that walking enables ethnographers to become attentive to the mundane and ordinariness of daily life. Focusing on the everydayness through the act of wandering or strolling is important because it enables researchers to experience and collect details about urban life and place-making practices. According to Tim Edensor (2010), "the rhythms of walking allow for a particular experiential flow of successive moments of detachment and attachment, physical immersions and mental wandering, memory, recognition and strangeness" (p. 70). One of the key concepts that emerges in relation to the everydayness of place is rhythm.

For example, Jo Vergunst's (2010) research on Union Street in Aberdeen, Scotland, attends to the rhythm and flows of streets, bodies, feet, and the sounds of urban life that create patterns and connections between places. Rhythm is also a means by which researchers think about the relationships of time and space to walking. The patterns and rhythms that emerge in walking ethnographic work "opened up possibilities for understanding everyday activity as a process of place making" (Vergunst, 2011, p. 387). Jennie Middleton (2009) similarly approached ethnographic research from the perspective of everyday rhythms. Participants in her project annotated their daily walking movements, which revealed to her the complex connections people make between walking and time. Rhythm becomes a means to order and frame urban experience and is negotiated through things such as pace, traffic rules, urban planning, and walking conventions. Pedestrianism, Vergunst (2017) writes, requires an analysis of "the political and material processes" that a walker is enmeshed within. Shifting his focus from research in rural Scottish landscapes, Vergunst's (2017) most recent work takes him along the banks of local urban rivers. Examining human flows, urban planning, and 'nature' regeneration, Vergunst describes the ordinary ways that humans transgress their environment through walking. An everyday pedestrian politics, Vergunst argues, presents "an alternative to the highly planned and strategised city" (p.,19).

Walking tours and ethnographies

Place also appears in research that uses walking tours as a method in ethnographic fieldwork. For example, using the form of a walking tour to examine the history of sex work in Vancouver, Canada, and Yokahama, Japan, Julia Aoki and Ayaka Yoshimizu (2015) incorporated walking methodologies to bear witness to the erased bodies of women in these sites. They write: "[B]eing part of the process of place production, ethnographic walks also potentially offer sites of intervention and negotiation into prevailing historical narratives and spatial configurations" (p. 277). The walks were as much about absent bodies, place, and memory as they are about the remains of place and the contested, negotiated, and resistant ways that people make sense of such remains in relation to history. *WalkingLab* partner, Kimberly Powell (2017) uses the form of a walking tour with intergenerational communities in Japantown in San Jose, California. Walking and talking with community members, Powell investigates migration and place. Walking tours are a means of understanding community and individual connections to place (Bendiner-Viani, 2005), and as collective or shared consideration of empathetic witnessing (O'Neill & Hubbard, 2010). Maggie O'Neill's (2017) research on walking borders uses the form of walking tours to examine place in relation to asylum, migration, and marginalisation. She writes: "Taking a walk with someone is a powerful way of communicating about experiences; one can become 'attuned' to another, connect in a lived embodied way with the feelings and corporeality of another. Walking with another opens up a space for dialogue where embodied knowledge, experience and memories can be shared" (np).

WalkingLab resident Elaine Swan's (2016) research focuses on ethnic food tours in Sydney, Australia. Examining how tour guides and tour participants move through place and negotiate the sights, smells, and sounds of ethnically designated urban spaces such as Chinatown, Swan carefully analyzes the ways in which place-making is mediated by race and gender. Informed by Sara Ahmed's (2006) work, Swan argues that walking as a process of place-making takes on "different forms for racialized groups, stopping or enabling movements, and impressing and shaping bodies as they take the shapes of the spaces they occupy" (np). Swan's feminist and critical race studies work is significant within the field of walking studies because she challenges neutralized views of walking, and emphasizes the need for walking studies to attend to race and ethnicity in the production and mediation of place.

The dérive has become one of the most ubiquitous forms of walking in relation to pedagogy and place. The dérive (see Chapter 3) is a 'drifting' on foot through urban space. This aimlessness disrupts the habitual methods people typically move from one place to another, and instead directs the walkers' attention to the sights, sounds, smells and other psychogeographic details of a place. Focusing on the socio-cultural dimensions of place, Marcia McKenzie and Andrew Bieler (2016) incorporated the dérive and other group walking practices such as night walks and trail walks, as part of a larger ethnographic study on student learning *in* place. Influenced by Ingold's (2000) wayfaring, the students navigate their way through and alongside streets, trails, and place-marking signs. McKenzie and Bieler note that walking "engages students in embodied and intuitive ways of finding their way through and alongside the nuances of place" (p. 70). Furthermore, urban dérives enable students to examine and understand the "co-production of power and place" (p. 70). Despite the focus on Treaty education and settler colonial legacies, these ethnographies *in* place suggest that more attention is required of walking's relationship to settler colonial histories and ongoing negotiations of place.

Mapping

Place is also materialized through the practice of mapping. Karen O'Rourke's (2013) extensive book on walking and mapping highlights the myriad techniques to map place including hand-drawn maps, collage, locative media like GPS, online data bases, and photography. A few examples worth noting here include Jeremy Wood's GPS drawing *Traverse Me*, where the artist walked for seventeen days to construct a map of the University of Warwick campus using GPS technology. Wood facilitated a workshop for *WalkingLab* where participants created a series of maps of the St. George campus of the University of Toronto. These walking maps emphasize both the body's relationship to space and also the interconnections between walking, place-making, and surveillance culture. Psychogeographer Tina Richardson (2014) has developed a mapping method that she calls schizocartography, which "enables alternative existential modes for individuals to challenge dominant representations and power structures" (p. 140). Schizocartography aims to create visual maps of place by revealing not only what is visually present or seen in a space, but the social history, alternative representations, and hidden or absent impressions.

In another, and quite different cartographic example, *WalkingLab* collaborator Linda Knight (2016) uses exquisite pencil lines to map young children's movements in playground settings. Shifting the focus from risk management often associated with children's play, her drawings, which she calls 'inefficient mappings' attend to the pedagogic forces of surfaces, light, time, bodily gestures, and sound as entanglements of place.

Nature and trail walks

Nature walks are not as pervasive in walking studies literature, but their findings inform how walking is conceptualized as both a practice of care of the environment, and a form of self-care. Walking is typically promoted by nature conservation organizations as a means by which people can experience place and as such embody empathy and care for the natural environment. From a health perspective perambulation in nature, such as on woodland trails, nature preserves, or in the country contributes to a person's emotional well-being. For example, researching user practices on the Croom Reserve, an urban nature reserve in Australia, Gordon Waitt, Nicholas Gill, and Lesley Head (2009) observe how walking is conceptualized as a practice of care, where place becomes therapeutic and restorative. Walking becomes a way of doing nature, as if nature is separate and distinct from humans.

However, nature, understood in this way, is exclusionary. Bodies marked out of place in nature – queer, disabled, racialized – trouble the narratives of who is "expected or allowed 'to go there'" (Kafer, 2013, p. 130). Crip scholar Alison Kafer (2013) argues that nature reserves and hiking trails are shaped around a compulsory neurotypicality, able-bodiedness, and normativity. Furthermore, environmentalism and even eco-feminism imply that the only way to know or understand nature is through immersion, which entails walking. This, she writes, ignores "the complicated histories of who is granted permission to enter nature, where nature is said to reside, how one must move in order to get there, and how one will interact with nature once one arrives in it" (p. 132). Normative understandings of able-bodiedness suggest that particular bodies are necessary to overcome the separation between nature and culture. Kafer's (2013) analysis describes not only the ways that disability is understood as 'out of place' in nature, but how 'access' is framed as being against environmentalism. For example, she discusses how environmental activists are often opposed to access because non-normative bodies and their support systems, such as wheelchairs, are harmful to the fragile ecosystem. She writes:

> The rhetoric of ecoprotection then seems to be more about a discomfort with the artifacts of access – ramps, barrier-free pathways – and the bodies that use them. Trails, which are mapped, cut, and maintained by human beings with tools and machinery, are seen as *natural*, but wheelchair accessible trails are seen as *unnatural*.
>
> (2013, p. 138, italics in original)

Environmental activists have even gone so far to talk about the noise of wheelchairs disturbing a hiking trail, a logic which Kafer cogently points out, is not applied to families and children. Nature trails are constructed around an ableist logic. Cripping the trail, Kafer (2013) argues, is not about accessibility but requires thinking about non-normative ways to encounter and experience nature, which "entails a more collaborative approach to nature" (p. 143).

Waitt, Gill and Head (2009) discuss the ways that Australian bushwalking conjures up notions of wildness and nation. Walking, they argue, "remains informed by the colonial logic of *terra nullius* and wilderness values. On other words, how most visitors walk through this place is informed by the assumption they have the right to go anywhere, ignoring the traditional owner's (Bininj/Munnguy) requests" (p. 45). In such an instance, bushwalking is a place-making practice that is "invested in settler futurity" (Tuck & Gaztambide-Fernández, 2013, p. 16).

Scholars like Pink (2009/2015) have used the term emplacement, which "attends to the question of experience by accounting for the relationships between bodies, minds, materiality and sensoriality of the environment" (p. 24). Here Pink is drawing on the work of David Howes (2005) who notes that emplacement "suggests the sensuous interrelationship of body-mind-environment" (p. 7). Emplacement, according to Pink (2011), locates the body "within a wider ecology, allowing us to see it as an organism in relation to other organisms and its representations in relation to other representations" (p. 354). However, emplacement, Tuck and McKenzie (2015) contend,

> is the discursive and literal replacement of the Native by the settler, evident in laws and politics such as eminent domain (and similar constructs), manifest destiny, property rights, and removals, but also in boarding schools, sustained and broken treaties, adoption and resulting 'apologies.'
>
> (p. 15)

Place continues to privilege "settler's views and values" and maintains a distinction between nature and culture, where land is merely a backdrop (Engel-Di Mauro & Carroll, 2014, p. 74). As such place-based research needs to be put into conversation with Indigenous knowledges, practices that 'unsettle' white settlers, and critical environmental studies to move place from the periphery of social science research. Tuck and McKenzie (2015) foreground the need for a "deeper consideration of the land itself and its nonhuman inhabitants and characteristics as they determine and manifest place" (p. 40). Drawing on Indigenous, postcolonial and de-colonial theories, Tuck, McKenzie and McCoy (2014) claim that any discussions of place should include an analysis of territory and settler colonialism; centre Indigenous realities; be infused with Indigenous metaphysics; and destabilize the local. Settler colonial states, according to Tuck, McKenzie, and McCoy are characterized by a "refusal to recognize themselves as such, requiring a continual disavowal of history" (p. 7). Therefore, there is a need to "attend to it as both an ongoing and incomplete project, with internal contradictions, cracks and fissures through which Indigenous life and knowledge have persisted and thrived despite settlement" (p. 8). Settler colonialism is composed of Indigenous people, who must disappear from the land, slaves that are to always be kept landless, and settlers who continue to make into property both land and bodies of Indigenous and slave peoples. What settler colonialism emphasizes is a complex relationship between "native-slave-settler" (Engel-Di Mauro & Carroll, 2014, p. 72). Place, writes Delores Calderon (2014), "has been inexorably linked to the genocide of Indigenous peoples and continued settler colonialism" (p. 25). La Paperson (2014) further remarks that place marks some sites as being wastelands to be rescued by settlers. His work, in what he describes as ghettos, underscores the way that place-based salvation narratives continue to enable the practice of settler belonging. Place, La Paperson (2014) writes, "becomes something everyone can claim, can tell a story about" (p. 124). Rinaldo Walcott (2016) likewise argues that neoliberal understandings of place assume that all bodies are connected to or have a place, and therefore assumes that everyone is a citizen of somewhere. We see this in walking research that guides participants on place-making walks to record their conversations and/or images of a local place. Such walking practices only lead to "restorying and re-inhabitation" (La Paperson, 2014, p. 124) and do little to account for the settler colonial histories and ongoing practices in place.

Stone Walks on the Bruce Trail: Queering the Trail

With these critical insights in mind, *WalkingLab* developed a research-creation event to purposefully connect walkers with the geological forces of place and Indigenous Land-centred knowledges. In contrast to walking practices that are framed through self-discovery, or where nature is a backdrop to be consumed or conquered, *Stone Walks on the Bruce Trail: Queering the Trail* ruptured and queered the trail, challenging the nature-culture binary, demanding that we think otherwise about human and more-than-human entanglements.

We discuss our use of queer in the Introduction of the book. Here, we additionally turn to environmental scholars who use queer in relation to place. For example, Catriona Mortimer-Sandilands (2008) argues that to queer the landscape is "to actively intervene in ideas and practices of nature (ecological and otherwise) to disturb its naturalizing and normalizing effects" (p. 458). Margaret Somerville (2016) takes up queer in relation to place as a strategy or method for research and writing. A queer method, she notes, disrupts and decenters the human, and emphasizes a new theory of representation. Somerville writes, "These moves that originate in the queer strategies that subverted the neat gender and sexuality binaries that structure heternormativity in the past are now applied to destabilize humanism's structuring nature/culture divide and to attend to human entanglement in the fate of the planet" (p. 25). *Queering the Trail* refuses an understanding of geology and Land from a human linear time-scale that can be reduced to heteronormative reproductivity.

The *WalkingLab* research-creation event convened on a wet, cold, grey morning in early April. We met our fellow walkers in the Chedoke Golf Course parking lot where the Radial Trail and Bruce Trail converge. More than 70 walkers joined us, happy that the previous day's rains had stopped and hopeful that the sun would come out, and that warmer temperatures would follow. We commenced the walk with a brief history on walking research and introduced the pop-up speakers: Katherine Wallace, a geology professor from the University of Toronto; Randy Kay, a community activist from the Hamilton region; Bonnie Freeman, Indigenous scholar from McMaster University; and Kaitlin Debicki, a PhD student and Indigenous scholar from McMaster University. Mary Tremonte, a queer feminist artist who works with the print making collective and activist organization *Just Seeds,* had made *Queering the Trail* felt pennants which we had mounted on a dozen bright pink stakes. These were passed around amongst the group of walkers on the trail. Mary had also designed a badge that we awarded to walkers once they had completed all 9 kilometers of the walk with us.

TH&B, an art collective of four artists from Hamilton, had already started up the trail, with the intent that the group of walkers would encounter their intervention along the walk. They had a bright blue painted wooden crate on wheels that was pushed and pulled along the trail. The crate contained something of great weight (which was revealed in a performance at the top of the trail) and walkers assisted TH&B in moving the heavy crate. TH&B is the name of the former railway that ran along the Toronto, Hamilton, and Buffalo corridor, and its initialism can still be seen marked on many of the railway bridges in the city of Hamilton.

WalkingLab gave two pop-up lectures during the event. We opened the walk with a talk on the history of walking, introducing walkers to our critiques of trail walking for fitness and health. Further along the trail, in a grassy meadow, we spoke about our use of the term queer, and its implication for thinking otherwise about walking-with practices.

Another pop-up lecture was given by Katherine Wallace, an expert on the geology of the escarpment of the Bruce Trail. Wallace spoke about the formation of the escarpment noting that the section of the trail where we were walking was once under an ancient tropical sea and closer to the equator. The escarpment was formed more than 450 million years ago under and beside these tropical seas. The rocks that we were standing amongst were carbonite sedimentary rocks, meaning that they contained evidence of having been created in salt water. Wallace noted that we had also walked past sandstone, which would have been formed at the shoreline. The dolestone rock, which is very hard, and is the top layer of the escarpment, is weathered and undermined by the softer layers of rock eroding beneath it. She humorously remarked that if we wanted to walk this section of the escarpment in 30 million years, we'd have to travel 100 kilometers further west as the escarpment is constantly moving in that direction.

In addition to introducing walkers to the escarpment formation, and the specificity of its rocks, Wallace noted that the rich biodiversity of the Bruce Trail is shaped by the geology of the area. Without such specific kinds of geological formations, the biodiversity of the escarpment would not exist. She also stated that in the past 100 years the escarpment has undergone more change than in the previous 9000 years because of human impact, such as quarrying, limestone kilns, and highways. Wallace's lecture impressed on the walkers that geology, while typically thought of as fixed and stable, is in fact moving and under constant change.

Cultural geographer Yusoff (2013) argues that we need to think of ourselves as "embedded in geologic temporalities (rather than just as authors of them)" (p. 786). This, she contends, has the potential to undo a humanist historicity "into thinking better with different geologic materialisms. This is to say that 'our' geologic force is not ours alone and owes a debt (of force) to the mobilisation of other geological materials: fossil fuels" (p. 786).

Yusoff's (2013) arguments require that we understand ourselves as geologic subjects, not only in the ways that we have acted on the earth and extracted use value from the land, but that we are geologically produced. This she contends re-imagines a sense of mineralization that entwines bios and geos. Yusoff (2015) evokes the term geosocial to call attention to the ways that the geological and the social are knotted, while also attending to different geologic scales. While the earth has typically been understood as a geologic surface upon which social relations occur, geosociality for Yusoff, insists on the imbrication of geological formations and social formations. In other words, both are materialized simultaneously.

Elizabeth Povinelli (2016) uses the term geontologies to refer to the entanglement of biology and geology, particularly in relation to how power is shaped.

Her arguments are particularly insightful for re-considering the boundary between what is conventionally classified as life and Non-life. While Yusoff's (2015) use of geopower and geontologies is somewhat different from Povinelli's, both, along with other scholars who take up the geologic, are asking that we question and re-think the categories of human and inhuman. Yusoff (2015) writes, "if we push beyond the boundary of life itself, to consider the inhuman as not a step beyond, but within the very composition of the human, then ecologically there exists the possibility to think different relations with the earth that – materially and conceptually – do not begin and end with the subject" (p. 389). These different relations, Yusoff (2015) would argue is not about how humans and nonhumans might or need to co-exist, which is a different ethical dilemma altogether. Rather, what the geologic impresses upon us is that the human is composed of inhuman forces, earth forces.

Katherine Wallace and Bonnie Freeman both spoke about the layers of rock as stories. These stories are told through traces of water ripples, ancient critters, and fossils that make up the different sedimentary rocks, and also stories of human and nonhumans who have lived *with* the land. Thinking this way invites us to "devise new procedures, technologies, and regimes of perception that enable us to consult nonhumans more closely, or to listen and respond more carefully to their outbreaks, objections, testimonies and propositions" (Bennett, 2010, p. 108).

Indigenous scholar Kim Tallbear (2012) reminds us that while current scholarship influenced by new materialism and posthumanism has turned to vibrancy and animacy, Indigenous peoples have always thought about the vitality and sentience of nonhuman entities including stone. The lack of animacy accredited to particular entities, she writes, is "linked to violence against particular humans [and nonhumans] who have historically been de-animated, made 'less-than-human,' made 'animal'" (np). Tallbear states that the problem with settler thinking is the way it attaches agency to humans. She provides the example of pipestone, which is extracted by Indigenous peoples to shape and create ceremonial pipes. She argues that settler frameworks understand the vitality of pipestone only in relation to ceremony, or in other words through human use or belief systems. Under the logics of settler colonialism, pipestone's animacy is dependent on humans.

Delores Calderon (2014) maintains that the alignment of vitalism with humans, is because of how Euro-Westerners understand land as non-Life. In contrast, Calderon argues for an understanding of Land that includes land, water, air and subterranean earth. Here she is drawing on the work of Dawn Zinga and Sandra Styres (2011) who advocate for Land as first teacher and Land as pedagogy. They write: "In this way, Land is at the core of Indigenous being and learning across diverse urban and rural landscapes and learning environments" (p. 62). Land, according to Zinga and Styres, is more than the physical earth and geography. Land, they write, "is a spiritually infused place that is grounded interconnected and interdependent relationships, and cultural positioning" (p. 63). Somerville (2013), an Australian settler, offers a perspective from her extensive research and intimate working relationships with Australian Indigenous peoples. She maintains that for Indigenous peoples, Land is a belief system and part of their social organization, and as such,

Land has profound implications for their understandings and materializations of place. Leanne Simpson (2014) articulates this through her understanding of Land as pedagogy, where land is "both context and process" (p. 7). For Simpson, Land as pedagogy is a radical break from educational systems that are primarily designed to produce and maintain settler colonialism and capitalism. In contrast, Land as pedagogy "comes through the land" (p. 9). Simpson uses the example of making maple syrup, where Land as pedagogy is not the procedure used to collect and boil sap, but the intricate and intimate web of relations between human and nonhuman bodies. Moreover, this web of relations does not take place on the Land, where Land becomes a background or place, but land is infused throughout this web of relations. Such a Land-centred education is "dependent upon intimate relationships of reciprocity, humility, honesty and respect with all elements of creation, including plants and animals" (pp. 9–10). Land as pedagogy enacts what Simpson (2011) calls Indigenous resurgence, which "requires a disruption of the capitalist industrial complex and the colonial gender systems (and a multitude of other institutions and systems) within settler nations" (p. 87). Resurgence centres Indigenous knowledges and Land.

Algonquin/Mohawk scholar Bonnie Freeman (2015), one of the pop-up speakers, writes that Haudenosaunee clans, which Euro-Western scholars have assumed is a human designation for groups of people, in fact is a Mohawk word that refers to Land, clay, or earth. Land cannot simply be substituted for Euro-Western post-human ecologies, rather "Land relationships," she writes, "are the basis of understanding clans and political structures. . . [and are] rooted in place, territory, and ecology" (Freeman, 2015, p. 72).

During the *Stone Walks on the Bruce Trail* event, Freeman spoke about her walking journeys with Indigenous youth and place-based knowledge that is Land-centred. She noted that place-based knowledge is knowledge that we receive from and with the Land, and that this knowledge is also collective and relational. She talked about Indigenous guardianship of Land, which comes in the form of inter-action with Land, not just care and maintenance of Land through systems of colonization and control. Freeman stated that as we "continue to speak and act upon the Land it becomes a reciprocal relationship to us – an active engagement that maintains a balance within all things." Walking, she noted, was an important part of place-based knowledge. "We learn as we walk," she said.

Freeman's lecture impressed upon the Bruce Trail walkers the importance of walking as a practice of decolonization for Indigenous youth. Her research with *The Spirit of the Youth Working Group*, who journeyed on foot over a period of four years, as an act of Indigenous resurgence, which "sought justice and self-determination" (Freeman, 2015, p. 219). For Freeman and the youth walkers, walking-with as a methodology became a "journey of decolonization and cultural resurgence" (p. 220) and performed an "Indigenous-based resilience [that] is innate, spiritual, and is relational to the land and environment" (p. 222). Such acts of decolonization, Zoe Todd (2014) contends are "concrete sites of political and legal exchange that can inform a narrative that de-anthropocentrizes current

Indigenous-State discourses" (p. 222). Walking-with research is not a metaphor for wider posthuman ecologies. Moreover, while *Stone Walks* walks-with place by acknowledging Indigenous knowledges of Land, as White settlers we do not view the walk as an act of decolonization. Rather, we use the term unsettling to describe our walking-with practice.

The Iroquoia Heights side trail descends a steep set of wood stairs and meanders through a forested and then grassland section of the trail. It was in this forested area that Kanien'keha:ka scholar Kaitlin Debicki spoke about the importance of a relational approach to Land. In her own research on Indigenous literature, Debicki has developed a methodology of reading trees. Trees she noted, slow down her temporality and demand that she become more in tune with 'tree time.' As we stood in the heavily forested section of the Iroqouia Heights Trail, Debicki talked about the three ways she reads trees: as metaphor, through oral histories, and as Place-Thought. Place-Thought is a concept developed by Aninishinaabe scholar Vanessa Watts (2013) that asserts the earth's aliveness and agency. She writes:

> Place-Thought is the non-distinctive space where place and thought were never separated because they never could or can be separated. Place-Thought is based upon the premise that land is alive and thinking and that humans and nonhumans derive agency through the extensions of these thoughts.
>
> (p. 21)

Earth, argued Debicki, "is not inanimate, earth is a person, has energy and ability to communicate, she has agency – can make things happen." Trees, Debicki stated, are Land. Trees don't simply grow out of or on the land, they are Land. Trees help her learn how to be Land-centred, as opposed to human or self-centred. Walking, she also reflected, is part of Place-Thought because it happens *with* Land. Tuck and McKenzie (2015) similarly advocate for relational validity as a way of doing critical place inquiry. "Relational validity prioritizes the reality that human life is connected to and dependent on other species and the land" (p. 636).

Relationality, Rene Dietrich (2016) argues, "is conceived of as a mode of being and living in the world, as well as a mode of political life and existence that can work to disrupt settler colonial logics and unsettle systems of thought in which biopolitical hierarchies are implemented that naturalize hetero-patriarchal White settler rule" (p. 5). This approach delegitimizes the taxonomies that categorize some things as human/nonhuman, living/nonliving. The Euro-Western logic that maintains a separation between geos and bios assumes that "land itself is not a living thing, is not animate, is not a form of life" and consequently excludes land from politics (Dietrich, 2016, p. 1).

Queering the Trail deliberately engaged with a relational politics that does not flatten all entities into equitable vitalism, but accounts for the ways that different phenomena come to matter as matter. As Watts (2013) states, "habitats and ecosystems are better understood as societies from an Indigenous point of view" (p. 23). Watts explains that this means that societies have "ethical structures, inter-species treaties and agreements . . . Not only are they active, they also directly influence how humans organize themselves into that society" (p. 23). Such relational ontologies rub frictionally against some posthuman scholarship that views vitality in nonhuman entities, but that their vitality is not the same as human vitality.

TH&B's intervention weaved in the industrial and working-class labour history of the town of Hamilton. As we walked along the Radial and Bruce trails, TH&B invited walkers to assist with pushing and pulling the blue wooden crate along the gravel trail and sometimes steep incline. Many of the teens and younger children would ask what was in the crate that made it so heavy and difficult to move. Often in the front of the pack of walkers, the efforts of those involved in moving the crate, set the pace for the walk. Sometimes we raced along quickly and at other moments, when the trail became steep or muddy, the crate became an obstacle that appeared to block the path. Its vibrant blue colour stood out against the grey cloudy weather and the early spring colours of mostly grey and brown. Yet, simultaneously the crate appeared to be part of the trail as walkers struggled to move it, the sound of its wheels vibrating over the gravel path. The 70-plus walkers created a critical mass on the trail which at times seemed in a kind of gravitational and frictional pull with the mass of the crate.

TH&B and participants pushed the crate to the top of the trail to an expanse of land populated by rusty fences, course grasses, and a soaring electrical pylon. In contrast to aesthetics of the forest we had just emerged from, this site is an important reminder of natureculture interfaces. Arriving at this destination, TH&B opened the crate, tipped it on its side, and proceeded to roll out a very large boulder, announcing the inauguration of the TH&B 'park.' On the boulder was a metal plate in the form of TH&B insignia. Over the past two weeks TH&B had rolled the stone towards the Chedoke Golf Course parking lot, where we started our walk. The rock had been moved from Bay Front Park, which could be seen from the top of the hill. After the performance, TH&B gave a short lecture on their collective art practice. They talked about how their projects investigate the entangled post-industrial ecology. Their gestures point to recent scientific research which has shown that rocks often contain evidence of industrial waste.[2] Many of TH&B's projects incorporate telephone poles or hydro-pylons, which are ubiquitous, yet overlooked markers of industrialization. These industrialized materials are fused with what might be more typically thought of as 'land-based' materials. Their work ruptures the natureculture binary, entangling together industrial symbols and objects with place. TH&B talked about place in relation to their practice, noting that when they formed as a collective in the 1990s, most artists were leaving Hamilton for more cosmopolitan art scenes such as Toronto, Vancouver, or New York. For them, Hamilton, a former industrial city, was important as a place to make work. They describe their practice as a form of fieldwork, and as such their projects, which range from sculpture, to installation, and performance, interrogate the de-industrialized landscape urbanism of place.

Trail walks: from conservation to a queer ethics of inhabitation

The Chedoke Radial Trail is a 2.7-kilometre section of the Bruce Trail. Unique to Hamilton, the trail draws on similar re-purposed infrastructures to create green spaces and parklands. The Radial Trail began in 1906 as an electric inter-urban railway that provided passenger and freight service. Four lines extended outward from Hamilton to neighbouring communities. The Chedoke Radial Trail was the Brantford and Hamilton (B&H) Electric Railway. Rock was blasted from the face of the escarpment to create a ridge for the track.

The railway closed in 1931 with the advancement of the automobile. In 1932 the tracks were removed and a highway was originally planned to replace the train. At the site where geologist Katherine Wallace gave her lecture is a long stone wall. This wall was built to keep bullets from the Royal Hamilton Light Infantry's rifle range located below the escarpment from bouncing onto the track and hitting the train. At some point in the 1950s the trail was taken over by the city and the hiking and biking trail opened in 1996.

The Radial Trail is similar to other urban efforts to re-naturalize de-industrialized space, often referred to as landscape urbanism (Beuglet, 2016; Foster, 2010). The aim of landscape urbanism is to "improve the functioning of urban ecologies and repurpose sites turning areas where ecologies have been destroyed and contaminated into naturalized urban green space" (Beuglet, 2016, p. 4). Dominant urbanization ideologies argue that re-designing former rail lines or hydro corridors into green spaces and public parks increases health and social benefits, public art and cultural innovation, and adaptive re-use of space (Foster, 2010). Despite such rewards, landscape urbanism functions as a normalizing process based on racialized, classed, ableist, and heteronormative ideologies that co-opt conservation in order to 'clean-up' and 'push out' different populations, or maintain settler colonial heteronormative elite spaces. Likewise, green restoration movements typically regulate the types of people and behaviours that use the trails. Jennifer Foster (2010) maintains that ecological restoration projects "are aesthetically configured to smooth away rust, graffiti, tracks and remainders of what came before, and ecological systems are not situated within regional or historical contexts" (p. 324). The industrial legacy of the rail line is obscured.

Engaging with the types of tensions that emerge in landscape urbanism, Randy Kay gave a short talk on the many uses of the Bruce Trail, including the ways in which people living on the margins of society occupy the many side trails in tents or even small caves, and youth who gather around 'illegal' camp fires. Kay intersected environmental issues with race and class, asking walkers "to consider what [and who] is ecologically displaced through restoration projects, and be alert to ways that ecology can be linked to forms of development that deepen social polarization and threaten marginalized people" (Foster, 2010, p. 335). Kay's talk highlighted the geosocialpolitical violence of landscape and its complicity with dehumanization.

While the movement to green can be seen as part of a larger response to human progress and climate change – where a re-naturalization of place is part of conservation efforts – this retreat, Jamie Lorimer (2015) argues, "relies on a linear understanding of time, configured around an axis of human progress and decline" (p. 3). Landscape urbanism and conservation emerge as geopolitical management and governance practices that are not only human-centred, they maintain distinctions between life and Non-life, human and inhuman. Moreover, as Lorimer (2015) states, such practices are "geared toward shaping good conservation subjects," who in turn continue to normalize such distinctions between nature and culture (p. 59). As such, conservation is about the continued human mastery and control of nature's wildness. It renders landscapes as inert resources that can be exploited and extracted. The idea of a re-turn and a re-naturalization neglects the ways that nonhuman species emerge from, and are dependent on, human entanglements (Myers, 2016; Yusoff, 2017a). The prefix re- signals a recurrence; an again and again. But, it also can mean a withdrawal or a backward motion, as in retype, remove, or retrace.

Rather than a retreat, Alaimo (2016) would insist on inhabitation. This inhabitation is not occupation, but rather a form of ethical action which arises "from the recognition of one's specific location within a wider, more-than-human kinship network" (p. 30). This she contends is an "ethics-in-place" that "counters the unsustainable romance of wilderness fantasies and the lure of ecotourism" (p. 30). Thinking place as geosocial and as Land demands that we consider the earth on which we walk and public parklands not as commodities to be owned, used and managed by humans for extractive profit. Rather sedimentation, fossilization, mineralization and the vitality of tree time and Land, demands a different response-ability (Haraway, 2016). As Alaimo (2016) states, "being materially situated in place holds in it possibilities that do not neatly replicate or privilege traditional geographic patterns of geometry, progress, cartography, and conquest" (p. 25).

In our introductory chapter, we asked 'what is to be done?' *Stone Walks on the Bruce Trail: Queering the Trail* takes up this question as a speculative walking event that "invites an expanded politics attentive to how the force of matter might participate in generating new associations and ethics" (Alaimo, 2016, p. 122). *Stone Walks on the Bruce Trail* aimed to intervene in the ways that place in walking research does not take into consideration the geologic, Indigenous knowledges of Land, and critiques of landscape urbanism.

Tuck and McKenzie (2015) maintain that place in qualitative research typically describes the surface upon which research happens and where data is collected. In Chapter 5, we attend in greater detail to how we understand research-creation events as 'speculative middles,' where methods are not determined as procedures or in advance of research. As a speculative research-creation event *Stone Walks on the Bruce Trail: Queering the Trail* sought ways to queer walking-with place by: bringing issues of the geologic and Indigenous knowledges of Land to bear on walking research, place, and the Bruce Trail; challenging landscape urbanism's re-naturalization and restoration, which continues to bifurcate nature and culture, human and inhuman; and queering the 'natural' beauty of the trail through artistic interventions as natureculture happenings.

Stone Walks on the Bruce Trail enacted what Tuck and McKenzie (2015) invoke in their understanding of critical place inquiry. They ask social science researchers to do more than simply collect data "on and in place, [but] to also examin[e] place itself in its social and material manifestations" (pp. 100–101). After each pop-up lecture we asked walkers to continue walking the trail and to use that time for questions and discussions with the guest lecturers, artists, and *WalkingLab*. As we left the Iroquoia Heights side trail after the final talk, and before the TH&B rock unveiling, we invited the group of walkers to walk in silence for an extended period of time. Unlike sound walks that might ask participants to tune into their sensory surround, the silence was intended as a form of Place-Thought, where the confluence of the days' events could come together. As a walking methodology *Stone Walks* enacts a conjunction between thinking-making-doing. Walking-with place insists on a relational, intimate, and tangible entanglement with the lithic eco-materiality of which we are all a part.

Notes

1 TH&B is the creative partnership of Simon Frank, Dave Hind, Ivan Jurakic, and Tor Lukasik-Foss. For more information on the arts collective, see: www.thandb.ca/
2 Scientists and artists have discovered a number of rock specimens that include human-made debris. One example, is Kelly Jazvac's Plastiglomerate, which are rocks discovered on the Hawaii shore and that are composed of plastic and other garbage from the sea. See here: www.kellyjazvac.com/Stones/Stones.html and here: www.geologypage.com/2017/03/rocks-tell-industrial-history.html

2   Sensory inquiry and affective intensities in walking research

Walking methodologies invariably invoke sensory and affective investigations. Despite the fact that sensory studies and affect studies emerge from different conceptualizations of sensation, both, we maintain, prioritize corporeal and material practices. Sensory studies and the various approaches to affect share an interest in non-conscious, non-cognitive, transmaterial, and more-than representational processes.

Sensory studies have prioritized the senses in research including methods that foreground touch, smell, and sound. This is, in part, informed by an appeal to explore "under-investigated non-visual modes of experience" (Howes, 2013, np). The bodily senses – touch, taste, smell, and sound – were historically viewed as subjective and intuitive, and as such rendered as illegitimate forms of knowing (Claussen, 1993; Howes, 2003, 2005; Springgay, 2008; Vasseleu, 1998). Vision, which was equated with reason and objectivity, was prioritized as a preferred method for qualitative research (Springgay, 2008). With the turn to phenomenology, poststructuralism, and feminist theories of the body – which ruptured the mind/body dualism – the proximinal senses became an important subject of study and increasingly valued as a method of investigation. Furthermore, the advancement in portable digital technologies, such as video cameras, smart phones, and voice recorders, and the shift to thinking about non-representational methodologies, also contributed to the prevalence and possibility of doing sensory research.

As the senses became increasingly entangled within the social sciences and humanities, many scholars noted their particular importance for qualitative research. Some of the most often cited include Paul Rodaway (1994), who argues that "everyday experience is multi-sensual, though one or more sense may be dominant in a given situation" (p. 4). Likewise, Paul Stoller (1997) suggests that sensory reflexivity be accounted for by researcher and participant. David Howes' (2003) work has significantly shaped the field, foregrounding a sensory approach to the study of culture, and the sociality of sensation. Sarah Pink (2009/2015), whose name is almost synonymous with sensory ethnography, argues that sensory perception is integral to social and material interactions, including walking research.

Affect studies similarly prioritized corporeal, pre-linguistic, and non-representational practices by asking questions about what affect *does*. Focusing on pre-, post-, and trans-individual bodily forces and the capacities of bodies to act or be acted upon by other bodies, the 'affective turn' signaled a means to theorize the social beyond the discursive (Clough & Halley, 2007). Affect studies emerged out of distinct theoretical frameworks and disciplines that often conceptualize affect in very different ways (Seigworth & Gregg, 2010). In qualitative methodologies, the most often cited affect theories extend from Spinoza's monism through scholars like Brian Massumi. Massumi (2002) maintains that affect is intensity that passes between bodies and affects the body's capacity to act. Massumi distinguishes between affect and emotion, where emotion occurs once an intensity becomes personal and is perceived as a particular quality – such as happy, sad, or fearful. Other scholars, like Sara Ahmed (2004), think affect through critical discourses of emotion where emotion works on the surfaces of bodies to structure how the body is lived and felt.

This chapter examines a number of *WalkingLab* projects and categorizes them as either sensory, haptic, or affective. This pedagogical exercise is arguably problematic and arbitrary, as many of the walks intersect sensory inquiry and affective understandings of corporeality. However, by structuring the chapter in this way, we are able to demonstrate the degree of complexity and the many variations by which sensory knowing and affective tonalities shape walking methodologies.

In the first section of the chapter, we focus on walks that isolate a particular sense. We then investigate walks that use synaesthesia to defamiliarize the ordinary, paying attention to visceral and immanent encounters of walking in urban space. Crucial to our examinations of walking research is a focus on critical sensory studies that interrogate the ways that walking and the senses produce gendered, racialized, and classed bodies. Furthermore, we take up various scholars' articulations of hapticality – a sense of touch felt as force, intensity, and vibration. We turn to Stefano Harney and Fred Moten's (2013) use of hapticality to articulate 'a politics of the feel' in order to think how walking constitutes a politics-in-movement (Gendron-Blaise, Gil, and Mason, 2016). This turn to 'a politics of the feel' is extended through our discussion of different affect theories, in particular we address recent scholarship on 'affecting subjectivities,' which attends to the affective messiness "of identity, representation, social construction, and experience" (Lara, Lui, Ashley, Nishida, Liebert, Billies, 2017, p. 33). Here intersectionality works with affective understandings of race, sexuality, gender, disability and additional forms of difference. In the final section of the chapter, we argue that 'feelings futurity' in walking methodologies requires that sensory inquiry, haptic modulations, and affective tonalities ask questions about 'what matters.'

Isolating a sense walk

Thinking-with Bark, a *WalkingLab* project initiated by Mindy Blaise and Catherine Hamm, experiments with multi-sensory and multi-species ethnography with early childhood teachers and students. The Bark Studio is an outdoor classroom in Cruikshank Park, Victoria, Australia, that occupies the traditional lands of the Marin Balluk Clan. Each week teachers and students go for a walk in the park along Stony Creek and think-with bark, specifically the varied Eucalyptus species (or Gum trees as they are commonly referred to in Australia). Gum trees shed their bark as part of their yearly cycle to rid themselves of moss, lichen, and parasites. The bark flakes off in interesting patterns, and colourful masses of texture. Blaise and Hamm's sensory ethnography attends to the tactility of multi-species inhabitation to counter the logic that tames, simplifies, and controls young students' learning. They ask: 'What happens when bark becomes the focus?' Their 'out and about' walking and sensory research aims to open "up possibilities for creating new ethical practices in light of human induced changes in the environment" (Blaise, Hamm, & Iorio, 2017, p. 32). In contrast to conventional early childhood research that would ask questions about children's development (e.g. Can they hold a pencil? Can they pick up the bark? Do they listen to instructions? Can they decipher one sense from another?), thinking-with bark as a sensory inquiry explores the ways that children's tactile experiences shape "lively stories" about human and nonhuman intra-actions (p. 40).

Kimberly Powell, one of the *WalkingLab*'s lead researchers, also uses sensory ethnography with young children. In her project called *StoryWalks,* Powell engaged a group of pre-school children on a series of walks in San Jose, Japantown. On one walk, the students were introduced to Ken Matsumoto's public sculpture. The children were invited to climb on and touch the stone, and to create stone rubbings. In a subsequent walk, the students visited a memorial that they banged on with their hands, allowing the vibrations of sound to become a way of knowing sculpture, memory, and place. Collaborating with artist PJ Hirabayashi, and in cooperation with the Japanese American Museum of San Jose, Powell's sensory ethnography examines walking, the choreography or movement of place, and migration (Powell, 2017).

Walking and sound have increasingly been combined in order to explore the sonic ecologies of place. Sound walks can take on many different forms and are known by many different names including sound walks, soundscapes, sonic walks, and audio walks. For example, one type of sound walk includes the method of walking in silence, while paying close attention to ambient sounds. The focus of these walks is not to record sound, but to listen more closely as one walks. An example is Hayden Lorimer and John Wylie's (2010) *Loop* walk. To execute this walk they each started walking – one from the north and one from the south – and converged in Aberystwyth, Wales. Walking alone and together, the activity of listening foregrounds their experience. Listening, they write "lend[s] intricate texture to experience" (p. 7). Walking as a listening body, the "movement within and through [landscape] becomes inhabitation – inhabitation of an implicitly wholesome, affirmative and even truthful kind, as opposed to the pre-occupied, artificial surfaces imposed by modernity" (p. 10). In Lorimer and Wylie's example of embodied walking, listening highlights a kind of aesthetic experience, or audible experiment in fieldwork, that attunes body to place.

Researchers sometimes combine other methods with the sound walk such as recording devices, mapping practices, or reflective journaling to capture the experience and understanding of sound. For example, Ozegun Eylul Iscen (2014) examines how immigrants translate sounds in a new environment with the sensory repertoires they brought with them from other places. In Iscen's research this is discussed as "soundscape competence," whereby a newcomer's experience of different sounds in a new urban context clash with previous sound habits and ways of knowing (p. 128). Soundscapes "may invoke intimate or intense relationships between people and places. For instance, the music coming from street musicians, local stores and coffee shops in a neighbourhood might facilitate a sense of belonging to a community" (p. 126). Iscen's (2014) fieldwork practices use walking and sound diaries (sounds recorded using a portable recording device), which are then mixed into an acoustic sound composition and played using loudspeakers in an installation-type setup. Each loudspeaker broadcasts the sounds of one of the participants, but because each soundscape varies in length and pauses "complex dialogues between speakers/narrative emerged throughout the installation" (p. 131).

Ethnographers interested in sound, such as Trevor Hagen (2014), invite participants to pay attention to soundscapes as they walk in their neighbourhoods, in order to examine people's relationship to and understanding of sound as place. David Paquette and Andrea McCartney (2012) maintain that soundwalks are important methods for qualitative researchers because they are immediate and adaptive.

Sonic or audio walks can be described as walks that use pre-recorded and choreographed audio tracks downloaded to phones or other electronic devices. Audio walks create a type of immersive environment and invoke a heightened sensory experience. *The Voice Exchange*, a *WalkingLab* collaborator, used both the method of a soundscape and a sonic walk. In their project, *The Ghost Variations*, they collected soundscapes from the University of Toronto's main St. George campus. They recorded audio from different types of spaces, particularly focusing on silent or quiet spaces such as libraries, chapels, and outdoor courtyards. After recording the soundscapes, they created five different audio compositions, which included single layers of sound, multiple layers from the same space, or many layers from different places. The compositions could then be played while repeating the walks. Walking and retracing the routes while listening to the audio files disorients the audience and conjures ghostly narratives of past lives, as well as heightens walkers' awareness to sound.

Writing about Canadian artist Janet Cardiff's sonic walks, Mirjam Schaub (2005) notes that "[y]ou can smell what she is describing and you can taste the salt from the sea air. Cardiff expands our sense of self-awareness by drawing our attention to the process of perceiving the immediate environment and talking candidly about our bodies as instruments of perception and their reactions to the world around us" (p. 132). Guided by the artist's voice, audio walks engender a form of "intimacy" (Gagnon, 2007) or what Andra McCartney (2004) describes as a sense of "sonic companionship" (p. 184). However, Angharad Saunders and Kate Moles (2016) argue that not all sonic walks create embodied experiences of place. Many audio walks that are produced for tourists re-inscribe normative narratives of place and as such offer neat, accessible, and power-laden stories. Creating community-produced audio walks in Cardiff, Saunders and Moles (2016) think alongside Ingold's (2007) meshwork and Deleuze's (1994) assemblage to suggest that audio walks should be "ragged and messy happenings that occur in the interstices of, or relationality between, self and world" (p. 69).

Michael Gallagher (2015), along with his research participants, records sounds from a place using the form of walking referred to as a drift. Participants, including himself, move through place, over time, recording ambient sounds and interviews. Recording devices are also fastened to feet and boots enabling the textures of footfall and the ground to be captured. Sounds guide their walks through place. These recordings are then mixed further into an audio track that is replayed when participants and audience members re-walk the place. These types of sonic walks he argues can "re-make landscape" (p. 468). For instance, he writes that the opportunity to walk in a place listening to pre-recorded sounds on an MP3 player "afford the possibility to fold the sounds of a place back into that same place" (p. 468). Similar to Janet Cardiff's sonic walks, Gallagher's (2015) sonic experimentation "doubles place back on itself, sounds returning as revenants that generate, at least for some listeners, uncanny affects of ambiguity, haunting and hallucination, especially in ruinous places, which often already have a ghostly feel" (p. 468). In Gallagher's sonic experiments, there is an entanglement between ambient sounds and audio walks. Gallagher (2015) writes that this kind of composition of sounds brings "a variety of voices back into the site [which] will help to unsettle an all-too-easy narrative" (p. 475). Using the sonic drift as a research methodology, Gallagher notes that "sound composition operates in a different emotive register . . . it is ephemeral, elusive. . . [and has] the power to move us in unpredictable ways" (p. 479).

Another *WalkingLab* example that attends to the proximinal senses is a smellscape walk in Kensington Market, in Toronto. J. Douglas Porteous (1990) introduced the term smellscape to suggest how smells are place related. The smell walk was carried out by students in Stephanie's graduate course on walking and sensory methodologies. Students walked and recorded smells using a variety of methods including colour annotations, descriptive words, and found objects to investigate the ways that place can be mapped using different sensory registers.

While the focus on the proximinal senses has disrupted occularcentrism, critical sensory studies argue that too often the senses are assumed to be neutral when in fact they produce racialized, gendered, and classed understandings of bodies and places (Drobnick, 2006; Springgay, 2011a; Tan, 2013). For example, fetid smells, particularly ones experienced in an urban city on hot days, are associated with infection and decay (Tan, 2013). These smells are then socio-culturally read as sticking to some bodies (Ahmed, 2006). Kelvin Low (2009) maintains that the sociology of smell is a process of othering. By "othering" Low (2009) means "that in smelling and perceiving the other's odor, an individual defines the self through a difference in smell, and also negates the other as a not-I" (p. 14). Particular smells become attached to particular bodies, not because that body emits a particular smell, but because of the racial and classed materializations between bodies, places, and smells.

In the Euro-Western taxonomy of the senses, smell and touch have been tra-ditionally relegated to the bottom of the hierarchy, and as such, associated with animality and primitivism. Foul smells have historically been linked to incivility, filth, and poverty. In his research on smoking in urban space, Qian Hui Tan (2013) considers how smoking is understood as malicious and malignant, and reproduces "intercorporeal distances between smokers and nonsmokers" (p. 56). Stephanie's smell walks examine the ways in which place is produced and negotiated through the senses. Students investigate how sensory experiences regulate and dehuman-ize particular bodies. For example, overly powerful smells, whether from exhaust fumes in dense urban areas, or the potency of 'ethnic' foods, are typically asso-ciated with pollution, and evoke sensory experiences of repulsion and disgust (Springgay, 2011a; Flowers & Swan, 2015). Jim Drobnick (2006) uses the term odorphobia to describe the xenophobia associated with particular smells. Con-versely, the lack of smell is often conceptualized as clean and sanitary. Some corporations brand particular scents that then become associated with class, for example, upscale hotels that defuse a scent in their lobbies. This smell is consid-ered palatable and pleasurable, and associated with Euro-Western understandings of class, cleanliness, and leisure.

The interest in the proximinal senses in walking research is significant for the ways that it has unsettled occularcentrism. In addition, sensory inquiry emphasizes the body and corporeal ways of knowing. However, such sensory turns need to account for the social, cultural, racial, sexual, gendered, and classed constructions of the senses. The senses are not neutral, but already exist as ethical and political demarcations of difference. In fact, as Pink (2011) suggests, the five-sense senso-rium is a cultural concept used by "modern western subjects as ways of ordering their world, rather than being a universal truth that can be applied to any context" (p. 265). Furthermore, sensory inquiry needs to take into account nonnormative sensory experiences. Alison Kafer (2013), writing about disability in relation to environmentalism, questions how chronic fatigue or deafness, as just two exam-ples, transform sensory inquiry. Consequently, while 'isolating' one sense can be a productive method in walking research, it simultaneously demands an account-ability of the ways that difference is materialized through sensory inquiry.

Synaesthetic walks

The senses, writes Kathleen Stewart (2011), "sharpen on the surfaces of things taking form. They pick up texture and density as they move in and through bod-ies and spaces, rhythms and tempi, possibilities likely or not. They establish trajectories that shroud and punctuate the significance of sounds, textures, and movements" (p. 448). Her articulation of sensation, as an intensive force and as an atmospheric attunement, manifests in a synaesthetic walk. Synaesthesia usu-ally refers to a psychological or neurological condition in which sensory stimulus from one sense is mixed up with another sense. For example, this can include a taste being associated with a colour, such as seeing red and immediately tast-ing licorice. Finish composer Jean Sibelius would hear F major when he saw his green fireplace. In walking research, synaesthesia can be deployed intentionally to defamiliarize a sensory experience of place and as a non-representational practice (Truman & Springgay, 2016; Truman, 2017). Synaesthesia was used by Sarah, coupled with the walking practice of the dérive, in her in-school research with secondary school students. Synaesthetic walks evoke, what Stewart (2007) calls ordinary affects, "an animate circuit that conducts force and maps connections, routes, and disjunctures" (p. 3).

The *Hamilton Perambulatory Unit* (HPU), a frequent *WalkingLab* collaborator, created a synaesthesia walk in the Hamilton Farmers' Market. In this walk participants strolled through the farmers' market, taking stock of the various smells on offer, which they mapped using words from another sensory register. For example, the smell of lemon might be recorded as screeching metal. Synaesthesia as a literary device uses words associated with one sense to describe another. For example, "loud yellow" (aural/sight), "bitter cold" (taste/haptic). Rather than describing a scent by using descriptive words that are typically associated with a smell, the synaesthetic walk forced participants to think about the scent using language more commonly affiliated with a different sense. For example, instead of describing a smell in the market as being 'oniony,' the synaesthetic description could be 'piercing sorrow.' In the HPU walk, synaesthesia was used to push language, to write as a way of becoming atmospheric. This is what Stewart (2011) would call a form of writing that is itself sensory and not about representation. This is a type of writing, she contends, that brings together incommensurate elements. On the HPU walk, the synaesthesia became overwhelming. Walkers talked about smell overload and the exhaustion of paying attention differently. As Stewart (2007) recognizes, ordinary affect "is a surging, a rubbing, a connection of some kind that has an impact" (p. 128). As opposed to a representative description of the world, synaesthetic walks attend to that which is palpable and immanent.

Derek McCormack (2010) has developed research methodologies that attend to 'atmospheres.' He contends that much social science fieldwork is concerned with "earthiness" and is "surface-based" (p. 40). In considering atmospheres in conducting fieldwork, McCormack attends to the affective intensities and relationalities between bodies, including air. Synaesthetic walks materialize a kind of atmospheric fieldwork that emphasizes density and surroundings.

Haptic walks

Hapticality relates to the sense of touch. In walking research, hapticality attends to tactile qualities such as pressure, weight, temperature, and texture. The haptic is sometimes organized around kinaesthetic experience such as muscles, joints, and tendons that give a sense of weight, stretching, and angles as one walks. It can also be described as physical where you feel things on the surface of your skin.

Hapticality has been theorized across a range of disciplines including visual culture and geography. For instance, Laura Marks (2000) writes about haptic visuality to emphasize the ways that intercultural cinema engages a viewer's sense of touch, smell, and taste. Here, she draws on the work of Gilles Deleuze and Felix Guattari (1987) who write " 'Haptic' is a better word than 'tactile' since it does not establish an opposition between two sense organs but rather invites the assumption that the eye itself may fulfill this nonoptical function" (p. 492). The haptic emphasizes the visceral register of sense events.

For example, walking scholar Hannah Macpherson's (2009) work with visually impaired walkers, and their 'sighted' guides, focuses on tactile knowledge through the feet rather than the hands. She writes: "As we ascend arm in arm the peat reso-nates beneath our feet" (p. 1043). Hayden Lorimer and Katrin Lund (2008) recount a group mountain summit walk as a process of encountering a trail through "toes, heels, and soles" (p. 186). Similarly, Jo Vergunst's (2008) ethnographic work in Aberdeen takes note of the corporeal ways that walking marks a bodily awareness of surfaces and textures. He writes about the gravel, pavement, and grass as embod-ied and sensory ways of thinking in movement. Perdita Phillips' (2004) project in the Kimberly region of Australia combines ethnographic, artistic, and scientific methods along with walking. She argues that the field or site of research is "re-corporealised" by walking because it is a bodily not a visual practice (p. 158). The bodily practice of walking, Deirdre (Dee) Heddon and Misha Myers (2014) main-tain, can be demanding, severe, and grueling. In contrast to embodied narratives of walking that extol the virtues of meditative drifting, writing about their *Walking Library* project they reflect on the arduous nature of walking across different land-scapes, carrying heavy packs, and in the blistering sun. They emphasize the ways in which the corporeality of knowledge is shaped through movement.

John Wylie (2002) describes the rhythm of walking as a corporeal event. Depths and surfaces – the topology of place – are distilled "into knees, hips and shoulder blades" (p. 449). Wylie's work speaks to the ways that walkers experience their own muscular consciousness on a walk, in relation to the slopes and peaks of a landscape. Lund's (2005) walking ethnographies similarly foreground haptical-ity such as postures, speeds, and rhythms, which "shape the tactile interactions between the moving body and the ground, and play a fundamental part in how the surroundings are sensually experienced" (p. 28). While Tim Ingold (2004) states that walking is a "more literally grounded approach to perception . . . since it is surely through our feet, in contact with the ground (albeit mediated by footware), that we are most fundamentally and continually "in touch with our surround-ings" (p. 33). He proposes that walkers "hear through their feet" emphasizing the proprioception of movement (p. 331). Ingold's embodied hapticality, however, foregrounds an individual's experience and understanding of surfaces and tex-tures, privileging the human. In Chapter 3, we extend these discussions of human embodiment through trans theories.

Haptic knowledge, writes Mark Paterson (2009), shifts sensory knowing towards a more complex, enfolded engagement with space. Commenting on Wylie's research walking the South West Coast Path, Paterson (2009) argues that Wylie's thick haptic descriptions "include a range of affects and somatic sensa-tions such as pain, weariness, movement, vertigo, bodily bearing, assurance, jou-issance, rhythm, rest, trudge-heavy joy, or exhaustive openness to the landscape that surrounds" (p. 783).

Hapticality emphasizes transcorporeal touching encounters. According to Hubert Gendron-Blaise, Diego Gil, and Joel Mason (2016) hapticality is *a politics of feeling* that courses and pulses through and between an event. Drawing on the work of Stefano Harney and Fred Moten (2013) they argue that the haptic exists as both modulation and force. The touching and feeling that Harney and Moten (2013) write about is inescapable, imperceptible, and unregulated. Writing about concepts such as the undercommons and the hold (the bowels of the slave ship; the neoliberal hold of capitalism) hapticality is a political mode of touching and being touched. This touching can be both physical (as in skin contact) but also relational or proximinal. For Harney and Moten (2013), hapticality is "the touch of the undercommons, the interiority of sentiment . . . the feel that what is to come is here" (p. 98). For them, hapticality is political because it marks the flows between bodies and objects, thought and feeling. Harney (2013) writes that normalized rhythms of capitalism, colonialism, and exploitation kill life. This is rhythm that he refers to as a 'line.' This is the assembly line, immaterial labour, and the middle passage. This is rhythm that is measured, managed, and controlled. Outside this line, though, are other rhythms that unsettle and struggle against the line. This is the rhythm of hapticality. Hapticality is not somewhere else or beyond the line. It is touching and proxminal and as such it offers possibilities for being together in dispossession, for feeling freely in confinement, for fantasizing about a different future. Gendron-Blaise, Gil, and Mason (2016) write: "To be haptic is to move with the modes of attention that an event needs, at the meeting point of the ever singular differences that weave the texture of the experience. Stretched over this exciting and intimidating landscape, we feel f(r)iction: the interaction of a troubling, a movement" (p. 2). Hapticality or a politics of the feel, lies below cognitive perception. Many *WalkingLab* projects could be framed as haptic or what Harney and Moten (2013) refer to as "skin talk, tongue touch, breath speech, hand laugh" (p. 98). While walking and other mobile methods are not necessarily more 'optimal' means by which to materialize hapticality – or for that matter any type of sensory inquiry – because some forms of walking emphasize movement as unmetered rhythm, as a vibrational flow, that takes place in a specific location, they can materialize a more haptic relationship to place.

Métis artist Dylan Miner's *WalkingLab* event *To the Landless*, which we discuss in more detail in Chapter 6, helps us think about a *politics of the feel*. *To the Landless* borrows its title from words spoken by anarchist Lucia Gonzáles Parsons (commonly known as Lucy Parsons) at the founding convention of the Industrial Workers of World (IWW). The walk speculatively brought together Lucy Parsons with Emma Goldman, another anarchist, who happened to live in Toronto in 1928. During the walk, participants read from Goldman and Parson's anarchist writings. Unable to separate history from the present and future, Miner asked participants to walk-with and converse with these two contentious and important activists and thinkers. Conversations incited by the walk focused on the politics of settler-colonialism, capitalism, patriarchy, and immigration.

During the walk, Miner talked about the tensions within artistic practices that tend toward the political. For instance, he wondered whether the fragments of text he had pulled from IWW publications from the early 1900s could be read as political during our walk through the streets of Toronto. Dylan also reflected on the ethical-political dilemma of reducing politics to an art form. He asked: 'How is the walk a politics, that isn't politics?' As in, how is it political when it might not look like a particular form of politics? It is here that hapticality is important for understanding the walk as a *politics of the feel* in that hapticality is the force and intensity of thinking-with, moving-with.

Hapticality is a kind of swarming political affect that courses between bodies. It lies below and within surfaces. Hapticality isn't about recognized political forms; it is a politics that is felt rather than identified. Walking, reading excerpts from the IWW publications, pausing, and talking hinted at this politics of the feel. It wasn't about grasping or concretizing a political form, such as the banners, but asked questions about how to tune into particular atmospheres. This is what Gendron-Blaise, Gil, and Mason (2016) call the 'affective tonality of an event.' They ask how we can create events that "train ourselves to attend to the affective tonality of the event, how the potential materializes itself. But also, what can – or cannot – potentially land in the concrescence of the event?" (p. 3).

To the Landless, as a politics of the feel, might also be understood through theories of affect, where affect is force and intensity. Affect has inflected qualitative research methodologies with an attention to matter as dynamic, energetic, and emergent. In the next section of the chapter, we continue to examine *WalkingLab* projects in order to consider the *affective* dimensions of walking. Admittedly, affect surfaces in the previous sensory experiments and walks, as affect circulates constantly. However, the focus in the previous experiments was on the ways in which walking shaped a sensory understanding of embodiment and place. Affect, we'll argue, although not synonymous with sensory experience, extends and complicates the ethical-political work of walking methodologies.

Affective intensities in walking research

Evaporation Walks, a *WalkingLab* proposition by Lori Esposito, is a group walking project where individuals carry broad dinner plates filled with pigmented water. Walking slowly across fields or urban spaces the water eventually evaporates leaving a trace or silt residue on the bottom of the plate. The project speaks to pain and grief, and the weight of carrying a dying body both literally (in the form of evaporation) and metaphorically (loss of a child). If affect demands that sensation be understood as intensities, vibrations, and forces that are transcorporeal, as opposed to located in a particular body, then pain and grief are palpable in the circulation of affects between bodies (Ahmed, 2004). As Manning (2012) writes: "Affect never locates itself once and for all on an individual body. Affect courses across, grouping into tendential relation not individual feelings but pre-individual tendencies" (p. 28). Affect signals a capacity for the body to be open to the next affective event, an opening to an elsewhere. Stewart (2007) writes that affect isn't about being positive or negative, but that it rests on an unpredictable edge where it can take on "the full charge of potential's two twisted poles – up or down, one thing or another" (p. 24).

Affect is about surfaces. Quivering, vibrating surfaces that affect bodies, sticking to them, or as Ahmed (2010) writes, how bodies become oriented. Affect, she writes, "does not reside in an object or sign, but is an affect of the circulation between objects and signs" (p. 120). Affect, argues Ahmed (2004), is contagious and contingent, where the passage of affects from one body to another circulate non-innocently. Affect is the unspeakable. For example, she notes that one can walk into a room and feel the atmosphere, but that what we feel depends on who we are and how we arrive. In other words, it's not that the room is fearful – the fear is not attached to the room or a body – but circulates and is contingent on bodies and spaces and their arrivals. Gallagher's (2016) sonic drifts, which we discussed earlier in this chapter, enact an affective, sonorous, composition of place, where place is materialized through the vibrations and flows between environment, landscape, bodies, rhythms, tempos, and sounds. Lisa Blackman's (2012) work on affect and rhythm is important here, particularly her accounts of affective thresholds. This threshold, she writes, is "at the interface or intersection of self and other, material and immaterial, human and nonhuman, inside and outside such that processes which might be designated psychological (are) always trans-subjective, shared, collective, mediated, and always extending bodies beyond themselves" (p. 23).

If, according to Deleuze, affects are not 'things' but created through encounters, which force us to thought, then in *Evaporation Walks* there is a difference between the walkers feeling emotions that are already recognizable – for example, grief – and pre-, post-, and trans-personal affects that unsettle and force us to resist identification. The affects that circulate might be anguish, but they could also be joyful. What arrives is dependent on contexts, histories, bodies, and affective encounters. Deleuze and Guattari (1987) state that we can't know anything about the body "until we know what a body can do, in other words, what its affects are, how they can or cannot enter into composition with other affects, with the affects of another body, either to destroy that body or to be destroyed by it, either to exchange actions and passions with it or to join with it in composing a more powerful body" (Deleuze & Guattari 1987, p. 257).

Evaporation Walks remain open to what might affectively arrive. Clare Colebrook (2002) states that "once something appears [eg. the emotion of grief] to us we have already organized it into a certain perspective" (p. 18). Colebrook (2002) provides the example of a poem in which the rhythms and pauses, the halting and hesitation creates an affect of fear; "a fear that is not located in a character nor directed to an object" (22). It is not that affectively we cannot sense fear, but that fear is not known or presupposed beforehand.

In another example of affective intensities in walking research, Rebecca Coleman's *WalkingLab* project *Encountering Temporality* focuses on the relationship between affect and time. Her project examines a series of walks taken between her home and office along Lewisham Way in London, UK. Blogging about one of her walks, she describes doorbells as anticipatory devices that are capable of bringing about affective encounters. Doorbells, she writes, are temporal and future oriented in that they announce an arrival. Writing about the relationship between futurity and methodologies, Coleman (2017) argues that futurity is unknowable and ineffable and thus complicated from the perspective of the present moment. Methodologies that engage with affect, such as walking, enable researchers to think about futurity. Doorbells highlight "both the (im)materiality of affect, and the ways in which an affective temporality complicates or confuses linear temporality, so that the future is not (only or so much) a distinct and/or far off temporality, separate to the present (and past), but is (also) experienced and felt 'in' as the present" (p. 527). If affect is an immediate intensity, then the future isn't somewhere off in the distance but is palpable on the body in the present (and the past). Temporality has affective resonances, where time undulates and contours rather than progresses linearly (Bertelsen & Murphie, 2010). Temporality enables affect to circulate, collect, and stick to bodies as a result of complex social and cultural processes.

Vincanne Adams, Michelle Murphy, and Adele E. Clarke (2009) write about a politics of temporality as a form of anticipation. Anticipation, they argue, is an affective state, "an excited forward looking subjective condition characterized as much by nervous anxiety as a continual refreshing of yearning, of 'needing to know.' Anticipation is the palpable effect of the speculative future on the present" (p. 247). Anticipation is how we organize ourselves temporally. As such it has long been part of political practices including anti-racism, decolonization, and feminist politics to name a few. Anticipation, they write, is also a form of governmentality, capitalism, and ongoing colonization. "Distributed anticipation – as mass fear or a politics of hope – can become politicized, mobilizing and sometimes creating states of war, nationalist communities, and economic productivity" (p. 249). Configured as both the logics of capital and against it, anticipation as affective temporality asks questions about how we can become accountable to a future orientation of time.

Affecting subjectivities

The political potential of affect lies in intensities – which can be either deliberate or incidental – and in the ways that intensities instantiate feelings. These feelings, while immediate and in the present, arrive with a past that is never in the past, and engender an indeterminate future. One of the dangers of establishing a binary between affect and emotion, Ahmed (2010) argues, is that in doing so emotion becomes aligned with a feminized subject. Aligning affect with autonomy, and emotion with the subject, re-colonizes the body. Other critiques emerge in affect studies suggesting that there can be a tendency to avoid the messiness of identity politics and a refusal to engage with issues of oppression. This neglects the ways that affect and feeling participates in the formation of subjects. However, many affect theorists have turned to affect precisely because affect enables a form of thinking about politics as "processes of circulation, engagement, and assemblage rather than as originating from the position of a sovereign subject" (Lara, Lui, Ashley, Nishida, Liebert, Billies, 2017, p. 34). Numerous scholars have attended to the entanglements between affect and politics, including the ways that power and control circulates and flows (Bertelsen & Murphie, 2010; Clough, 2008; Puar, 2012) and the formation of animacy hierarchies that condition corporeal threats (Chen, 2012). Feminist, queer, trans, disability, and critical race theorists stress the importance of affective subjectivity to take up disability, class, race and other sites of oppression (Ahmed, 2004; Blackman, 2017; Nishida, 2017). The politics of affect resonates with the ways that queer, trans, Black, and Indigenous scholars have politicized flesh, the body, and feelings. What affect theory helps us do is re-think the assumption that agency and politics begins with the human subject, and that the human is the only animate agent.

Affecting subjectivity offers possibilities for exploring material and visceral processes of subjectivity, re-thinks categories previously associated with identity, and considers the emergence of subjectivity as an assemblage of conscious and non-conscious matterings (Lara, Lui, Ashley, Nishida, Liebert, Billies, 2017). Affectivity becomes a practice and process of defamiliarization, where subjectivities are not flattened or erased but neither are they fixed, known, or assumed.

Turning to two water walks, we consider the ways that affecting subjectivities contributes to the scholarship on the intersections between affect and politics. *Lost River Walk* is a walk that Stephanie executed with her walking and sensory methodology class. The city of Toronto is built on top of a number of creeks and rivers that at one point flowed through the city towards Lake Ontario. The lost waterways speak of industrialization, urban planning, and settler colonization. The rivers and creeks are still present under the city sidewalks and streets, and in some cases surface periodically, in subway tunnels and in small ravines. As a micro-research event Stephanie and her class followed *Taddle Creek*, which begins north of St. Clair Avenue and meanders through the Annex neighbourhood and the University of Toronto campus, until it finally reaches Lake Ontario. *Taddle Creek* was used by Indigenous peoples as a navigation route and for drinking water. The current *Philosopher's Walk* that stretches through the University of Toronto campus is one of the few spots where the topology of the former creek bears the traces of banks and a shore. This was a site of importance for Indigenous people, but this history has been erased from its current use. As the city of Toronto grew, the creek became a popular place for settlers to fish or skate in the winter, and other recreational pursuits. In 1859, a part of the creek became a pond near what is now Hart House on the University of Toronto campus. However, because sewage drains from University buildings and houses from the Annex neighbourhood flowed into the creek, in 1884 efforts began to bury the creek in pipes and underground conduits. The idea of 'out of sight and out of mind' merely shifted the sewage to Lake Ontario. Even today, Toronto's sewers that serve both homes and storm water runoff are not separate and thus, after major storms, the city's sewage and rainwater overwhelm treatment facilities and the overflow pours untreated into the lake becoming a major source of contamination.

Walk to Windermere Basin is a walk organized by Astrida Neimanis for *WalkingLab* that lead us to the East Harbour of the post-industrial city of Hamilton. The area now known as Windermere Basin was a polluted mess due to chemical run offs, sewage overflows, and eroded sediment. In 2012, the city of Hamilton and the province of Ontario combined efforts to build the largest man-made coastal wetland in Canada in an effort to clean up the area. Situated in a section of the city between Lake Ontario, a major highway, and in view of smelting furnaces, today Windermere Basin is growing back into a wetland – populated by migratory birds, Indigenous and non-Indigenous plants, and fish. On a blazing hot summer day, Neimanis, who has been conducting ongoing research in this area, lead *WalkingLab* on an exploratory walk of the Basin, as a mode of performing what she calls a hydro-logics.

Neimanis' hydro-logics are ethically and politically attuned to how water – as power – flows through, across, and between human and more-than-human bodies politically, socially, and environmentally. Neimanis (2009) writes, "our bodies of water open up to and intertwine with the other bodies of water with whom we share this planet – those bodies in which we bathe, from which we drink, into which we excrete, which grace our gardens and constitute our multitudinous companion species" (pp. 162–163). This hydro-logics was also palpable on the *Lost River* walk affectively, as loss, fear, and moistness that flowed through and clung to our bodies in its presence/absence. Affect, Lone Bertelsen and Andrew Murphie (2010) remind us, is not a fixed state. Affect is transitive, and in constant variation. It passes between things shaping temporal contours that intra-act, link up, and entangle with other affective tonalities.

Animacy hierarchies, Mel Chen (2012) contends, are ontologies of affect. For example, toxicity needs to be understood not as a 'thing,' such as lead in toys, but how the affective dimensions of lead poisoning (fear), are sexually and racially instantiated. The taxonomy of affect, or what Ahmed (2004) calls the 'economies of affect' work to regulate and dehumanize particular inhuman bodies. Analyzing the ways that toxicity flows highlights for Chen (2012) the porosity and fluid boundaries of bodies. Toxicity, Chen argues is intimately linked to queerness and disability, where pollution threatens the human or proper body.

In the water walks discussed in this chapter, toxic waters have been contained and managed. *Lost River Walk* is a reminder of the governmentality that manages water through concealment and erasure. Yet that water still flows beneath the city and into the lake. It bubbles up, threatening order. In *Walk to Windemere Basin*, environmental maintenance attempts to regenerate and revive 'nature,' where nature is in opposition to culture and exists as a state that can be returned to. In both instances hydro-management tries to control affect, reduce it, and stabilize its intensity (Bertelsen & Murphie, 2010). Maintenance is a practice of separation where nature and culture are rendered discrete. In the *Lost River Walk* human effluence is obscured and masked, while in the Basin human pollution is camouflaged through regrowth and rehabilitation. In both instances management is a practice of concealing human nature entanglements and as Chen (2012) would argue, about the regulation of animacy. Toxicity, Chen contends, is sexually, racially, and able-bodily instantiated, where particular bodies are under threat from 'other' bodies. Race, gender, sexuality, and disability are not identity markers, but dynamic processes that circulate, accumulate, and stick to bodies. In the case of the Windemere Basin restoration project such management becomes an emblem of stability where affect is reduced to moralism and emotion. This is what Stacy Alaimo (2016) claims as an anthropocentric model of sustainability, which is an "environmentalism without an environment" (p. 176). Foregrounding the ontological and relational connections of bodies – human bodies, water bodies, toxic bodies – subjectivity becomes known and felt, like moist water droplets of air. Affects "help us tune into the sometimes flat, sometimes fuzzy, sometimes painfully-sharp sense experiences that loom up around matter" (Shomura, 2017, np). As Akemi Nishida (2017) states, affect has the potential to build more power-ful co-compositions, co-capacities from which to act. This is affect's politicality. As an ethico-political tending, walking demands that we respond beyond sys-tems of management, containment, and concealment, to think-with the affective entanglements of which we are all apart.

Feelings futurity

There is no denying that sensory experiences, haptic feelings, and affective inten-sities course through walking research. What matters, we contend, is how we *tune into* sensation, hapticality, and affect. As Ahmed (2008) so cogently states, "there is a politics to how we distribute our attention" (p. 30). This is the politics of the feel. Over the past few decades, qualitative research has been re-shaped by sensory studies, non-representational theories, and affect studies making way for non-visual experimentations and techniques. The expansion of digital technolo-gies has also enabled different kinds of sensory investigations to emerge. From sensory walks with early childhood educators and students, artistic experiments that isolate an individual smell, soundscapes and sonic walks that render place as acoustic and sonorous entanglements, to everyday pedestrianism that tunes into affective anticipation, walking is an important and significant mode by which the senses, the haptic, and the affective can be mapped, conditioned, and material-ized. It is our contention however, that *feelings futurity* in walking methodologies not only lies in these meaningful and vital contributions to qualitative research, but in the politicality of sensation and affect. This means that walking methodolo-gies need to account for the ways that more-than-human sensations and affects circulate, accumulate, and stick to different bodies and spaces in different ways.

Smell, as we have outlined, is not neutral. How smells flow, how they become attached to bodies or places, and the kinds of encounters such flows generate are important as part of sensory research. The kinds of surfaces or atmospheres that walking methodologies evoke can be captured or managed and therefore partici-pate in power and control. As such feelings can be easily harnessed and moralized – we are expected to feel particular ways – and continue to demarcate some bod-ies as inhuman. The management of affect, in the examples of the water walks, serves to continue the separation and reification of culture from nature. The con-trol of affect, in the water walk examples, functions to maintain the human in the centre of the natureculture entanglement. But affect, because it leaks and seeps like the *Lost River* flows beneath the city, can resist capture and as such has the potential to defamiliarize, destabilize, and resist the boundedness of the human subject. *Feelings futurity* arises as forces that act through and upon us. The future of walking methodologies requires not only innovative techniques to experiment with and account for sensory and haptic understandings, but must also attune to affecting subjectivities and the ways that affect flows and sticks to different bodies and spaces. *Feelings futurity* insists that we turn our attention to how matter comes to matter.

3 Transmaterial walking methodologies

Affective labour and a sonic walk

Walking researchers insist that walking is embodied because it is immediate, tangible, and foregrounds the bodily experience of moving. As we walk we are 'in' the world, integrating body and space co-extensively (Pink, 2009/2015; Ingold, 2004). However, the linkage between walking and embodiment is contentious because particular ways of walking might not be embodied, such as mindless daily commutes to work. Likewise, when walking is described as embodied, it is typically assumed to be productive, lively, convivial, and therefore positive. However, mass refugee flights experienced globally enact vulnerable, exposed, and brutalized embodiment. Normative understandings of embodiment are framed as affirmative, but do not take into consideration antagonism or power.

Feminist environmental humanities scholar Stacy Alaimo (2010) contends that embodiment does little to account for "networks of risk, harm, culpability and responsibility" within which humans find themselves entangled (p. 3). Rejecting a model of embodiment based on individual experience, Lindsay Stephens, Susan Ruddick and Patricia McKeever (2015) argue that embodiment theories need to account for more politically emplaced and spatially distributed understandings of bodies and space. Eve Tuck and Marcia McKenzie (2015) likewise note that particular accounts of embodiment are too often expanded on to make universal claims about the emplaced subject and as such neglect "the situated realities of historical and spatial sedimentations of power" (p. 36). Theories of emplacement, they contend, have perpetuated ongoing settler colonial practices.

Alaimo (2010; 2016) proposes the concept *transcorporeality* to describe more-than-human embodiment that includes "material interchanges between human bodies, geographical places, and vast networks of power" (Alaimo, 2010, p. 32). Transcorporeality posits humans and nonhumans as enmeshed with each other in a messy, shifting ontology. Transcorporeality cleaves the nature-culture divide and asserts that bodies do not pre-exist their comings together but are materialized in and through intra-action. Feminist scholar Astrida Neimanis (2017) provides a poetic example of transcorporeality in her scholarship on water. She describes her bedside glass of water's leaky entanglements with bodily effluence, amniotic fluid, climate change, and all bodies of water. Human bodies, she notes, are 60–90 percent water, further entangling humans and nonhuman 'water.' Water is transcorporeal. As such, transcorporeality demands an ethics that does not centre the human but "is instead accountable to a material world that is never merely an external place but always the very substance of our selves and others" (Alaimo, 2010, p. 158).

This chapter conceptualizes walking methodologies as transmaterial. To develop a transmaterial thesis, we think-with a sonic walk called *Walking to the Laundromat*, created for *WalkingLab* by Rebecca (Bek) Conroy. The sonic art performance consists of a 106-minute audio track that participants listen to while doing their laundry at a public laundromat, interspersed with walks around the neighbourhood in between cycles. To begin, we describe the sonic walk and a form of transversal writing that we use to engage with the project. Following this, we unfold various conceptualizations and understandings of trans. Commencing with Alaimo's transcorporeality we draw on different trans theories to disassemble and disturb taxonomies, and confound the notion of an embodied, coherent self. In the next section, we discuss the sonic walk, and affective and gendered labour to question how some bodies are perceived as disposable in order for other bodies to thrive (Mbembe, 2003; Puar 2007). Here we critique normalized and universal references to the flâneur, a man of leisure, who is able to walk, detached and privileged in a city. The flâneur, we argue, is a problematic emblem for walking methodologies. Following this we introduce transspecies and viral theories to further complicate humanist conceptualizations of embodiment. In the concluding section of the chapter, we discuss the ways that sounds, in laundromats and other places of service work, can be normalized and sanitized, and as such continue to render some bodies as inhuman. Transmateriality, we contend, enlarges understandings of corporeality and takes into account more-than-human movements and entanglements that are immanent, viral, and intensive.

A sonic walking art performance and transversal writing

Walking to the Laundromat is a 106-minute audio track that participants listen to while doing their laundry at a public laundromat, interspersed with walks around the neighbourhood in between cycles. The audio track parodies the form of a 'self-help' audio book. Produced as a binaural sound file, the participant is greeted by a voice that instructs them when to walk and how and when to do their washing. Intersected with this masterful and controlled voice are sounds that emerge as part of neoliberal life, including a 1950s laundry detergent commercial, and new-age mindfulness music and well-being affirmations. Another layer intersperses intensive matterings about capital, money laundering, and affective labour, particularly the gendered and domestic/service labour performed by those who clean, wash and perform care in underpaid, often violent domestic or service jobs.

In this chapter, we introduce trans theories cut together with paraphrased excerpts from the audio file, to transduce and shape the writing *with* rather than *about* the sonic walk. In thinking trans, we invoke a transversal writing practice that attempts to rupture a reliance on lived description of artistic and bodily work. A challenge of writing and thinking-with more-than-human methodologies, and their experimental, material practices, is how to attend to their fleeting, viral, multiple, and affective intensities without reducing walking and art projects to mere background. There is a tendency to 'interpret' contemporary art practices, privileging the researcher's voice over the artists.' Rather, we approach Conroy's sonic walk as an instantiation of theory. The walk enacts and engenders the concepts that we attend to in this chapter. As such the theories are immanent to the project, not outside of it. The audio walk soundtrack can be accessed at www. walkinglab.org. We encourage the reader to listen to it while doing a load of laundry and taking a series of short walks between cycles.

Trans theories

In using the prefix trans, we understand that trans and non-trans people have different stakes in the field of trans studies (Elliot, 2010). Viviane Namaste (2000) warns that queer and feminist theorists often use the term trans while simultaneously ignoring and consequently erasing the material and social conditions of transgendered people's lives. Namaste (2000) argues that when transgendered and transsexual people are "reduced to merely figural: rhetorical tropes and discursive levers invoked to talk about social relations of gender, nation, or class" there is a real possibility of rendering them invisible (p. 52). The prefix trans was put to work in a special issue of *Women's Studies Quarterly*, to counter the logic of trans as a move from one fixed location to another. Susan Stryker, Paisley Currah, and Lisa Jean Moore (2008) in their guest editorial invoke the prefix trans to consider the interrelatedness of all trans phenomena. "Transing," they write, "is a practice that takes place within, as well as across or between, gendered spaces. It is a practice that assembles gender into contingent structures of association with other attributes of bodily being, and that allows for their reassembly" (p. 13). Similar arguments are made by Rosi Braidotti (2006) who describes transpositions as "intertextual, cross-boundary or transversal transfer, in the sense of a leap from one code, field, or axis into another" (p. 5). Transpositions are not a weaving of different strands together, but rather of "'playing the positivity of difference' as a theme of its own" (p. 5). Transpositions are non-linear and nomadic, and as such accountable and committed to a particular ethics. Transpositions occur by "regulated disassociation" of bonds that normally maintain cohesiveness (p. 5).

Trans is a prefix that denotes across, through, or beyond. Transversing from embodiment to trans theories of walking requires us to move beyond questions that position particular kinds of human experience at the centre. Participants in the audio walk not only listen to a sonic element, they walk and wash and fold clothes in a coin operated public laundry, thereby generating the performance through their own bodily labour. The mechanics of washing and folding are composed on the audio file so the actions become routine, conditioned by the habits of domestic soils and capitalism.

Jasbir Puar (2015) articulates trans, following Deleuzian thought, as "an ontological force that impels indeterminate movement rather than an identity that demands epistemological accountability" (59). As Eva Hayward and Jami

Weistein (2015) write, trans shifts the focus from a being or a thing to intensities and movement. Eva Hayward and Che Gossett (2017), like many of the scholars cited in this chapter, insist on a refusal of trans as a 'this to a that.' Such an understanding of trans is about a linear understanding of transition. Rather, trans, they argue, "repurposes, displaces, renames, replicates, and intensifies terms, adding yet more texture and the possibility of nearby-ness" (p. 21). Trans refutes the nature-culture divide proliferating in nonhuman forms. More importantly, Puar (2015) contends, trans includes the interventions of critical race studies and post-coloniality in posthuman or more-than-human conceptualizations of difference, where difference is not between entities, but constituted through movement and affect: a trans touching materiality. If the human is predicated on anti-Blackness, and slavery and settler colonization founded on animality and 'flesh' (Spillers, 2003) then trans as an undoing of animacy categories, foregrounds Black and Indigenous Studies (Hayward & Gossett, 2017). Abraham Weil (2017) writes that trans and Blackness are always associated with animality. He argues that therefore it's not an issue of one or the other, but their entangled linkages, or transversality. Trans for Weil becomes a process of pollination and murmuration, or what we'll refer to later in this chapter as viral.

Affective labour

Labour is addressed in the sonic walk through the intersections of reproductive labour, capitalism, and affective labour. Affective labor refers to the relationship between emotion and work (Vora, 2017). Affective labour is performed in the service industry and by maids, nannies, and sex workers. Affective labour produces commodities of care and comfort that are not physical objects but still circulate and are consumed. Affective labour, which is often performed by women and people of colour is linked to exploitation. Hochschild's (2012) work on emotional labour is significant here. Women, she contends, in the service of being kind and generous, make emotional work into resources that are then made profitable by patriarchy and capitalism. One example often given of affective labour are the smiles that service workers must deploy, which add value for their employers. The smile becomes the emotional product that circulates (Flowers and Swan, 2015; Hochschild, 2012).

WalkingLab collaborator Elaine Swan writes about the form of affective labour that is produced by walking tour guides. Walking tour guides, according to Swan, map out a safe route, facilitate comfort, and monitor the pace of the group. As "body work," a term Swan uses to discuss the affective labour of those in the service industry, this:

> entails specific types of gestures and bodily movements: such as walking in varying tempo and intensity: for instance, marching, setting the pace, leading from the front, walking backwards turning round to check everyone is there, slowly stopping, moving from a stop to ambling to striding.

> (2016, np)

These affective bodily labours, Flowers and Swan (2015) contend, are materialized along racialized, gendered, and ethnic axes.

Affective labour, Sara Ahmed (2015) writes on her *Feminist Killjoys* blog, is tricky business. For example, the labour of working against and to expose violence (such as naming institutionalized racism) might in fact render particular bodies to be perceived as causing violence. To labour against violence means you are going against institutionalized norms. To publicly interrogate institutional sexism means that you are against the institution. This labour, Ahmed states, is emotional and uncomfortable, but necessary. Thus, while some forms of affective labour, such as in the service industry, are exploited to make a profit, other forms of affective labour become obstacles in the production of neoliberalism and capitalism.

One of the ways that labour gets circumnavigated in walking research is the reliance on two specific tropes: the flâneur and the dérive. The flâneur emerged as a distinctive figure in early 19th-century Paris. He was portrayed as a disinterested, leisurely observer (invariably cis male) of the urban scene, taking pleasure in losing himself in the crowd and becoming a spectator. As an elite figure, the flâneur was able to wander the city, with no purpose or destination in mind. Strolling through the city the flâneur "stands apart from the city event as he appears to 'fuse' with it; he interprets each of its component parts in isolation in order, subsequently, to attain intellectual understanding of the who as a complex system of meaning" (Burton, 1994, p. 1). As Edmund White (2001) writes, "the flâneur is by definition endowed with enormous leisure, someone who can take off a morning or afternoon for undirected ambling, since a specific goal or a close ration of time is antithetical to the true spirit of the flâneur" (p. 39). The flâneur enjoys a tremendous amount of spare time, is free to move in urban space, and possesses the detachment of a scientist, although he often writes poetically. The flâneur remains anonymous and detached from the city and thus is supposedly able to observe the world around him. Walter Benjamin (2002) wrote extensively on, and popularized the anaesthesia of the flâneur. In the decades since, qualitative researchers, particularly those interested in urban ethnographies, use the flâneur as a methodology informing their practices. As Jamie Coates (2017) argues, the flâneur has taken on mythical qualities in research. He writes: "The rise of the flâneur in academic circles is often conflated with the practice of walking in the city in general and is used to describe any form of agency adopted to negotiate the flux of contemporary mobile urban life" (pp. 29–30). The flâneur's popularity, Coates (2017) insists, is due in part to mobile fieldwork practices, where the flâneur "became an icon of movement in the city and a methodology for understanding themes of embodiment and the urban" (p. 31). The flâneur, it is important to note, and his practice of wandering often referred to as flânerie, privilege the visual as a mode of observing and knowing the city. Moreover, as Coates (2017) notes, the flâneur is an alienated figure, part of the city and detached from it. As such, scholars like Sarah Pink (2009/2015) and Tim Ingold (2004) suggest the need to develop other walking practices that account for non-visual modes of being emplaced.

The idealized flâneur is a problematic genealogy for walking methodologies. In the 19th century it would have been impossible for a woman to walk the streets in the manner of a flâneur. In fact, had a woman taken up the same wandering she would have been marked as licentious and immoral, and associated with the figure of the prostitute – a 'street walker' (Wolff, 1985). Thus, the flâneur is consequently both gendered, racially, and geographically marked. Coates (2017) cautions researchers who use the flâneur as the basis for their ethnographic work, asking that they question their position (and those they walk with) in terms of race, class, gender, sexuality, and ability.

Instead of the flâneur, we need different conceptualizations of walking that deterritorialize what it means to move. For example, Eliza Chandler (2014), in her research into crip communities, recounts a story of walking in the city and the ways that her body is figured intersectionally as being in-place and different at the same time. Rather than an understanding of walking that normalizes particular movements, 'walking differently,' Chandler, contends, offers affirmative and relational ways of creating different communities, and as such re-image possible crip futures. Chandler's (2014) and Kafer's (2013) critical disability research emphasize the problematic images and representations, including those offered via walking, that need to be disrupted. Instead, of the strolling flâneur, Chandler's walking narratives of 'dragging legs, and tripping toes' enacts a different narrative of moving in the city. Much like Kafer's (2013) disruption of cripping nature and hiking trails, that we discuss in Chapter 1, Chandler problematizes the built environment with its uneven sidewalks and surface cracks. In another example, Garnett Cadogan (2016) details his experience of walking in New York City and the list of 'tactics' that as a Black man he has to employ: no running, no sudden movements, no objects in hand, no hoodies, and no loitering on street corners. Quite unlike the invisible and detached flâneur, Cadogan's 'tactics' emphasize the material realities of 'walking while Black.' These crucial contributions to walking research disrupt embodied understandings of walking as a meditative flow and as being co-extensive with place.

Throughout the 20th century, aesthetic and critical approaches developed in tandem with the flâneur, including work by the Dadaists and Situationists in France, and later with the psychogeographers in Britain. Psychogeography describes the effects of the geographical environment on the emotions and behaviours of individuals. In the 1920s, in Paris, the Dadaists staged a series of provocative 'events' in theatres and halls, and in the streets exploring on foot the banal places of the city (Sanouillet, 1965). In the 1950s the Situationists gave these practices a distinctive twist, changing the passive spectator into an active participant they sought to abolish the separation of art and life (Debord, 1958). One of the practices the group developed was known as the dérive, a 'drifting' on foot through urban spaces that would in turn produce alternative patterns of exploration and protest against the alienation of life under late capitalism. In the dérive walking becomes a means of shaking one's perception of everyday urban space while creating new meaning within it.

Deirdre (Dee) Heddon and Cathy Turner (2012) contend the history of walking research engenders a 'fraternity' in that it tends "towards an implicitly masculinist ideology. This frequently frames and valorizes walking as individualist, heroic, epic and transgressive" (p. 224). They remark that the legacy of the flâneur, the Romantic poets, and naturalists were founded on the ideas of adventure, danger, and the new. To walk was to "release oneself from the relations of everyday life" (p. 226). Henry David Thoreau, they observe, describes the walker as a crusader and errant knight, traversing the wild. Thus, walking is inscribed in ideologies of the human walker conquering nature. In such instances, the walker is presumed to be uninflected by gender and thus male, reinforcing the position of the autonomous male walker who leaves behind everything in order to tap into the wildness of place. An "uncomfortable undercurrent of misogyny and neocolonialism lurks within much psychogeography and has since its inception" (Rose, 2015, p. 150). Alexander Bridger (2009), working in the area of psychogeography and psychology, writes that a "feminist psychogeography should aim to study how the structure and content of gendered experience of place is determined by the nature of places themselves, and how our gendered experiences and behaviours can shape those places in turn" (p. 288). Yet, psychogeography, Heddon and Turner (2012) argue, has been burdened with detachment "without much concern for the specificity of one's own body and cultural position" (p. 227). There are a number of feminist psychogeographers and collectives that use the practices of the dérive to critique and subvert the myth of urban detachment.

Walking to the Laundromat resists the tropes of the visually privileged flâneur and queers the dérive, underscoring the labour, violence, and structures that enable some bodies to walk more freely. The audio track emphasizes the violence of labour and transnational mobility, and the performance, of washing clothes, walking, and returning repetitively to the laundromat, further positions the performance as itself a form of labour. Unlike the dérive, which is normalized as a strategy to transgress the city, Conroy's sonic walk was restricted, in the sense that one had to return to the washing machines periodically. While the Situations sought walking as a method to cast off usual relations, *Walking to the Laundromat*, through the labour of walking and washing, embodied affective labour.

We insist that walking researchers need to stop returning to the flâneur to contextualize their work, and instead consider transmaterial walking practices. Researchers must recognize that walking is not always a leisure activity, and that particular bodies already labour over walking as work. Additionally, while there are important strategies deployed by the dérive, it is imperative that researchers who use this technique in their work, remain critical and not assume that it is automatically radical. Some bodies literally walk on foot for miles carrying laundry, water, or other commodities. Examples of this kind of critical walking research can be found in Maggie O'Neill's (2017) 'methods on the move.' O'Neill uses walking and mapping to examine borders, risk, and belonging. Her extensive website and blog detail her transmaterial walking practice that is participatory and collaborative. Walking-with women in North England, who make use of a women's hostel, O'Neill notes that walking enables researchers and participants to think differently about marginalization and space. Physically moving through a city, participants reflect on borders, real and imagined, and articulate different practices of resilience and access.

Conroy's sonic walk, although quite different from O'Neill's ethnographic practice, similarly thinks about urban space, access, and labour associated with walking, borders, and mobility. The sonic walk disrupts the occularcentrism of the flâneur, focusing instead on sounds, bodies, and transmigratory spaces. Conroy's sonic walk connects to her ongoing work into labour and economy. She writes:

> There is something deceptive about the humble washing machine that makes it hide in plain sight. Is it the manner in which something dirty and experienced with life could be returned to its owner with a sweet smelling new lease on life; a fresh start, sans stains – a new you? The same threaded garment, now with micro particles of soil extracted, ready to start again. Each time, less innocent than before.
>
> (2017, np)

One of the many projects Conroy is working on is an artist-led laundromat, where money generated through the laundromat would feed back into artistic funding and support. Reconfiguring the laundromat as a collective labour, is a subversive device. She writes:

> More than this, the idea of 'folding into' and symbiotically hosting an arts practice and arts space within a functioning artist-run business brings with it all the interesting complications and connotations that come with gendered labour, the rise of affective and intangible capital, and the entrepreneurial zeal that is rampant neoliberalism.
>
> (2017, np)

On the audio track we hear:

> *prepare your laundry detergent and reflect on the nitrogen infused waters that will soon empty into the sea. Increasing the algae swarms and killing plankton.*

Walking to the Laudromat interrogates the ways that capitalism and neoliberalism render some lives disposable, and asserts the violence and Whiteness of colonial sovereignty. The laundromat is both a space of care and cruelty. Conroy describes her project through three threads: mindfulness and penetration; invisible leaking bodies; and viral strategies. The mindfulness soundtrack questions the ways in which mental illness and the internalization of labour impacts productivity. Women's bodies and labour are foregrounded on the soundtrack and in the physical walk to and from the laundromat. Washing clothes, for instance, is outsourced labour that is shifted to racialized and poor bodies. These gendered laboring bodies are perceived as excess matter, and as such function as surplus value. The laundromat as a subversive performance space becomes a viral strategy.

The audio walk takes up the issue of necropolitics, where queer, trans, and racialized populations are subject to occupation, conquest, and elimination.

Necropolitics asserts that the ultimate expression of sovereignty is the power and capacity to decide who can live and who can die (Mbembe, 2003). Elijah Edelman's (2014) research into 'walking while trans' underscores how brown trans feminine bodies are constructed and articulated through heteronationalistic understandings of a viable life. Brown trans feminine bodies are marked simultaneously as dangerous and in need of regulation. They are perceived as threats to social order because they are perceived as 'sex workers,' and should therefore be controlled, while at the same time rendered disposable and open to attacks, which are often underreported or erased by the very forces that should protect them. Bodily labour – whether it's laundry, care work, or under paid service work – "permits the healthy life of some populations to necessitate the death of others, marked as nature's degenerate or unhealthy ones" (Clough, 2008, p. 18). The performance of doing laundry while walking and listening to the audio track further emphasizes the hapticality of gendered labour and disposable bodies. Public laundromats, unlike private and often 'sanitary' private home washing facilities, emphasize the toxicity of laundry detergents through the strong odors and the intensive hum of multiple machines. These affects, as we described in Chapter 2, stick to certain bodies – labouring bodies, immigrant bodies, gendered bodies – rendering them smelly, noisy, and toxic. Other contemporary artists, like Tarsh Bates (2017) explore transmateriality in artistic practices, baking bread with the yeast *Candida alicans* that is then served to public audiences. Similar projects, like Jess Dobkin's *Lactation Station Breast Milk Bar* (Springgay, 2011b), and Dobkin and Springgay's *The Artist's Soup Kitchen* (www.theartistsoupkitchen.com) speak to the ways that trans underscores the viral intra-actions between multiple bodies.

As a sonic walk, the project, also emphasizes the relationship between sound, movement, and labour. Walking between washing and drying cycles, participants listen to various recorded sounds and are simultaneously confronted with the sounds of traffic, street crowds, and the occasional sirens. In the laundromat, the intense hum of the machines press upon the participant bodies the intensity and force of the sounds of labour. Sounds operate in contemporary society to regulate and code bodies. For instance, the sounds emanating from gentrified urban spaces, such as hotel lobbies and trendy clothing stores, are markedly different from the ones that feature prominently in Conroy's sonic walk. Corporations often market particular sound tracks that are played over and over again as part of their branding. These sounds convey a sense of orderliness and conviviality. An example, could be the sound track played in the lobby of the W Hotels worldwide. In addition to a branded scent that greets visitors the minute they step into the hotel, particular sounds (a compilation of easy music) are used to suggest cleanliness, uniformity, and regulation. These are directly linked to neoliberalism and White supremacy, where the sounds, smells, and leakages of inhuman bodies are made to disappear. The laundromat, whether in the basement of a large hotel, or a public facility on a street corner, contradicts these sterilized sounds.

Transspecies and the viral

Building on Alaimo's (2010; 2016) transcorporeality, we turn to Julie Livingston and Jasbir Puar (2011), who summon the term interspecies to refer to "relationships between different forms of biosocial life and their political effects" (p. 3) Interspecies theories and research insists that the human can no longer be the dominant subject of analysis. Referring to the body of literature within animal studies that traces anthropocentrism, anthropomorphic projection, incorporation and invasion, transmutation, and exotic alterity, Livingston and Puar (2011) write about the productive tensions between the growing body of scholarship called posthumanism and transspecies theories. They note that while posthumanism seeks to "destabilize the centrality of human bodies and their purported organic boundedness," not all posthuman scholarship attends to a posthuman politics in that they "unwittingly reinscribe the centrality of human subject formation and, thus, anthropomorphism" (Livingston & Puar, 2011, p. 4). Consequently, an optimistic reading of posthumanism proliferates another version of humanism where some bodies remain less than human. As a transmaterial project the extra-sensory sounds and smells of the laundromat signal migratory crossings of domestic (illegal) labour, further troubling terms like transnationalism, translation, transmigration, and transspecies.

In opposition to posthumanism, which Livingston and Puar contend, is grounded in neoliberal Western European conceptualizations of subjectivity, interspecies "offers a broader geopolitical understanding of how the human/animal/plant triad is unstable and varies across time and space" (Livingston & Puar 2011, p. 5). Interspecies also departs from privileged sites in posthuman work – the human and the animal – or what Donna Haraway calls companion species, to include "'incompanionate' pests, microscopic viruses, and commodified plants – in other words, forms of life with which interspecies life may not be so obvious or comfortable" (Livingston & Puar 2011, p. 4).

Aristotle's animacy taxonomy continues to render some entities as alive and others excluded from the hierarchical chain (Chen, 2012). According to Aristotle, things that eat, reproduce, and grow can possess a soul and are therefore 'alive.' What transspecies emphasizes is that the human and nonhuman entanglements stretch beyond human and animal, or human and already considered forms of 'life,' to include the animacy of Land, water, and other entities that have traditionally be denied of life. Eliza Steinbock, Marianna Szczygielska, and Anthony Wagner (2017) in their editorial introduction on *Tranimacies*, write that trans "enmeshes . . . transgender, animal, amimacy, intimacy" (p. 1). The frictional intimacies of trans undoes the animacy hierarchies. The voice on the audio file states:

> *Transformation of salary to employee into human capital . . . facilitated by contemporary management techniques: individuation . . . subjectification and exploitation . . . capital reaches deep and penetrates soul*

In one instance, the audio file suggests an openness to neoliberalism, echoing the techniques used on self-help audio books and by meditation specialists. But other discordant sounds sweep in and the viral penetration undoes these tidy, human-centric narratives. 'Being open' becomes transspecially linked to exploitation and environmental degradation.

Colebrook (2015) introduces another trans concept – transitivity – which emphasizes the linkages and intra-actions between entities that are non-linear. For Colebrook 'transitive indifference' undoes the notion of difference 'from.' When things are set against one another, and are different from each other, one entity remains in the centre, and is the basis for comparison and measurement. For example, when a human is said to be different from an animal, this continues to structure a binary or a taxonomy of difference. Indifference for Colebrook (2015) stresses the self-differentiating singularities of becoming. The audio track and performance of walking and washing is an instantiation of transitive indifference: the dirty laundry, washing machines, water, laboring bodies, dirt, and money are not distinct and different entities from one another, but together they create various flowing assemblages. These assemblages have vectors, speeds, rests, modes of expression and desiring tonalities (Deleuze & Guattari, 1987). Kathryn Yusoff (2013) uses the idea of indifference to suggest that our responses to events must be indifferent. By this she means response-ability cannot position the human as the axis by which or through which we care.

Carla Freccero (2011) uses the term transpecies to invoke a form of becoming that breaks down species taxonomies questioning origins and materializations of classification hierarchies. Trans is less 'place bound,' and more like the concept of ecology often invoked in posthuman discourse, and as such interrogates the logic of human exceptionalism and heteronormative reproduction (Livingston and Puar, 2011). This is enacted in the sonic walk through the following narrative:

> *centuries of exploitation – recycled as share economy that turns out to not care at all – dirty female bodies violated in capital's time – bio-political context is a ground to investigate the relationship between affect and value.*

Karen Barad (2015) forms another reading of trans as a process of self-touching animacy, regeneration, and recreation. Drawing from studies in quantum field theory, Barad deconstructs the reductionist ontology of classical physics and describes instead how indeterminancy is entangled through all being. For Barad, matter operates agentially, "where trans is not a matter of changing in time, from this to that, but an undoing of 'this' and 'that,' an ongoing reconfiguring of space-timemattering" (2015, p. 411). Trans unravels a reliance on difference that situates something as *different from*, which emphasizes a fixity of one term over the other. Trans for Barad is about a "radical undoing of 'self,' or individualism" (2015, p. 411). Trans, as we're building in this chapter, emphasizes movement as flows, vectors, and affective tonalities. Trans shifts the focus from a being or a thing, to intensities and movement.

Listening to Conroy's sound track while doing laundry transcorporeally connects affects with amniotic fluids, menstrual blood, and breast milk, bodily effluences that also stick to some bodies and demarcate them as less than human (Springgay & Freedman, 2010). Molding the clothes into soppy bundles, participants listen to audio compositions that connect laundry detergent to fish, finance capitalism, and menstrual blood. As participants drop their coins into the coin-operated machines, Conroy's voice links biopower to forms of financialization that obscure material bodies and labour. We hear:

Women's laboring bodies are made to disappear. Birthing labour – giving birth to bodies that are transformed into human capital. Financialization. Promise of salvation lies in the return in investment – get out more than what we put in!

Although she does not evoke the prefix trans, Lisa Blackman's (2012) work on mediation and affect underscores rhythm's transmutation, as gaps are created between relational connections and affective intensities. *Walking to the Laundromat* operates at this affective threshold. Rather than a sonic walk that represents affective labor, the threshold operates affectively, pushing the force of movement (walking and doing laundry) against the sonic vibrations on the audio file. This creates a temporal space between the actions and what one hears during the walking performance.

Enacting transmateriality the sonic walk asks questions about a more-than-human conceptualization of embodiment. Like Chen's (2012) work on animacy hierarchies, Colebrook (2014) maintains that the limit of a humanist conceptualization of embodiment is that it excludes that which is "in a form of rampant and unbounded mutation" (136). She notes that a virus cannot be defined as "embodied" because it's not a living system: it exists only as a parasite. Viral life is a "process of invasion, in flux and (to a great extent) non-relation" (Colebrook, 2014: 136). For Colebrook, an understanding of humanistic embodiment does not move us towards an ethics of the future. She speculates on how to re-think embodiment in such a way as to consider in-organic potentialities, a kind of trans viral politics where there's no self-defining body, only mutant encounters.

Walking to the Laundromat enacts a virality of mutation through intensities of affect – sounds, vibrations, and repeated rhythms – and by thinking transmaterially across different bodies and spaces. The audio walk demonstrates how humanist critiques of capitalism are inadequate to the task of explaining the history of exploitation or the consequences of neoliberalism. As Puar (2013) states, virality underscores the "multiplication and proliferation of difference, of making difference and proliferating creative differentiation: becoming otherwise of difference" (p. 41).

Puar (2013) notes that virality, as "intensified speed," most notably that of the internet, "also refers to indiscriminant exchanges, often linked with notions of bodily contamination, uncontainability, unwelcome transgression of border and

boundaries while pointing more positively to the porosity, indeed the conviviality, of what has been treated as opposed" (p. 42). The audio track emphasizes this
bodily contamination – bodies leak, money is laundered, water bodies are toxic,
each penetrating the other. The voice on the audio track hints at the impossibility
of removing these contaminations. They are permanent stains. The voice over
says emphatically:

> *Out, dammed spot!*

Puar (2013) uses the idea of the viral to untether sexuality from identity and het-
ero reproduction, in order to think about sexuality "as assemblages of sensations,
affects and forces" (p. 24). The viral, Puar and Clough (2012) note, is important because it is an assemblage that transforms through replication as difference
(where difference is indifference not difference from). They write:

> In its replications, the virus does not remain the same, nor does that which
> it confronts and transits through. Viral replication swerves from the perfor-
> mative "repetition with a difference"; it is replication without reproduction,
> without fidelity, without durability.
>
> (p. 14)

Hayward's (2010; 2015) use of the term 'tranimal' similarly reconfigures heteronormative sexuality and reproduction. For Hayward, tranimal perverts an understanding of embodiment that relies on bounded and distinct entities, to consider
reproduction as "excess, profusion, surplus" (p. 590). Trans, for Hayward, like
many of the scholars we include in this chapter, is about a kind of viral movement.
This isn't a movement from one point to another. Rather it replicates as difference.
In the viral, difference is affective and affecting modulation. It is speculative, activating potentiality and futurity through mutant replication. Conroy's performance
operates transitively with her other current projects, which re-think artistic production and capital. As viral strategies, the sonic walk and her many laundromat
projects, shift from a critique of 'what is the matter with capitalism?' to a mutant,
virally reproducing, affective site that has the potential to re-imagine labour in
different terms. While viruses operate parasitically and they penetrate a host, they
are not adjacent to or simply touching a host, but alter and stretch the host. The
voice and sounds on the audio track are viral, linking together neoliberalism, environmental degradation, rampant individualism, and reproduction for profit. As we
fill our washing machine with dirty clothes, the corporate mindfulness voice on
the audio track states:

> *Don't think about all the well-known politicians, thugs, rapists, international
> businessmen getting away with the money laundering – it's just business as
> usual. Don't think about the great barrier reef, hospitals under austerity
> measures.*
> *Breathe. Gratitude.*

I'm known for my positive energy and abundant lifestyle ... money flows freely and abundantly into my life ... I love having a prosperous career ... I'm surrounded by people who are eager to contribute to my abundance ...

In shifting from embodied theories that perpetuate a coherent sense of subjectivity, trans theories insist on an ethical-politics of walking. Thinking alongside transpeciation, Myra Hird (2006) argues that trans interrogates the idea that there is ever a natural body – the one we are born with – which must also parallel particular normative behaviours and desires. Trans, according to Camille Nurka (2015) "radically reinvigorates posthumanism as a decentering exercise, in which the human vis-a-vis nature is repositioned in terms of fluid relationality" (p. 220).

Personal growth and wellbeing are mapped on the logic of capital accumulation. Self-realization means maximizing our capacity to be productive, to accrue social, cultural and sexual capital.

Dislodge affective labour from capitalism.

Feminists have long argued that bodies' capacities to think and act are affected by the environments in which they move, or are prevented from moving. Furthermore, biocapital insists that bodies are never enough – healthy enough, wealthy enough, relaxed enough – and thus are "always in a debilitated state in relation to what one's bodily capacity is imagined to be" (Puar 2009: 167).

Service economy. Human form – bent over. Fordism (1930s) new industrialism – not previous capitalism of before but a new kind of man. An assembly line man. Gendered division of social labour. Supportive wife. Fordist labour. 9–5. Factory time – bend to demands of capital.

Women's bodies the most flexible, bendable, prone.

Mould clothes into shape of a small human put it in dryer (furnace)

As Puar states, while some bodies are prevented from, for example, poor health, other bodies are offered, or made available, for injury precisely because they are expendable in order to "sustain capitalist narratives of progress" (Puar 2009, p. 168). Cycling back through our load of laundry, the bodies of immigrant labor that operate coin laundromats or work as domestic workers in private homes, often for long hours and for inadequate pay, are disposable labor because they are never fully human. The voice over asks the participants to 'separate and sort,' to become part of the 'devastating tangle of clothing.' The invisible labourer – in their shops, laundromats, and restaurants – press on our soapy, soggy, pile of clothes. If washing your clothes is part of a particular notion of what it means to have a viable life, of maintaining a particular understanding of what it means to be human, Conroy's transmaterial sonic walk ruptures the common place understandings we have of the sounds and smells of clean laundry. The discordant sounds on the audio file, the loud drone of the industrial washing machines, and the toxic smells of too much detergent, pressed upon the walkers an intensity that was not easily remedied.

Trans theories are invested in thinking about assemblages and viral replication rather than heteronormative future-oriented reproduction. Trans insists that the transitive state is not that some bodies matter while others continue to perish. Rather, "what is reproduced is not the human subject, identity, or body, but affective tendencies, ecologies of sensation, and different ontologies that create new epistemologies of affect" (Puar, 2013, p. 43). Trans emphasizes movement and vectors.

Clean garments: create a cloth uterus

Walking to the Laundromat as a transmaterial practice emphasizes the underpaid, repetitive, and bodily labour of service work. The project intervenes into the comfortable ways that walking is described as relational and convivial, recognizing that not all bodies move freely and that walking itself is a form of labour. Departing from the privileged strolls of the flâneur, whose approach to cosmopolitanism is feigned detachment, Conroy's sonic walk emphasizes the specificity of bodily labour, and the violence and necropolitics of capitalism and transnational movements. If the flâneur symbolizes a universal method of seeing and experiencing the city, *Walking to the Laudromat*, as situated and accountable to networks of risk and harm that constitute our world, enacts an opposition.

The soundtrack for the sonic walk combines narratives regarding transmaterial gendered labour with narratives that parody mindfulness meditation, self-help audio books, and holistic healing dogma. For example, we hear in the tone of mindfulness affirmations:

> *I believe in me . . . I am swimming in a sea of wealth . . . and money keeps flowing to me . . . I am open to receiving money now . . . I am brilliant . . . I am open . . . I am mentally willing to receive . . . I am following my intuition . . .*

What Conroy's audio track makes clear is the way that embodiment, as a form of mind-body awareness and mediation, has been co-opted by neoliberalism. Self-actualization and awareness runs parallel to neoliberalist ideals of independence, autonomy, and success. Using the methods from relaxation techniques – which include stillness, breath work, and visualization – the sonic walk points at the ways these techniques in fact discipline, regulate, and render bodies compliant. Embodiment manifested as self-help, acts to transform the human from the inside and does little to account for wider social, economic, and political networks. As the soundtrack affirms our place in capitalism, *I am swimming in a sea of wealth*, participants drop their dirty underwear into a soapy washing machine. The automatic and repetitive acts of doing laundry simultaneously enact life affirmations of becoming clean and free from burdens. We hear on the audio track:

> *Say goodbye to your dirty deeds . . . Let the great unwashed be washed.*

Swan (2016) uses the term 'body work' to talk about affective labour in the service economy. Body work can also denote the corporatization and whitening of bodily practices such as yoga, meditation, and tai chi, which aim to bring about a greater unity between mind and body. This is the body work that is valued in neoliberalism. But body work continues to render a distinction and divide between different bodies. Not all forms of body work are embodied, mindful, and affirmative, and not all body work is valued on a personal level. Embodied affirmations as escape mechanisms render other forms of bodily labour invisible, and create a distinction between valuable lives and pathological lives. 'I' am worthy, useful, productive and prosperous. 'I' am important.

> *I manifest more abundance . . . my prosperity thoughts create my prosperous world . . . I have a large and steady permanent financial income . . . Breathe in servitude. Breathe out longitude*

In bringing trans theories to bear on walking research we open up and re-configure different corporeal imaginaries, both human and nonhuman that are radically immanent and intensive, as an assemblage of forces and flows that open bodies to helices and transconnections. Trans activates a thinking-in-movement. By conceptualizing walking methodologies as trans, we shift from thinking of movement as transition (from one place to another) or as transgression (that somehow walking is an alternative and thereby empowering methodology), towards trans as transcorporeal, transitive, transspecies, and viral in order to activate the ethical-political indifferentiation of movement. Trans activates new ways to talk about, write about, and do walking methodologies that take account of viral, mutant replication, and recognize the intra-active becomings of which we are a part.

4 An immanent account of movement in walking methodologies

Re-thinking participation beyond
a logic of inclusion

This chapter engages with mass forms of walking such as processions and group movement practices informed by parkour, wayfinding, and orienteering to consider *participation* from a vital and materialist perspective. Participation is typically framed as democratic interaction where individuals come together by choice, and as a convivial mode of collectivity. Participation is valued as emancipatory, liberatory, and transformative. The problem with this understanding of participation is that while it seems to promote diversity and equity, it operates as a symbolic gesture that fails to undo the structural logics of racism, ableism, homophobia, and settler colonialism. Furthermore, participation in contemporary art practices assumes audiences become active in the work versus passive spectators. This produces a false binary between active participation and passive viewing. Despite these challenges, participation, we contend, is important in walking research and as such we need different ways to think about participation's potential. In this chapter we ask: *How might vital, material, and immanent theories ask different questions about the* how *of coming together and taking part?*

This chapter considers three different walking projects in order to think about participation beyond a rhetoric of inclusion. The first walking project is *Ring of Fire*, a contemporary art event that resulted in a procession for the opening of the Parapan American Games – a multi-sport event – held in Toronto in 2015. The second, *The Warren Run*, was a running-orienteering race executed in an urban neighbourhood in Sydney, Australia, which took participants through private properties, inside houses, through backyards and over fences. The final project we think-with is *White Cane Amplified*, a performance in which a cane used by a walker who is visually impaired is replaced by a megaphone. Projects like *Ring of Fire*, *The Warren Run* and *White Cane Amplified* are commonly understood as participatory art projects because groups of people come together to participate in the work alongside the artist; participation makes the work function.

The main thesis of this chapter is a critique of participation as inclusion. To do this, we use a number of exciting and valuable walking projects. In the first section of the chapter we analyze how inclusion operates to normalize and commodify difference. We use Heather Sykes' (2016; 2017) concepts "taking part" and "taking place" (p. 55) and critical disability scholars Jasbir Puar (2017), Margaret Shildrick (2015), and Alison Kafer's (2013) critiques of rehabilitation, to examine the ways that inclusion in events like *Ring of Fire* and the Parapan Am Games produces and maintains settler colonialism and White ableist homonationalism. In the next section, we discuss *The Warren Run*, and the ways in which participation framed as inclusion in public art projects diffuses conflict, dissension, and difference through convivial notions of relationality. Our critiques aim to demonstrate the failure of thinking about participation as inclusion, rather than the limits of these particular projects. Following the crucial critiques of inclusion, we draw on theories of immanent movement, to ask questions about how we might think differently about participation. Participation, we contend, is important to walking research but needs to be understood beyond a rhetoric of inclusion. To do so, we return to *Ring of Fire* and *The Warren Run*, and introduce a third project, *White Cane Amplified*, to argue that participation begins before the invitation of inclusion commences. To conclude we offer an analysis of participation that is composed from within, is immanent, vital, and of difference.

Taking part and taking place

Ring of Fire was a 300-person street procession created by Trinidadian artist Marlon Griffith and performed for the opening of the Parapan Am Games in Toronto, August 2015. Griffith's project, commissioned by the Art Gallery of York University, was a two-year residency, where Griffith worked with a number of diverse groups in the city to develop, create, and eventually perform the procession. *Ring of Fire* used the form of a Trinidadian Carnival 'mas' and the 'mas camp' as a site of collaborative and pedagogical exchange. Mas, as we discuss next, are large-scale performances, processions that incorporate movement and costumes. *Ring of Fire* brought together disability dancers from Picasso Pro (a non-profit organization working with deaf and disabled artists), Equal Grounds (a social enterprise group that works with individuals with accessibility needs), and the Mississaugas of the New Credit First Nation (an Ojibway First Nation located in Brantford, Ontario). Alternative Roots, a youth group based in New Credit, created the music for the procession in collaboration with the SKETCH band (a community-arts-development initiative based in Toronto that engages young people who are homeless or on the margins), and the movement and spoken word poetry developed across the project as a whole. Members from Escola de Capuera Angola, and Toronto's Capoeira community, along with youth spoken word poets from the Jane-Finch, Malvern, and Regent Park areas of Toronto also collaborated on the project.

The mas tradition has its roots in Trinidadian culture, when plantation owners would host masquerade balls in the days leading up to Lent. Slaves, who could not take part in these festivities, created their own counter-colonial events, which became the precursor to the Carnival. While music, dancing, and drumming are important components to Carnival, elaborate costumes, often designed and assembled in 'mas camps' by artists, designers, and local community members, are key aspects of the Carnival aesthetic. Mas refers to both the costumes and the performance, which is often denoted as to 'play mas.' The mas form was already a common practice in Toronto because of the annual Toronto Caribbean Carnival 'Caribana,' which has run since 1967. This event includes a grand parade, mas bands, costumes, and performances.

During the two-year-long participatory project, performative forms of cultural resistance – such as the Pow Wow, capoeira, and spoken word poetry – interrogated issues related to access and mobility. Movement workshops, music and dance, Pow Wows, and spoken word poetry shaped the methodological practice by which the concepts for the procession emerged. While the final procession manifests as a public and visible component of the project, the workshops and other micro projects, many of which included movement and walking, compose the project as a whole. For the purpose of this chapter, we focus on the culminating procession, and its more public dimension of participation.

Ring of Fire is inspired by the Anishinaabe Seven Grandfather Teachings: Wisdom, Courage, Respect, Honesty, Humility, Truth, and Love. These teachings serve as the basis for the organizational structure of the procession as well as guide the methodologies of participation. Young spoken word poets played the roles of orators in the procession. The procession also featured seven large-scale, elaborately costumed Sentinel characters. A costumed Entourage of over 70 individuals accompanied the main Sentinel characters and were played by members of Picasso Pro, Equal Grounds, the Mississaugas of the New Credit First Nation, Capoeira Angola, and youth artists who had worked on the project at each of the community-driven mas camps. In addition, a call was put out for members of the Toronto community, or those coming to Toronto for the games, to participate in the 300-person procession.

The Parapan Am Games began in 1999 in Mexico City, and included 18 countries and four sports. The games function as a regional qualifying event for the Paralympics. In 2007, the Rio Pan Am and Parapan Am were held in the same city and organized by one overarching committee. The impetus behind the Parapan Am Games are to elevate the Paralympic status and to promote accessibility within sport. The 2015 games were held in Toronto, and four additional communities including Markham, Mississaugua, Milton, and Whitby, which are located adjacent to Toronto and together compose the 'Golden Horseshoe.' Some 1608 athletes from 28 countries participated in 15 sports, and the total budget for both Pan Am and Parapan Am was $2.4 billion.

Sport mega-events like the Olympics and the Parapan Am Games operate as corporate, neoliberal sites of homonationalism, crip nationalism, and settler colonialism (Puar, 2017; Sykes, 2016). Homonationalism, according to Jasbir Puar (2007) is the patriotic inclusion of Western liberal gay subjects that produces "convivial rather than antagonistic relations" (p. 49). Homonationalism, writes Richard Fung (2013), appears in Canadian policies that oppose gay rights, while simultaneously using gay rights to criticize countries such as Iran and Uganda. LGBTQ2S rights are "being appropriated and deployed" for nationalist agendas (Fung, 2013, np.). Heather Sykes (2016) provides the example of Pride Houses, in the Vancouver 2010 Olympics. These houses were developed as spaces for gay and lesbian supporters to watch and celebrate events. However, while marketed as creating safe and inclusive spaces, and used to promote diversity in the Olympics, they also contributed significantly in generating revenue and spectators. In this instance, Sykes (2016) notes, the Pride Houses were both symbols of equity and neoliberal consumption. The inclusion of LGBTQ2S individuals normalizes queer bodies to promote Canada as a multicultural and tolerant nation. Inclusivity becomes a symbolic gesture, but does not interrogate the systemic structures of state violence against queer bodies.

Sykes (2016) offers the useful concepts of "taking part" and "taking place" to analyze the logics of inclusivity (p. 55). 'Taking part' celebrates queer, disabled, and Indigenous participation in mega events. In 'taking part,' participation is understood as a form of inclusion. Different subjectivities are invited to take part in the event to make the event appear multicultural and diverse. However, 'taking part,' Sykes contends, fails to undo the structural logics of racism, homophobia, ableism, and settler colonialism. Inclusivity, in this sense, is a form of tokenism.

'Taking place,' Sykes's other concept, perpetuates the displacement of Indigenous peoples from their traditional territories. For example, while queer and Indigenous Two-Spirit people were invited to take part in the Vancouver 2010 Olympics, Indigenous peoples were displaced in order for the sporting event to take place. Sykes (2016) provides the following comment: "Two-Spirit youth were displaced from their community services; Indigenous communities were displaced from their unceded traditional territories by ski resorts; and settlers' property laws about owning land displaced indigenous principles of shared responsibility for the land" (p. 55). In addition to critiques of homonationalism, Sykes (2016) contends that mega sport events are linked to settler colonialism. Settler colonialism, write Kate McCoy, Eve Tuck and Marcia McKenzie (2016), is the ongoing practice of settler occupation, which results in the forced removal and the disappearance of Indigenous peoples from traditional territories. Sykes (2016) writes that the Olympic celebration: "draws attention away from ongoing Colonial realities in Canada" (p. 55).

Ring of Fire was part of the opening events for the Parapan Am games. Participating in the procession were the Mississaugas of the New Credit First Nation, youth from under-served communities in Toronto, capoeira and disability dancers, and members of the general public. Opening ceremonies, argues Sykes (2016), "allow host nations to momentarily display histories of colonial contact and even conflict, quickly and colorfully moving into nationalist, multi-ethnic scenes of inclusion and reconciliation" (p. 50). *Ring of Fire*'s inclusivity functioned symbolically, joining together different regions of the city and different communities, and celebrated different cultures, races, and bodies. This is what Janice Forsyth (2016) would call the "illusion of inclusions" (p. 23). The inclusion of Indigenous people serves to regulate the debilitating relationship between Indigenous peoples and the Olympic committee.

'Taking part' operates as an "absent presence" (Sykes, 2016, p. 60) where the inclusion and visibility of diverse bodies naturalizes and neutralizes their ongoing oppression and debilitation. Inviting Indigenous people to participate in mega sports events and the procession is in fact a practice of managing dissent (Adese,

2012). Working in conjunction with 'taking part' is the way that mega events 'take place' from Indigenous peoples. Although the Mississaugas of the New Credit First Nation were invited as official hosts to the Parapan Am games in Toronto, and collaborated with the artist Marlon Griffith to create and perform *Ring of Fire*, the development of new sports centres and event spaces throughout the greater Toronto region, continued to 'take place' from the Mississaugas of the New Credit First Nation and other Indigenous peoples. Sporting events and the art and cultural events of the opening and closing ceremonies give visible "bodily form to the nation" (Zaiontz, 2016, p. 75).

Rehabilitation as inclusion

Puar (2017) has similarly argued that crip nationalism privileges some forms of disability and mobilizes disability in order to maintain White supremacy. Shifting from a disability rights discourse that understands disability as an exception that can be overcome, epitomized by the inclusion of the 'super crip' athlete in Mega sporting events, Puar turns to the biopolitics of debility. Racism, lack of medical care, settler colonialism, occupation, and incarceration are all tactical practices deployed by the State to create and maintain precarious populations through debilitation. Debilitation as such is endemic rather than exceptional. Debilitation is necessary and required for profit and expansion of the nation. In this sense then inclusion functions to produce and sustain debility.

Disability studies scholars are similarly critical about inclusionary logics whereby non-normative bodies have to be re-habilitated as part of their participation (Shildrick, 2015; Titchkosky, 2011). For example, normative discourse around disability and mega sports suggests that prosthetics (e.g. prosthetic limbs) enhance mobility and performance, thus rendering the disabled body able. The disabled body overcomes and transcends limitations through the use of technology. Similar to homonationalism that normalizes queer bodies to serve the Nation, mega sport events promote the 'supercrip,' the athlete who against all odds has successfully risen above their disability (Kafer, 2013; Puar, 2017). "Supercrip stories," writes Kafer (2013) "rely heavily on the individual/medical model of disability, portraying disability as something to be overcome through hard work and perseverance" (p. 141). In overcoming their disability through the use of prosthetics and sport, the disabled athlete becomes normalized and thus able-bodied.

The 'absent presence' then of disability within mega sports continues to undermine and dehumanize differently abled bodies. Deana Leahy and Jo Pike's (2015) work in education, similarly critiques the ways in which different bodies are made to conform and to avoid risk in order to support neoliberal notions of a happy and healthy body. The continued pathologization of difference, and the inclusionary politics of diversity, require differently abled bodies to appear able and useful.

Kafer (2013) argues for a political/relational model of disability that focuses less on the individual or medical approach to inclusion and more on the political materialization of disablement. This is similarly explained by Shildrick (2015) who writes:

for many disabled people, rehabilitation to normative practice or normative appearance is no longer the point; instead, the lived experience of disability – with its embodied absences, displacements, and prosthetic additions – generates, at the very least, its own specific possibilities that both limit and extend the performativity of the self.

(p. 14)

For example, Sunaura Taylor (2010) who navigates the city in an automatic wheelchair due to a disability went on a walk with Judith Butler through San Francisco's Mission District and had a conversation about accessibility. Taylor (2010) uses the term *walking* to describe her mobility in a wheelchair. She states: "I use that word even though I can't physically walk. I mean. To me, I think the experience of going for a walk is probably very similar to anybody else's: it's a clearing of the mind, it's enjoying whatever I'm walking past. And my body is very involved even though I'm physically not walking" (p. 186).

Rather than a 'taking part,' which continues to pathologize the differently abled body, critical disability and crip scholars like Kafer (2013) and Shildrick (2015) insist that the body-technology-environment be understood not as a supportive device that helps an individual overcome limitations, but as moving assemblage that has different configurations and rhythms. Wheelchair users and those who use other mobility and assistive devices were encouraged to participate in the *Ring of Fire* procession, and to work with Marlon over long periods of time to co-develop the choreography. Their participation countered the idea of 'absent present' by inserting new representations and images which offer expanded possibilities for what a body can do (Rice, Chandler, Liddiar, Rinaldi, & Harrison, 2016).

If *participation as inclusion* continues to normalize and pathologize different bodies, maintaining White, ableist, heteronormative, settler colonialism then what other ways can we think-with participatory projects like *Ring of Fire*? What gestures will create new trajectories, as Erin Manning (2016) states, from which "the potential of the *what else* emerges" (p. 203)? It is crucial, we argue, that participation move beyond the logics of inclusion, but in doing so we must find ways to think about the affirmative potential of participation.

Rosi Braidotti (2013) continually argues for an affirmative politics and feminist posthuman ethics. For Braidotti affirmative politics generates possible futures. This is a mode of thinking-doing that is anticipatory and creative rather than destructive. But affirmation should not be understood as the opposite of critical or as celebratory. Affirmation is not comforting. Affirmation "invent[s] conditions for new ways of activating the threshold of experience, new ways of experimenting in the complexity of what does not easily fold into a smooth surface" (Manning, 2016, p. 202). If participation as inclusion closes things in on itself, keeping things tidy, cohesive, and comfortable, then we need a way to think about participation that "keeps things unsettled, a push that ungrounds, unmoors, even as it propels" (Manning, 2016, p. 202). We attend to these matterings later in the chapter, in the section on movement. In the next section, we examine another project, *The Warren Run*, a parkour-influenced orienteering run to further explore the inclusionary rhetoric of participation as it surfaces in art writing.

Conviviality and conflict-free participation

The Warren Run explores movement through running races such as marathons, orienteering activities, and parkour. *The Warren Run*, created by artist Matt Prest, was a participatory art event in a residential suburban area called 'The Warren,' in the suburb of Marrickville in Sydney's inner-west. 'The Warren' was first a Victorian-Gothic mansion in Marrickville south built in 1857. It was given that name because its owner stocked the grounds with rabbits for hunting. In 1884, the land was subdivided and sold off, taking on many different buildings and identities until 1922 when the land was further subdivided to build a housing estate for returned soldiers from WWI. The area is still referred to as The Warren, although for many of the locals the history of the original mansion is lost. 'The Warren' remains an apt term because the houses are tightly packed together, the streets run at odd angles, and one can get easily disoriented or made to feel like you are in a rabbit hole. This is the land of the Cadigal Wangal clans of the Eora nation.

The concept for the art project was to have a running race in a suburban area, which took participants through residents' private properties, inside houses, through backyards, and over fences. The work aimed to disrupt the normal flow of human traffic through a typical suburban area, breaking some of the rules of this type of residential space and how we engage with it physically. Additionally, Prest wanted to create an event that would bring the otherwise disparate neighbourhood and community together. Permission was sought and granted from homeowners who were present to cheer on racers and hand out water and treats, and thus the orienteering event resembled a small community parade.

The race worked like a simplified version of orienteering. The orange and white markers used were official orienteering markers and sixteen of these were placed as checkpoints at different locations along a route approximately 2.5 km in distance. Prior to the race, each runner (or group of runners) received a simple map with a list of addresses and some basic directions for each address. For example, 'Julia and Bernie's, 38 Cary St, Location: Backyard Cubby House.' They also were given a punch card, which they could punch at each checkpoint with a unique imprint to prove they had made it to each checkpoint (this is also official orienteering equipment, albeit 'old-school' as they mostly use electronic tags these days). Runners left at one minute intervals, with their departure and arrival times recorded. So, effectively the race was a time trial. Runners could take whatever route they liked, just as long as they made it to each checkpoint.

Twenty participants consisted of: experienced runners, infrequent runners, artists, and families with kids aged seven to twelve, and a pair of dads who carried their toddlers on their shoulders the whole way. The route included: a cubby house stop at Julia and Bernie's, where the hosts had supplied oranges and jellybeans; a run straight through Josh and Carlie's living room; a rushed visit through a local art gallery at 'Airspace Projects;' and a home childcare space in 'Branco's

Backyard.' The race was won by locals Adam and Geoff with a time of around 32 minutes. Second place was a group of five boys age 9 to 11, Warre, Archer, Tom, Les and Ubu and chaperoned by Mirabelle. *The Warren Run* was organized to create a sense of community for a short period of time. Disrupting common orienteering practices and the typical approach to trespassing in parkour, Matt Prest contacted local residents to gain access to private property inviting them to also participate in the race as they saw fit.

The practice of incorporating orienteering into artistic projects is not new. For example, Canadian artist Hannah Jickling has developed similar projects in Portland, Oregon; the Yukon, Canada; and in Rauma, Finland. In *Portland Orienteering Museum* (2010) and *Featured Features, Rauma* (2012) she collaborates with local orienteering clubs, sometimes in museum spaces and sometimes in the outdoors. Typically, orienteering involves navigating between points with the aid of a map and compass. The sport uses creative decision-making, physical strength and endurance, and speed in order to complete the course in a record time. Maps, visual symbols, and markers are also common in museums and urban neighbourhoods, like Marrickville. *The Warren Run* also incorporated parkour, a form of movement which was developed from military arts obstacle training. Like orienteering, parkour involves getting from one point to another, except here there is no equipment and might involve rolling, running, leaping, climbing, and jumping. It is seen as a novel and subversive way of interacting with the environment.

Walking art projects like *The Warren Run* that include communities and groups of people in the work, are often described using an assortment of terms including socially engaged art, social practice, relational, and participatory. There have been numerous contentious debates in art scholarship about relational, participatory, and antagonist art practices that are far too numerous to take up in detail in this chapter. We tease out a few of these critiques to further examine the problem with framing participation as inclusion.

First, is the critique that participatory art projects can be naïve and celebratory (Bishop, 2012; Helguera, 2011). Appraisals of this sort contend that most participatory practices are often "diluted or weak," and "simply a strategy for an audience to consume art without a qualitative or meaningful engagement with it, or, put another way, offers a form that does not actually change any aspect of the art system" (Reed & Goldenberg, 2008, p. 6). Critics have argued that participatory art offers nothing more than convivial relations that do not outlast the artistic event. Participation does not guarantee an audience's ability to "alter the work's structure, only to assume [their] role within it" (Bishop, 2012, p. 224).

Second, participatory art is often rationalized as being non-hierarchical and collaborative. While many participatory art projects are concerned with power and are created with marginalized groups, the assumption with participation is that there is a unified, pre-existing, and self-determining subject who participates, which obscures the complex ways that humans and nonhumans intra-act (Ellsworth, 1989). The dilemma of participation is that under the guise of collaboration, sociality, and inclusion participation becomes a method of appeasement as opposed to any real process of transformation (Miessen, 2010). Participation is often instrumentalized to minimize conflict and friction, and reifies utopic notions of emancipation, voice, and agency (Springgay, 2013a; 2016a). For Chantal Mouffe (2000), antagonism is an inescapable part of a participatory or political process, and requires a plural or heterogenous understanding of difference. Participation, according to Mouffe, is not about consensus building.

Third, as Bishop (2004) has argued, the issue isn't participation, but that the kinds of relationships that are generated are under examined. She asks: "What types of relations are being produced, for whom, and why?" (p. 16). As Jason Miller (2016) contends,

> It is one thing to champion relationality as a conceptual tool for making sense of art works that don't necessarily seem like art work . . . But it is quite another to praise relationality as a good in itself, given that exploitation, humiliation, and physical or psychological abuse are also human relations, but presumably not the sort that relational artists want to endorse or enable. So it turns out we can't simply collapse the ethical and the aesthetic under the rubric of "relational" art.
>
> (p. 170)

Enmeshed within these critiques, we would add, is the assumption that we know what participation is, what it looks like, how it operates, and what it does. The belief that we can recognize and represent participation is problematic.

Laura Cull (2011) has remarked that naming some art as participatory sets up a false binary between active participation and passive viewing. She contends that participation exists in all encounters with works of art at an on-going, pre-, post-, and trans- subjective level. If as Cull (2011) maintains, participation is on-going, and the distinction between active and passive participation is a false binary, then how would an immanent perspective contribute to a different understanding of participation in walking research? According to Gilles Deleuze (1990) inclusion "usually appears as an accident supervening on what is participated from outside, as a violence suffered by what is participated" (p. 169). Instead Deleuze proposes an immanent model, where difference proliferates, with attention to singularity, newness, and potentiality. Brian Massumi (2002) argues that participation occurs prior to cognition, before the act of thinking about taking part. Participation comes first, while organization or stratification is second. Thinking-with theories of movement in the next section of the chapter, we tease out an immanent conceptualization of participation, arguing that such an ontology of participation might propose a more ethical-political understanding of taking part and coming together.

Relative and absolute movement

Rhythm in Western thought is typically linked to meter and is structured by recurring movements that creates patterns of particular frequency (Ikoniadou, 2014). Operating this way, rhythm is regular, continuous, and enables predictions of what is to come. Rhythm as a metered movement makes things or events knowable because you can anticipate their next recurrence. Throughout its history, rhythm has "meant both regularity and unpunctuated flow; symmetry and motion as well as the confinement of movement and pause" (Ikoniadou, 2014, p. 148). While commonly associated with music, and as such time and duration, in walking and mobilities research rhythm has been affiliated with space. Following Henri Lefebvre (2004), walking scholars have focused on rhythmanalysis to examine how rhythm produces environments.

For Alfred North Whitehead (1978), rhythm depends on novelty and is thus concerned with potentiality, immanence, and newness. Other accounts of rhythm conceive of it as "force that resists systematized or exhaustive capture" (Henriques, Tiainen, Valiaho, 2014, p. 16). Here scholars draw on the work of Deleuze and Guattari, where rhythm is not metric, but formed through a repetition of difference. Rhythm is a differential patterning that emerges through the relations between things. Rhythm, according to Deleuze and Guattari (1987), is repetition within difference. Rhythm is the transcoding that passes between milieus, a kind of communication or passage between space-times that is never metric or measured. Deleuze (1994) distinguishes between cadence and rhythm, where cadence is the envelope of repetition of the same, while rhythm is variation, characterized by speeds and rests. Deleuze and Guattari (1987) write:

> Movement has an essential relation to the imperceptible; it is by nature imperceptible. Perception can grasp movement only as the displacement of a moving body or the development of a form. Movements, becomings, in other words, pure relations of speed and slowness, pure affects, are below and above the threshold of perception.
>
> (pp. 280–228)

In other words, participation is a constantly differing process that unsettles recognition. This imperceptibility of movement might be understood through Manning's (2012) articulation of absolute movement, which she argues is different than relative movement.

Movement, particularly when discussed as a component of walking, is typically described as an act of changing one's physical location. In this definition, the body consciously moves between fixed points. This is what Manning (2012) refers to as relative movement. In relative movement the body moves, while the street, sign posts, and other nonhuman objects remain inert. Tim Ingold (2011) calls this "transport" (p. 151); a movement that is directional. Manning (2012) notes that relative movement is where "form preexists matter" (p. 15). In such an instance body and street are pre-given and ontologically distinct and movement is something that happens in-between, designating an interim between two points that maintains and respects the individuality of these points. Movement is what passes between the points.

Absolute movement, on the other hand, is a form of movement that proliferates endlessly (Springgay, 2014; Springgay & Zaliwska, 2016; Truman & Springgay,

2015). In absolute movement, motility does not pass between points. Manning (2016) gives the example of a yoga pose where the body appears to be in stasis, but is in fact a composition of ceaselessly moving micro-movements. Walking performs both relative and absolute movement. In relative movement, one walks between two different points. As absolute movement both the point and bodies are multiplicities. For example, in walking, not only are the feet being propelled from one point to the next, each foot, kneecap, thigh, arm, wheel, cane, sidewalk, tree, and wind are in an interminable array of micro-movements that are both a component of the overall perambulatory movement, and shape other assemblages of movement that may in fact function counter to the walking movement.

Ring of Fire can be instructional in distinguishing between relative and absolute movement. As relative movement, the various participants moved along University Avenue towards City Hall. As the Sentinels and Orators walked their movement passed between various points along the route. The points, such as a lamp post or the doors of the City Hall, remained fixed and the procession merely moved between one point and the next. This would describe the relative movement of the event.

However, if we think of the procession from the proposition of absolute movement then the ambulatory relations change and bodies become more-than themselves. Not only was there a movement along a street, there was a multiplicity of "non-conscious inflections," which are not external to the event of walking (Manning, 2016, p. 18). As the runners in *The Warren Run* leaped over fences and charged through living spaces, movement becomes "the vibrational force within actual movement that agitates within every displacement, within every figure or form. It is what makes movement multiple and complexly active" (Manning, 2014, pp. 170–171). Bodies, jellybeans, mouths, orienteering flags, cubby house, legs, running shoes, and water bottles are all vibrating in endless movement.

Rhythm is comprised of vibratory micro-movements that are constantly in flux and change. These vibrations of micro-movement are imperceptible and molecular. A vibrational account of rhythm provides a means to interrogate how encounters that are imperceptible produce affects across diverse entities. Thus, vibratory accounts of rhythm enable different kinds of analysis that attend to the immanent and affective dimensions of participation.

Volitional and decisional movement

Building on her prior writings on relative movement and absolute movement, Manning (2016) offers two new concepts: volitional and decisional movement. Conscious, or often called volitional, movement is directed by humans, or nonhuman agents, from the outside of the event. An example of volitional movement is the choice to 'take part' in a procession or other such event. Volitional movement, directed by an agent, is denotative of choice, freedom, and inclusive participation, and as we discuss earlier, is immersed in particular neoliberal accounts of politics. For example, when we think of inclusion as the freedom to choose to participate, participation then becomes the human power to act. This is strategized or relative movement.

Decisional movement is unconscious, intuitive and non-neurotypical movement. The term decisional is complicated by our common usage of the term. While we think of decision as a conscious act, here Manning is using the term in contrast to volitional, which is about choice. In decisional movement, a body reacts and moves, in relation to other decisional movements. Decisional, she writes, refers to "the cut, in the event, through which new ecologies, new fields of relation are crafted" (p. 19). She provides the example of an athlete making decisional movement on a soccer field. While an athlete has prior training and knows how and when to move in relation to the ball, where the ball moves and how the players move and respond to each other and the ball, cannot be determined prior to the game-event itself. The player makes decisions on the field, in the game, based on the continuous absolute movements between bodies-field-ball-posts-turf, etc. Decisional movement is not mapped in advance, but according to Manning, is "capable of altering the course of the event *in the event*" (p. 19, italics in original). Decisional movement is activated by "mobile cues" (p. 18). Mobile cues affect how an athlete moves in the event itself. For Manning, volitional or conscious movement gets in the way of decisional movement. Decisional movement is necessary because it "cleaves the event, in the event" (p. 20). In other words, decisional movement leaves room for mutation.

Movement is "constantly inflected by improvisatory quality of a response, in the event, to cues and alignments" (Manning, 2016, p. 21). For instance, in *The Warren Run*, the participants were running a course that they had not preplanned. Living room chairs and sofas become mobile cues, and decisional movement shapes movement from within the event itself. When a running body encounters a sofa, and moves with the sofa – bending, leaping, stumbling, or even resting – this is decisional movement. If that same body-subject approached the sofa, already knowing before the event of the sofa that they were going to summersault over it, that is volitional movement. How to bodily move-with the sofa was determined before the event of sofa took place.

'Taking part' understood through inclusionary logics requires difference to be normalized. For example, the disabled athlete is included when they overcome their disability and perform as a 'super-crip.' This is relative movement where a body moves into the centre. This is movement from the outside. Rather, what we need is to conceive of participation as rhythmic, created as a pattern of difference, and which is composed of endlessly moving decisional vibrations. Writing about non-neurotypicality and autism, Manning (2016) states that decisional movement is crucial because it takes into account different ways that bodies move and are inflected.

The problem with volitional movement is that it conceives of participation through inclusionary rationalities and, as we have demonstrated, these continue to support White, ableist, setter, and heteronormative logics. Volitional movement as 'taking part,' while inviting different subjects and different bodies to participate, supports and reinforces norms. Furthermore, this rhetoric of inclusion is in fact exclusionary, where certain bodies are always marked as different and only included by conforming.

However, if participation is composed of absolute and decisional movement, where bodies – human and nonhuman – are rhythmically moving in variation and difference – then we can begin to think of participation beyond the rhetoric of inclusion. This is crucial. We need different ways to conceive of and understand participation, and think about participation's political potential. This is where absolute and decisional movement become important.

If participation isn't reduced to the volitional act of an individual, but is rendered in rhythmic terms of assemblage and composition, participation engenders a politics of potentiality. Rather than get bound up in critiques of sociality, collaboration, and antagonism, participation becomes the incipient worlding of potential, or what Massumi (2015) calls the "power to form us" (p. 18).

Instead of 'taking part,' which privileges inclusion, and evaluates the kinds of interaction inclusion creates, we ask: *how to tend to the proliferation of difference, the immanence of participation*?

Inclusionary participation implies volitional movement, a form of free will or choice. This is then linked to individual agency, rationality, and mastery. Furthermore, it continues to render some bodies outside of an event, or outside of what it means to be human. Inclusionary logics reinforce an inside and an outside.

Decisional movement engenders variation and difference. As Manning (2016) states, this is participation that is "gesturing always toward a futurity present in the act, but as yet unexpressed. This is its force, this is its call for freedom" (p. 24). Decisional movements are rhythmic relations that are produced in and of the event. They are immanent to the event itself. This is a knowing in the event (not before the event) that is composed of both conscious and unconscious movements. Participation becomes intensive, it is internal to itself, and constituted through movement and affect. In other words, participation is produced without knowing what that production will look like. It is creative and experimental.

Immanent participation

'Taking part' in an event assumes that any negative limitations have been removed and that by being included the subject is now transformed, empowered, and liberated. However, inclusion continues to render an outside and an inside. Furthermore, inclusion implies a degree of choice. Elizabeth Grosz (2004) maintains that this understanding of inclusion or freedom renders the existence of choice intact. When subjects are included in an event, nothing has changed. Subjects are brought into the event but both the event and the subjects remain separate. Drawing on the work of Henri Bergson (1988), Grosz (2004) argues for the idea of "free acts" (p. 46). Free acts, she writes, "come from or even through us" (p. 46). Freedom, or what we are naming participation, is not about rational choice and individual agency. Rather, it is a "freedom of action that is above all connected to an active self" (p. 147). This action, however, is not about human mastery, but indebted to decisional movement, to cleaving, cuts, intra-actions and transcorporeal entanglements between all bodies. Moreover, this understanding of participation, Grosz contends, is material. It is not 'of' the mind, but engendered through material-discursive relations. We turn to our final example, to tease out immanent participation and the capacity to act.

The white cane, which is commonly used by individuals with visual impairments, was invented by an English photographer, James Biggs, in the 1920s. After losing his sight due to an accident, he was working in his darkroom where, despite his visual impairment, white photopaper glowed and was highly visible. Inspired by the white in the darkroom, Biggs painted his cane white for increased visibility by motorists. Carmen Papalia's project *White Cane Amplified* replaces the white cane with a megaphone, which the artist, who himself is a 'non-visual learner,' uses to instruct other pedestrians and vehicles about his presence and to request help from participants in crossing streets and navigating urban spaces. Papalia performed *White Cane Amplified* for *WalkingLab* in Vancouver, Canada.

Papalia uses the term 'non-visual learner' to describe himself as opposed to terms like blind or visually impaired, which refers to body parts that are lacking or not working. Using terms associated with learning, as opposed to reductive language of disability, Papalia works "to generate spaces and experiences of agency for himself through his creative practice; from his choice to identify as a non-visual learner, to works that playfully confront disabling perceptions around who, and how one, might lead" (Garneau, 2016, np). Carla Rice, Eliza Chandler, Jen Rinaldi, Nadine Changfoot, Kirsty Liddiard, Roxanne Mykitiuk, and Ingrid Mündel (2017) argue that ableist logics and normative representations of bodies condition art history and contemporary visual culture. As such, a disability-art ethics, they contend, requires different curatorial and academic scholarship, that does not simply include work like Papalia's into an already problematic canon. For example, the white cane renders Papalia visible as an individual with a 'disability' but simultaneously invisible as a specific person. The megaphone, on the other hand, disrupts how people perceive him in public space. Walking, he repeatedly calls out through the megaphone "hopefully you can see me. I can't see you." Disability art, Rice et al. (2017) contend, disrupts and re-orders futurity. Crip futurity, they argue, imagines a different future, not based on inclusivity, and normativity, but difference.

Papalia, in contrast to heteronormative notions of a self-reliant male strolling through the city, requires participation from others to navigate safely. Although dressed in dapper clothing reminiscent of the historical figure of the flâneur, Papalia queers the notion of a flâneur who is described as an incognito spectator who strides effortlessly through crowds in detached anonymity. Papalia instead continually speaks through his megaphone, "Is anyone there? Can someone help me cross the street? Is it safe to cross? I can't see. I can kind of see shapes." Papalia requests assistance from strangers, yet the megaphone rather than serving as a device that provides assistance, "amplifies his anxiety and vulnerability" (Garneau, 2016, np). While people and nonhuman objects such as lamp posts, curbs, and bushes, get 'called' to participate in his performance, via the megaphone, Papalia is not asking them to participate so that they are included in his project as an act of community building or empowerment. Rather, the participants – much like the megaphone, the sidewalk, and other obstacles he encounters – are deci-sional in that they become inflexions that alter his movements discretely.

White Cane Amplified as decisional participation "punctures" an event "leading the event elsewhere than toward the governant fixity of the major, be it the major in the name of normative political structures, of institutional life, of able-bodiedness, of gender conformity, of racial segregation" (Manning, 2016, p. 7). The participa-tory event composes-with, it is indeterminate and ineffable, and makes perceptible what can be felt, in the event, but not measured or categorized. This perceptibil-ity of feeling is affective, and affect according to Massumi (2015) is participatory "because affects . . . are basically ways of connecting, to others and to other situa-tions. They are our angle of participation in processes larger than ourselves" (p. 6). This perceptibility is not coded or structured. It cannot be represented but it can be mapped. Participation as such, is not based on logics of inclusion or belonging, but pulses through life as affect, force, and variation.

Participation is in the event and of the event. Manning (2016) writes that par-ticipation "is not the way the outside adds itself to a process already underway, [e.g. inclusion] but the operational multiplicity of a practice in its unfolding. Par-ticipation is not what the artist wishes the public to do, but the activity of the work's potential as opened up by the process itself" (p. 55). *Ring of Fire, The Warren Run*, and Carmen Papalia's projects, including *Mobility Device* exemplify this notion of participation as the work's potential.

In *Mobility Device*'s walking performance, Papalia replaces the white cane with a marching band. Working over a period of months, Papalia and the band composed a multiplicity of sounds that would signal to Papalia when he should turn right or left, obstacles, different elevations on the ground, and other things that a person navigates when walking. *Mobility Device*, however, doesn't simply replace the white cane with a marching band. Rather the assemblage between band, sounds, obstacles, Papalia, and walking confounded the logic of orientation through an intensive, rhythmic force. Adopting a definition of participation as immanent and affective changes how we understand the work.

In each example discussed in this chapter, if we think about participation from the perspective of inclusion, we are actually thinking about participation as out-side of the event, or something that is added to the work. For example, adding First Nations houses to the PanAm Games; adding disability dancers to an artist's procession; including publics in a work of art; all of these additions or inclusions render collectivity as having an inside and an outside, and continue to demarcate some bodies as belonging and others not. Inclusion suggests that there exists a work that individuals can be included in. But in all of the research-creation proj-ects engaged with in this chapter, participation is what makes the work *work* from the inside. If participation is immanent to an event, then participation asks how collectivity conditions the work, how it is activated or modified.

Derek McCormack (2014) contends that participation begins with potenti-ality. He writes participation "is never reducible to the intentional act of indi-vidual human actor. Participation takes place through relational assemblages of bodies, materials, concepts, and affects: participation in these terms is always a cofabrication, a coproduction that involves more than the individual human participant" (p. 188). Participation cannot be known in advance of its eventing. As a speculative gesture it activates the work from the inside.

Walking methodologies are commonly understood as participatory. Scholars and artists frequently argue that walking is social and interactive, whether you walk with others, or commune with your senses on a solo walk. But the inclusionary logics of participation, as we have outlined, normalize, commodify, and stratify particular bodies. Additionally, they establish an inside and an outside that are distinct. To participate means to move from the outside into the inside. In this regard, participation would appear to be a concept that stifles a work. But if participation is immanent to life, to walking, to events, and as such to research, different questions can be asked about what participation does, or how it operates. Participation as immanent proliferates and multiplies endlessly. Participation as relational, always taking part, emphasizes movement and rhythm as difference.

5   On the need for methods beyond proceduralism

Speculative middles, (in)tensions, and response-ability in research

```
Walk as SLOWLY as you can.
FEEL the air against your SKIN as you MOVE.
Move with an irregular rhythm.

        ~

Walk DIAGONALLY through the city.
Cross the road. Cross a threshold.

        ~

Keep your eyes CLOSED while walking.
Change the length of your STRIDE.
Remove your shoes. Trust the earth.

        ~

Follow lines, smells, the colour red.
```

This chapter responds to agitations that are occurring in qualitative research, particularly issues related to: the incompatability between new empiricist methodologies and phenomenological uses of methods (St. Pierre, 2016a; Vagle & Hofsess, 2016); the preponderance of methodocentrism (Weaver & Snaza, 2016); the pre-supposition of methods (Manning, 2016); a reliance on data modeled on knowability and visibility (Lather & St. Pierre, 2013; Maclure, 2013); the ongoing emplacement of settler futurity (Tuck & Mckenzie, 2015); and the dilemma of representation (Lorimer, 2005; Thrift, 2007; Vannini, 2015). While enmeshments between ontological thought and qualitative research methodologies as shaped by affect theory (Springgay, 2016b; Springgay & Zaliwska, 2016), new materialisms (Barrett & Bolt, 2013; Blaise, Hamm, Iorio, 2017; de Freitas & Curinga, 2015; Coole & Frost, 2010; Mazzei & Jackson, 2016; Snaza, Sonu, Truman & Zaliwska, 2016), the new empiricism (St. Pierre, 2016b), and posthumanism (Snaza & Weaver, 2015) have rigorously interrogated the logic of anthropocentrism in conventional humanist research methods, questions remain about concepts such as research design, methods, procedure, data, and analysis. We appear stuck, writes Elizabeth St. Pierre (2016a), between new empiricist theories as methodologies and traditional phenemenologically informed methods. And while scholars are eager to suggest that we can do away with method, this chapter will address some concerns we have with this proposition.

First, there is an assumption that methods are particular things, such as interviews, participant observation, or video ethnography. Yet, as we'll elaborate, methods themselves have been playfully interrogated and experimented with in ways that already resist representation (Thrift, 2007; Vannini, 2015). Second, although we agree with a radical empiricist understanding that posits thought as a form of inquiry, for us – as qualitative researchers who conduct large, multisite, durational research projects with others, including groups of students and teachers, artists and community members, but also nonhuman entities like rocks – methods are significant and very much present in a research event. Thus, rather than a refusal of methods, the remaining sections of this chapter propose that particular (in)tensions need to be immanent to whatever method is used. If the intent of inquiry is to create a different world, to ask what kinds of futures are imaginable, then (in)tensions attend to the immersion, tension, friction, anxiety, strain, and quivering unease of doing research differently.

The chapter commences with a short review of arguments emerging in qualitative research, particularly around the viability of methods and data, within the turn to more ontologically nuanced research. The problem, we contend, isn't the types of methods researchers use, or that new methods need to be invented. There is already an abundance of methods and experimental practices of doing research! We approach methods propositionally, speculatively, and experimentally and maintain that it is the *logic of procedure and extraction* that needs undoing. Research methods cannot be framed as a process of gathering data. Understood relationally, methods become "a distributed, immanent field of sensible processuality within which creative variations give rise to modifications and movements of thinking" (McCormack, 2014, p. 25). Research methods become a practice of being *inside* a research event. We attend to the *how* of research by thinking-with various walking projects from *WalkingLab* and beyond. We use the idea of the *walk score* as a catalyst for movement. Influenced by the tradition of Fluxus event scores,[1] they enact what Erin Manning and Brian Massumi (2014), following Alfred North Whitehead (1978), call propositions. Propositions are different from research methods or a research design in that they are speculative and event oriented (Truman & Springgay, 2016). They are not intended as a set of directions or rules that contain and control movement. Scores emphasize chance and improvisation. Justy Phillips (2015) writes that "scoring is a technique of eventing through lines of writing" (p. 133). Invoking a number of artists and thinkers that engage with propositions as scores, Phillips maintains that the score does not have a set order of activation. The score events the middle and "is the mechanism which allows us all to become involved, to make our presence felt. Scores are process-oriented, not thing-oriented" (Halprin, cited in Phillips, p. 133).

The propositional form of the walk score invites us to 'begin' in a speculative middle, where rather than the "making-reasonable of experience" (Manning, 2016, p. 31) research "must be reinvented at every turn and thought must always leap" (p. 45). We need to shift from thinking about methods as processes of gathering data towards methods as a becoming entangled in relations. This requires a commitment to methods in which experience gives way to experimentation, where it "becomes a field of variations in which to experiment with the questions of how felt difference might register in thinking" (McCormack, 2014, p. 11). The question of movement is at the heart of this endeavor. Not a movement from one point to another, but rather a thinking-in-movement. Through examples from our many research projects we'll discuss how research needs to be understood as speculative eventing, and how within the speculative middle, methods need to be (in) tension so that research becomes attuned to ethico-political matters and concerns.

```
Walk a familiar path repetitively
Listen to what is no longer there
```

John Weaver and Nathan Snaza (2016) argue that traditional qualitative approaches to research fetishize methods, and in so doing maintain an understanding of methods as predetermined entities that exist separate from the research event. The givenness of method is exactly what Manning (2016) confronts when she states that method "is a static organization of preformed categories" (p. 31), an "apparatus of capture" (p. 32) that "stops potential on its way, cutting into the process before it has had a chance to fully engage with the complex relational fields that process itself calls forth" (pp. 33–34). If method is pre-given and known in advance, it also suggests that data is an already presupposed entity that is waiting to be captured, extracted, and mined. Method, writes Maggie MacLure (2013) treats data as if it were an "inert and indifferent mass waiting to be in/formed and calibrated by our analytic acumen or our coding systems" (p. 660). Methods, write Weaver and Snaza (2016) that rely on processes of data gathering privilege sight and its concomitant certainty, truth, stability, and representation. As a move to unfurl methodocentrism and neo-positivism in qualitative research, Patti Lather and Elizabeth St. Pierre (2013) proposed a 'post' conceptualization of research. They contend that researcher's prior training in qualitative methods might in fact "normalize our thinking and doing," where a research design that follows conventional protocols of questions, literature review, methods, data analysis, and representation assumes that the "human is superior to and separate from the material" (p. 630).

Writing about the politics of method and, in particular, the effects of interpretive analysis on Māori-settler relations, Alison Jones and Kuni Jenkins (2008) insist on strategically foregrounding material events over interpretation. Using what they call a "materialization reading," which gives a speculative account informed by "Maori recognition . . . of the 'shape' of the events" (p. 132), Jones and Jenkins argue that methods need to attend to their material effects.

Furthermore, St. Pierre (2016a; 2016b) draws attention to the gap between new empiricist methodologies, particularly those informed by Gilles Deleuze and Felix Guattari, and what is often now referred to as new materialisms, and phenomenological uses of methods. St. Pierre argues that too often researchers still design, implement, and gather data based on phenomenological understandings, or conventional empirical methods, which are incommensurable with imma-nent theories. In a "leap to application" researchers utilize ontological theories to analyze and code existing data collected using dominant phenomenological methods (p. 111). St. Pierre (2016a) asserts that one can't deploy Deleuze and Guattari's rhizome to interviews collected through standard phenomenological methods, because "they are thought in different ontological arrangements" (p. 2). The resulting confusion is in part caused by the perpetual theory/practice divide. Privileging practice, she states, has resulted in normalizing methods and problem-atically assumes that the 'how' of research is separate from the theory or think-ing of research. We see evidence of this in the overuse of diffractive analysis on decades-old data, or arts-based practices such as cutting, stitching, and collaging together transcripts in an attempt to 'perform data differently.' Neither diffraction or collage are necessarily problematic, but iterated in these ways data remains as something that can be "abstracted from experience into a system of understanding that is decipherable precisely because its operations are muted by their having been taken out of their operational context" (Manning, 2016, p. 29). The idea that data is a 'thing' that sits in the world and can be isolated and extricated by a method, while remaining separate from that method, is impossible if, as Karen Barad (2007) states, "relata do not precede relations" (p. 334). The insular way in which data and methods are divorced from one another is also common to how theory and methods are conceptualized as detached. Addressing the enmeshment between theory and practice, St. Pierre (2016b) encourages researchers to "*read and read and read* until its concepts overtake us and help us lay out a plane that enables lines of flight to what we have not yet been able to think and live" (p. 122, our italics). Her encouragement to read as a practice of pushing thought to its edge, to where thought thinks thought, is necessary and productive. Radical empiricism insists that thinking and experimenting are both material gestures and, consequently, reading is an encounter that brings "into being that which does not yet exist" (Deleuze, 1994, p. 139). According to Manning (2016), radical empiri-cism begins in the middle of a mess of relations not yet organized in terms like subject/object. "Neither the knower or the known can be situated in advance of the occasion's coming to be- both are immanent to the field's composition" (p. 30). In the same way that methods cannot be known in advance and used as pre-established procedures, thought must also arrive in the middle and be immanent to the event itself. In the example of collage, collage then would not happen after the event of research as a way to creatively entangle data, but rather collage must become a thinking-making-doing, where collaging and thought exist simultane-ously. This means that a researcher can't extract data from a research site using phenomenological methods and then make a collage out of that data. Such a model is based on a process of extraction. The collage isn't the issue, it's the idea that there is inert data that can be mined.

Counter to St. Pierre's (2016a; 2016b) arguments, Mark Vagle and Brooke Hofsess (2016) ask questions about the productivity of bridging phenomenology with post-qualitative methodologies, insisting that a playful "putting together" of phenomenology and Deleuze and Guattarian concepts provoke a post-reflectivity.

However, our own new materialist and speculative conjectures about method-ologies and methods are more in line with St. Pierre's convictions that reflexiv-ity (humanist) and radical empiricism (more-than-human) are incommensurate. Reflexivity, even as an entangled practice, presupposes a subject and is founded on interpretive practices. For example, Margaret Somerville (2016) notes that while the crisis of language and representation has troubled qualitative research-ers for decades, the focus on the materiality of language that new materialism offers, attends to data "that defies representation, data that commands attention precisely because it cannot be explained" (p. 1163). This is what MacLure (2013) calls data that 'glows,' where glowing speaks to the intensities and forces that can-not be interpreted or understood through conventional meaning-making practices.

Standard approaches to qualitative research conceive of methodologies as the theoretical orientation of research, and methods are the procedures by which empirical materials are collected and interpreted. While conventional qualitative methods, such as interviews, can be used on their own, more often researchers combine a number of approaches, including idiosyncratic experimental practices to generate both observed and ephemeral 'data.' For example, walking on its own can be a method of doing research such as long walks, dérive, and psychogeogra-phy. Or it can be merged with various other methods like photography and video, drawing, sensory methods, different mapping techniques including GPS, and per-formance. Walking is distinguished as either ordinary, and thus simple, or as an 'innovative' strategy that utilizes new technologies.

But even amidst innovation and experimentation there is a risk that methods are determined in advance of research and that they are intended to aid a researcher and/or participant in gathering some kind of evidence. Innovative or arts-based methods can also fall into a logic of proceduralism that can be validated, codified, and represented. Walking is sometimes figured as one of these counter methods, but as Manning (2016) argues

> any ordering agenda that organizes from without is still active in the exclu-sion of processes too unintelligible within current understandings of knowl-edge to be recognized, let alone studied or valued. Despite its best intentions, method works as the safeguard against the ineffable.
>
> (p. 32)

In instrumentalizing walking as a method there is the presumption that walk-ing is going to do something specific before the event occurs, and that walking is uniquely situated to discover and gather data. The problem, we maintain, is that instead of attending to the ecologies of research, or what we prefer to call the thinking-making-doing of research, researchers fall into the trap of believing that creating *new* methods will offer different solutions. This, as Manning (2016) contends, cuts "into the process before it has had a chance to fully engage with the complex relational fields the process itself calls forth" (pp. 33–34). In taking up the question of how to do immanent research, it is no longer sufficient to engage with representation and interpretation (reflexivity). Rather we must consider speculative eventing as a research practice that provokes an ethics that is accountable to a material world. We posit that methods are not the issue. Methods must be engaged with in the speculative middle and (in)tensions must be brought to bear on them. In what follows we discuss these agitations.

```
Follow a thought in the direction of the wind
CROSS (m)any lines
```

Research begins in the middle. For Deleuze and Guattari (1987), the middle is where things grow, expand, and pick up speed. The middle is not an average nor a zone between the beginning and the end. The middle passes between things as a "transversal movement" (p. 25). In the middle, immanent modes of thinking-making-doing come from within the processes themselves, rather than from outside them. In the middle, the speculative 'what if' emerges as a catalyst for the event. The middle is a difficult place to be. Deleuze and Guattari (1987) write that it's hard to see things clearly in the middle. That is the point. The middle can't be known in advance of research. You have to be 'in it,' situated and responsive. You are not there to report on what you find or what you seek, but to activate thought. To agitate it. The speculative middle "seeks to energize new modes of activity already in germ" (Manning & Massumi, 2014, p. 87). In the speculative middle, "experience is not an object out there to be acted upon. Rather, it is a field of variation in which thinking is another variation" (McCormack, 2014, p. 9). The speculative middle shifts methods from a reporting on the world to a way of being in the world that is open to experimentation and is (in) tension. Celia Lury (2012) names this approach "live methods," which she contends

> must be satisfied with an engagement with relations and with parts, with differentiation and be involved in making middles, in dividing without end(s), in mingling, bundling, and coming together. The objects of such methods – being live – are without unity, un-whole-some; put another way, they are partial and undivisible, distributed, and distributing.
>
> (p. 191)

Situated and partial knowledge, of course, has its antecedents in a long and pressing history of feminist research. Moreover, the affective, expressive, intra-active, and precognitive underpinnings of what Lury calls 'live methods' intersect with 'new materialist' methodologies that insist on the way agency flows through relational networks and is mobilized through human and nonhuman intra-actions. This liveness is quite different from phenomenological understandings of 'lived experience' that enfolds human subjectivity into the event. Rather this liveness, or incipient subjectivity of a sense-event remains open, incorporeal, virtual and exists in a time that is always past and always about to come, but never happening (Deleuze & Guattari, 1987). Research thought in this way, as an event of becoming, emphasizes doing rather than meaning-making.

The becoming incipient event of research, a becoming-intense, engenders a politics of imperceptibility and offers the potential for unravelling anthropocentric models of research.

What has become increasingly clear is that rather than trying to collect data or represent an objective reality – methods that privilege the human and treat data as existing phenomena – we need to think about inventive practices that "intervene, disturb, intensify or provoke a heightened sense of the potentiality of the present" (Sheller, 2014, p. 134). This requires a different orientation to methods.

```
WALK backwards without looking over your SHOULDER.
Perform a sun DIAL.
```

The Walking Neighbourhood directed by artist Lenine Bourke, and a featured *WalkingLab* project, is an interactive walking tour lead by children and/or youth that explores local communities on foot. The project has been enacted in more than eight different cities in Australia, Europe, and Asia. Each iteration begins with a series of propositions and problems that are then further attended to in workshops between the artists facilitating the project and the young people involved. Different methods are brought to bear on the workshops which activate the various ideas that surface. For example, propositions and problems in the project in Chiang Mai, Thailand, focused on the immediate neighbourhood block that the young people lived within, the different kinds of relations and encounters that were (im) possible, and how different ways of walking and moving in their neighbourhood could enact different forms of responsibility. Methods included storytelling, walking, sound recordings, drawing, photography, and games. While each of these examples are known, in the sense that we know what a photograph is, the methods themselves were not planned in advance of the research event. Bourke did not know before she and the other artists started working with the young people, what methods would be generative to the practice of working together. The methods emerged out of the collaboration between the artists and the young people and responded to the immanence of the event itself. Furthermore, the methods were not a means by which the young people collected data from their neighbourhood. The methods were not used to extract a sense of what already existed in the neighbourhood or the young people's personal experience of place. Instead, the young people and the artists created minor public walking interventions that were not about recording or capturing their environment, but about activating problems and concepts in the midst of the event. Research methods create new concepts, new knowledges, and new practices of relating. This inventive and experimental process becomes a process of exhausting terminology and what is already known. The speculative middle and the problematizing altered the method of the walking tour. Typically, walking tours impart information about a particular place. On a tour, you learn about the topology of a place, the history, or significant landmarks. Walking tours are both planned – as in the leader has information they wish to instruct participants about – or explorative – as in participants discover something new. Examples include the international movement called Jane's Walk and food tours (Flowers & Swan, 2015), where walking tours become particular kinds of pedagogical practices.

Over weeks of eventing, *The Walking Neighbourhood* artists and the young people, use various methods to problematize further problems, and to creatively produce a response. The response is a series of youth lead walking tours. These performances are themselves speculative middles, contingent on entanglements between tour leaders and participant-audiences. The audience does not simply watch the tour. Rather, participant-audiences are invited to become attentive to and to meaningfully respond within the event. Artist-researchers recognize there is a politics and ethics to how we come to know others. As performative experiments the methods of the walking tours "probe speculative dimensions" (van Dooren, Kirskey, Munster, 2016, p. 9). Artist-researchers don't describe research events but engage with the event as a speculative practice. This is similarly addressed in the project *Nightwalks with Teens*, a performance-based project where teens lead groups of strangers on a series of walks, in the dark (Springgay, 2013a). In contrast with Jane's Walks (which impart information), or guided hikes (where participants are encouraged to become attuned to 'nature'), *Nightwalks*, whether performed in urban cities or rural areas of Canada, disrupts any pre-given assumption about how the walks can be consumed or experienced.

Other examples, of speculative middles include Stephanie's multi-year project *The Pedagogical Impulse* (see www.thepedagogical.com) where artists worked on a diverse range of projects with students in K-12 schools and community centres (Rotas & Springgay, 2014; Truman & Springgay, 2015; Zaliwska & Springgay, 2015). While the focus of the projects was not specific to walking research, in many instances walking methods were used as speculative practices.

In speculative middles a practice is engendered "that puts relations at risk with other relations," or "in the presence of those who will bear their consequences" (Haraway, 2016, p. 12). In a speculative middle a,

> charge passes through the body and lingers for a little while as an irritation, confusion, judgement, thrill, or musing. However it strikes us, its significance jumps. Its visceral force keys a search to make sense of it, to incorporate it into an order of meaning. But it lives first as an actual charge immanent to acts and scene – a relay.
>
> (Stewart, 2007, p. 39)

A speculative middle does not stop a researcher. It's a thrust, a future provocation for thinking-making-doing. As Manning (2016) writes: "in the midst, in the event, we know the object not in its fullness, in its ultimate form, but as an edging into experience" (p. 48). Speculative middles, through processes such as walking, reading, and writing, emerge as agitations and as affective force. Donna Haraway (2016) writes that "it matters what matters we use to think other matters with" (p. 12). In the speculative middle, which is not a place, but an event, (in)tensions, concerns, and gnawings continually emerge. As the agitations take shape, it is the (in)tensions that incite further action, which elicits additional propositions, and enables new speculative middles to emerge.

```
Notice
the turn of the feet,
the lock of knee,
the shift of the hip
```

(In)tensions arise in the speculative middle and alter the *how* of methods and the research event.

The prefix 'in' can signify the negative of a concept, for instance, inattention or inexpensive. But 'in' can also be used to express a towards or a within, in such words as insular, intake, inside, and intimacy. In, writes Jeffrey Cohen (2014), signals both abjection and inclusion and is therefore "full of affect" (p. i). If conceived of as the opposite of the human, the prefix becomes enmeshed with nature, signifying the nature-culture divide. But in, Cohen, poses, is far more complex, and is also a "designation for excesses of scale (too vast or miniscule for familiarity); a separation within incorporation; negation belied by production; an antonym that fails" (p. i). (In)tensions are attuned to ethico-political concerns that emerge in each speculative middle. If methods are not pre-determined in advance, and arise in a speculative middle, then they become ways of thinking about problems. Todd May (2005) writes that "solutions present themselves as stable identities whereas problems (at least the worthwhile ones) present themselves as 'open fields' or 'gaps' or 'ontological folds.' Problems are inexhaustible, while solutions are a particular form of exhaustion" (p. 85). To begin in the speculative middle means to let go of agendas and embrace "conditions to come" (Uncertain Commons, 2013, np). In that regard, problems are always virtual, while solutions are actual in the Deleuzian sense. To think in terms of problems – to problematize – rather than find solutions keeps a method (in)tension.

Deleuze's (1994) ontology is not concerned with what is (with discrete forms of identity as being) but is an approach to experimentation, a way of probing what *might* be. Deleuze's *might be* exists virtually in all instances, but as a virtuality, cannot be known until after it emerges. For Deleuze, whatever emerges as an event in turn has the ability to modify *virtual* potentials: a process that he calls *differentiation*. For Deleuze, the virtual "possesses a full reality by itself" it is *"real without being actual, differentiated without being differenciated, and complete without being entire"* (pp. 211; 214). Although Deleuze was not a quantum theorist, and Barad (2015) does not seem to cite Deleuze, her recent journal article exemplifies the dynamism between the virtual actual when she states, "virtuality is the materiality wandering/wonderings of nothingness; virtuality is the ongoing thought experiment that the world preforms with itself" (p. 396). Or as Manning (2016) states, "[t]he virtual is never opposite to the actual – it is how the actual resonates beyond the limits of its actualization" (p. 29). For Manning this operates as a "relational field of emergent experience" where there is no pre-established hierarchy and no preconstituted subject-positions, there are only "emergent relations" (p. 29).

All relations, and the events they constitute, have virtual potential. What emerges in actuality *stirs* the virtual, and vice versa.

Deleuze's thought compels researchers to experiment with *problems* rather than seek *solutions*. Similarly, rather than political activism rectifying problems of the past, Elizabeth Grosz (2004) argues that it should be "augmented with those dreams of the future that make its projects endless, unattainable, ongoing experiments rather than solutions" (p. 14). As such methods become an experimental site for *posing new questions as speculative middles (in)tensions*. Methods push us to ask questions differently, to problematize problems, rather than collect data or seek solutions. In the speculative middle, problematizing is a mode of defamiliarization that ruptures taken-for-granted habits, tropes and common assumptions about *how* methods perform (Truman & Springgay, 2016).

A few summers ago, Sarah set up a darkroom in her basement. It was a time when many of our colleagues were experimenting with GoPro cameras and other wearable technologies as a way to record movement, and we wanted to reconsider more analogue approaches. We built several pinhole cameras out of coffee tins, shoeboxes, and a Chinese tea chest. Pinhole photography is a lensless process. In the case of a coffee tin, a small hole, or aperture, is punctured in the wall of the tin, allowing light to pass through onto photographic paper that is sealed inside. Once the paper is exposed to light, it needs to be processed in the darkroom. Because they typically require long exposure times, pinhole cameras are usually mounted in one place for the duration of the shot. Moving the camera during the exposure time can produce ghostly gestures; a palpable effect of rhythm and light. We took our shoebox and coffee tin cameras on walks and their long exposure time forced us to pause, to attend to our thinking-in-movement. But the darkroom chemicals are toxic, so we have traded the analogue process for a pinhole mount on a DSLR camera. These digital pinhole pictures don't require long exposures, and as no photo paper is needed we can record a series of images in a short amount of time. Wearing or holding the camera as we walk, the walking pinhole images become indistinct shadows of light and movement. They disorient perception of space and time. They evoke what Kathleen Stewart (2007) calls ordinary affects through their quivering surfaces. Ordinary affects, she states, "provoke attention to the forces that come into view as habit or shock, resonance or impact. Something thrown itself together in a moment as an event and a sensation; a something both animated and inhabitable" (p. 1). The images, which undulate and animate assemblages of human and nonhuman encounters do not represent the walks but incite new modes of thought and different practices of relating. As a method, the pinholes set the event of thinking-making-doing in motion. They are a thinking-with practice.

If the idea is that methods are a way to pose problems differently, the pinholes became, for us, a way to think about how to wrestle with methods as affective ecologies. How do you work a method that is infused with movement and affect? How to think movement moving? Anthropologist Natasha Myers (2016) has similarly experimented with walking and photography to think-with plant sentience in an Oak Savannah in Toronto's High Park. Methods, she contends, are practices for cultivating "*modes of attention* that might help *tune in* to the deep time of these lands and the *naturalcultural happenings* shaping its present" (italics in text, p. 2). Modes of attention ask questions about what matters to the land. To tune into, is not the same as to capture, or to document. It is a bending and folding, or what Carla Hustak and Natasha Myers (2012) call "involutionary momentum." Involution, as opposed to evolution, is a relational movement, a coupling, or co-mingling. Involutionary readings, they write, "give way to livelier ontologies and intra-active worldings" (p. 105). (In)tensions tune into and attend to not knowing, asking "what modes of embodiment, attention, and imagination would we need to know this place well?" (Myers, 2016, p. 3). Thus, the issue isn't what methods are used such as walking or pinhole photography but the kinds of problematizing, or tuning into, that matter. Linda Knight, a *WalkingLab* collaborator, has invented a method she calls 'inefficient mapping' to think-with the movement of playground spaces. Like the pinholes, Knight's multi-layered tracings do not represent space, but activate different modes of attention.

Our pinhole walks habitually take place on the Bruce Trail behind Sarah's house in Hamilton, Ontario. The Bruce Trail opened in 1967 and stretches from Niagara Falls to Tobormory (see Chapter 1). At almost 900 kilometers it is the oldest and longest marked hiking trail in Canada. It was created to draw attention to the geologic formation called the Niagara Escarpment, and stretches through Haudenosaunee territory. The escarpment is a horse-shoe shaped ridge of rock from Rochester, New York, through Lake Ontario to Hamilton, north to Tobermory, beneath Lake Huron, surfacing again on Manitoulin Island, where it then moved across northern Michigan. It was shaped over 400 million years ago and is composed of sedimentary rock, which is under continual erosion as soft rocks underneath the limestone caprock are worn and weathered by streams. The gradual removal of soft rocks leaves a cliff or escarpment. It is this escarpment over which the infamous Niagara River plunges at Niagara Falls.

The Bruce Trail Conservancy (BTC) is committed to improvement, maintenance, and/or protection of the trail. Based on humanist notions of stewardship and land care, the BTC is not only involved in the preservation of the biosphere but continues to purchase land in order to expand the 'park's' rights and access to the trail. However, as Myers (2016) writes, conservationist practices "participate in an ongoing colonial project that has enforced the dispossession of Indigenous peoples from their lands" (p. 3). Walking-with pinhole photography as a method, entangled with an (in)tension of problematizing what matters, demands we reimagine 'land care.' Conventional conservation practices see the need to preserve nature in a 'natural' state. But as Leanne Simpson (2014) argues, learning comes through Land. Rather than approaching care as a settler colonial act of maintenance and capitalism, imposed on from the outside, care becomes intimate and relational between all entities. Learning-with the Land is important here. The ghostly images of trees, rocks, and human bodies in our pinhole photos reminds us of our continual entanglements and the conflicting understandings of the Bruce Trail. Our methods of *walking-with* insists that the Land, the sediments of the escarpment that consist of rocks and Indigenous peoples, stays with us in unrestrained full-ness. Research methods that pre-determine what can exist, and as such what can be extracted, reproduce particular ontological certainties. Methods (in)tensions with themselves, as relational, unsettle givens, and attend to being otherwise.

```
Walk with a friend who lives in another city
Walk on the same street, at the same time, but in
    your respective cities
Walk in companion
```

Speculative middles escape order. They are in excess. Stewart (2007) writes that in the middle it's the "fragments of experience left hanging" (p. 44) that are of most interest. As agitations proliferate, questions need to be asked in order to "cultivate the capacity of response-ability" (Haraway, 2016, p. 35). These ques-tions don't require idealized or utopic solutions, rather they force us to engage with the world and to create conditions for ongoing provocations.

As part of *WalkingLab*, and one of the many projects executed for her doc-toral dissertation, Sarah developed an in-school project in a secondary school in Cardiff, United Kingdom. The focus of the project was the relationship between walking or a thinking-in-movement, writing, and youth cultural production as emergent 'literacy' practices. These are documented at www.sarahetruman.com. In much the same way that *The Walking Neighbourhood* emerged out of specula-tive middles, continuously problematizing problems, the in-school methods Sarah used, materialized as a series of minor events. Drawing on Deleuze and Guattari's (1986) minor literature, Manning (2016) explores what she calls a minor gesture, a speculative middle infused with ecologies of practice. The minor, she writes, "is a continual variation on experience" (p. 1) that "invents new forms of existence" (p. 2). While the 'major' tends to organize itself according to predetermined understandings of 'value,' the minor is a "force that courses through it, unmooring its structural integrity, problematizing its normative standards" (p. 1). The minor seen in this way, is varied, open to flux, and indeterminate. Minor gestures are everywhere and happen all the time. It is through ongoing minor punctuations of events that new things occur and are inherently political. And, because the minor occurs in the indeterminate phase of an event, the minor functions speculatively, and can reorient the direction of experience.

For example, many artists, writers, and qualitative researchers draw on the idea of a dérive to set thought in motion. As outlined in Chapter Three, a dérive is a walking strategy that originated with the Situationists International in the 1960s, in Paris. While the dérive is often conceptualized as a playful experimental prac-tice, the intent of the dérive was to move about the city, without a focused trajec-tory, but with an intensive consciousness of the environment. Current approaches to the dérive take on many different forms, but are typically marked by an active awareness of place.

Feminists have critiqued the dérive's tactics for producing a tourist gaze that per-petuates a separation between observer and observed (Massey, 2005; Richardson,

2015). This, we argue, further exploits the nature-culture divide and marks some bodies as inhuman or 'out of place.' Some contemporary forms of the dérive play with its form as a means to counter this heteronormative logic. For example, artist Diane Borsato's *Chinatown Foray*, led groups of amateur mycologists on urban forays through a city's 'Chinatown,' identifying Asian mushrooms using a variety of guidebooks, many of which featured species from North America. Identification practices included visual and other sensory modalities, and as such, the forays, while intended to be creative and experimental practices, resulted in further abjectification of particular bodies and spaces (Springgay, 2011a). In this example, walking and paying attention to things out of synch with habituated practices might actually reinforce power relations and reterritorialize bodies. What is at stake then, with the dérive as a method, is not a matter of form (eg. a mushroom foray), but *a matter of (in)tension.*

The dérive was a propositional catalyst for some of the in-school walks, in Sarah's study, where students were encouraged to use defamiliarization to attend to what was present and absent. Students were encouraged to tune towards what matters, and what is excluded from mattering (Barad, 2007). In the speculative middle, different minor techniques problematized the dérive including mapping using literary devices, writing poems that examined the spatial politics of their walks to and from school, and writing exercises that activated rhythm in conjunction with movement. What these minor gestures opened up for the dérive was a place for different (in)tensions to matter. But a dérive inflected with minor gestures is infused with intimacy where knowledge of place is not something grasped from a distance but emerges through proximity; where proximity is not a voyage of discovery, but where one bears the consequences for the things that are not even known yet (Springgay, 2008).

Too often researchers get fixated on experimental methods such as a dérive. However, when these creative practices are used to generate data that appear nonconventional there is a tendency to see the creative method as a practice of deterritorialization. But being experimental in itself is not enough. On a dérive, for example, we need to ask the question, "what is being worked here?"; meaning, not just what are we paying attention to that we might not typically experience, but what response-abilities arise from such tending towards. Haraway (2016) urges researchers to act inside ongoing trouble and, as such, methods must exist in conflict frictionally (Springgay & Truman, 2017c). Moreover, methods cannot assume to be 'one size fits all.' For instance, not all bodies move in a city in a similar way. Some bodies are already marked by particular inheritances. Sara Ahmed (2006) demonstrates how some spaces or places, such as the city street, are barred from the experience of certain bodies, even as those spaces co-produce such bodies, particularly racialized bodies. She states, "[t]he 'matter' of race is very much about embodied reality; seeing oneself or being seen as white [or brown] or black or mixed does affect what one 'can do,' or even where one can go, which can be re-described in terms of *what is and is not within reach*" (p. 112). Garnette Cadogan (2016) similarly writes "walking while black restricts the experience of walking, [and] renders inaccessible the classic Romantic experience of walking alone" (np). In Sarah's in-school study, one student wrote a poem about the politics of surveillance she encounters on a daily basis, because she wears hijab. Her poem, which deploys the clichéd refrain of 'walking on eggshells' is, in effect, an argument that psychogeography and the dérive are privileged practices. Liberal humanism presumes that psychogeography is an activity of paying attention to the corporeality of walking in space, casting off usual relations, in order to become more 'enlivened' by walking and place. But race, gender, sexuality, and ability are not corporeal skins that are attuned into only at particular moments, such as on a dérive, nor can they be flung aside innocently. Writing about exceptionalism in relation to queerness, Jasbir Puar (2007) states that transgression "relies on a normative notion of deviance, always defined in relation to normativity, often universalizing" (p. 23). The dérive, as an act of transgression, coheres and regulates bodies.

Methods are "non-innocent knottings" (Haraway, 2016, p. 29) and mobilize what Stacy Alaimo (2016) calls an ethics of inhabitation, which entangles the situatedness of corporeal knowledge, the movement of walking, and the large geopolitical realm of White supremacy and nationalism. Methods, like the dérive, used blindly and without (in)tensions stifle "the very opening through which fragile new modes of existence can come to expression" (Manning, 2016, p. 9). The issue, as such, is not that we abandon methods, such as the dérive, nor methods altogether, but that (in)tensions remain immanent to the speculative middle, which consequently alter the response-ability we have for the methods we use.

Another example of an (in)tension coupled with walking methods is addressed in *The New Field* project. This project, organized by *Public Studio*, a Toronto arts collective and *WalkingLab*, used the method of the long walk to walk the 900 kilometres of the Bruce Trail with various community groups and individuals. The (in)tensions inhered in this long walk project included questions about how landscapes, such as Provincial trails are mapped and produced, advocacy for Land and Indigenous sovereignty, disability and 'crip' resistance, and ethical political concerns for more-than-human ecologies that are not based on human-centric conservation practices of care.

```
Walk (in)tension
Practice an ethics of invention
```

Despite the ubiquitous concerns in qualitative research about the role and place of methods, we are convinced that methods themselves are not the issue. Whether you practice more conventional methods such as interviews or experiment with mobile technologies is beside the point. Call them methods, or techniques (Manning & Massumi, 2014; Phillips, 2015), or whatever you want. Invent, experiment, queer them. Methods are necessary for thinking-making-doing. This of course requires the idea of a method becoming an ecology of practices that are generated in a research event.

Regardless of what methods are incorporated, they i) cannot be pre-determined and known in advance of the event of research; ii) should not be procedural, but rather emerge and proliferate from within the speculative middle, as propositions, minor gestures, and in movement; iii) should not be activities used for gathering or collecting data. Instead methods must agitate, problematize, and generate new modes of thinking-making-doing; and iv) methods require (in)tensions, which trouble and rouse ethical and political matterings.

Initiating a research event in the speculative middle and with (in)tensions might seem like a daunting proposition to graduate students and experienced researchers trained in conventional qualitative research. Yet, the kinds of post methodologies that Lather and St. Pierre (2013) demand already proliferate in many different fields including education, human geography, visual arts and performance studies, and anthropology. Stephanie's work inside and outside of schools, with large groups of participants, or in small artist community settings, provides one such example. Sarah's research with using creative non-fiction *as* the research practice (Truman, 2013; Truman, 2016a), and her PhD projects such as *Intra-textual Entanglements* (Truman, 2016b), which invited participants to create and intervene with a Nietzsche text, are other examples of speculative middles. These examples, are funded by research grants and have gone through research ethics board approval. Rather than training students in conventional methods, through coursework, and then expecting or rather hoping that they find ways to speculatively invent, we need to develop alongside our students' experimental practices. Of course, this requires, as St. Pierre (2016b) suggests, reading and reading and reading in order to push thought to its edge, but this reading, we contend, must also be accompanied simultaneously with a thinking-making-doing.

Additionally, we have begun to imagine methods moving frictionally across all aspects of a research event, from its inception, its execution, and its dissemination. In the final section of this chapter, we discuss the entanglement of methods with practices of documenting and mobilizing knowledge. Rather than conceive of methods entering into a research project only at the stage when a qualitative researcher is 'in the field,' methods permeate research in its entirety. They are "extensive and permanently unfinished," writes Haraway (2016) and require "the cultivation of viral response-abilities, carrying meanings and materials across kinds in order to infect processes and practices" (p. 114). Methods are contagious: they mutate, and infect each other, which as Haraway (2016) contends is a feminist practice of care. This care, we understand from her writing, is not a moralizing gesture, but one that puts bodily ethical and political obligations (in)tensions where they become accountable "to the specific materializations of which we are a part" (Barad, 2007, p. 91). This, Barad argues, requires research practices that are "attentive to, and responsive/responsible to, the specificity of material entanglements in their agential becoming" (p. 91).

Methods can be practices of generating research *and* methods for dispersing the research with different publics simultaneously. In what follows we consider three aberrant examples. Aberrant means atypical, irregular, anomalous and deviant, and underscores the idea of ecologies of practice rather than models that can be replicated. The three aberrant examples we use to conclude this chapter stray and wander, unfolding frictional tensions that are capricious, indeterminate, and in constant variation. Characteristic, however, within these anomalous examples is the insistence that methods are generated both as a means to produce, create, and materialize knowledge *and* practices of dispersal, collective sharing, and activation of knowledge *at the same time.*

There are a number of ways we consider methods interwoven with research dissemination. One example is that walks themselves are methodologies. They are also methods of thinking-making-doing research, and they become events where knowledge is shared. In the *Stone Walks* project we detail in Chapter 1, different groups of people walked with us including different speakers and artists. Rather than approach research as an event of data gathering followed by analysis and dissemination, the walk becomes an event of research where the generation of research and its knowledge dissemination cannot be separated out.

Another iteration might be the creation of discursive events that are both sites to problematize research and as a means to work with different publics around the knowledge flowing through the research event. For example, *WalkingLab* curated an event in collaboration with the University of New South Wales Art Gallery called *Live Art, Social and Community Engagement: Interrogating Methodologies of Practice.* This event was not intended to be a space for artist-researchers to report on, or describe, previous research. Instead panelists were provided a series of provocative questions, as methods, that shaped the conversations. While the panel discussions were happening, and during the afternoon breakout sessions, 'Live Writers' used various methods or 'writing machines' to further enter into the event. Their 'live writing' was not intended to capture the speakers' words but to respond, engage, antagonize, and problematize the ideas, theories, concepts, and provocations put forth by the panelists and the small group discussions. Some writers used laptops and data projectors, another created a series of haikus, another wrote on the floor of the gallery space, which had been covered in cellophane paper, and yet another created a counter-archive as an appendix of concepts, words, and agitations from the day. The *Live Art* event was open to the public and more than 80 people from the arts, including practicing artists, curators, and scholars, participated. The production of knowledge and the communication or sharing of said knowledge occurred in situ. Phillip Vannini (2015), writing about similar concerns emerging in more-than-representational methodologies, states that research needs to "enliven rather than report, to render rather than represent, to resonate rather than validate, to rupture and reimagine rather than faithfully describe, to generate possibilities of encounter rather than construct representative ideal types" (p. 15).

A third example is the *WalkingLab* website. The website works in multiple ways, including the aim to share research through open access models of 'publication.' From the outset, the research has sought ways to mobilize knowledge to vastly different audiences. So, while in some cases (e.g. the projects page) the website functions as a repository or an online archive, other methods built into the website are simultaneously research and dissemination oriented. Here we point readers to the residency portion of the website. While each resident is 'in' residence virtually with the *WalkingLab*, they simultaneously enact minor gestures to problematize different (in)tensions about walking research, and by blogging about their methods and practices they share their thinking-making-doings with audiences.

In closing, we think-with Manning and Massumi's (2014) words of caution, that even inventive practices have the potential to become institutionalized "in accordance with established criteria, [which] would boil down to little more than grouping traditional disciplinary research methodologies under the same roof" (p. 88). Methods are multifarious and contagious, and exist throughout the duration of a research event, propelling thinking-making-doing forward into the next speculative middle.

```
Bring nothing but words
Walk from one BODY of water to another
```

Note

1 The international artist group called Fluxus created 'scores' for live performances where the process of creating was privileged over completed works.

6 'To the landless'

Walking as counter-cartographies and anarchiving practices

Walking and mapping have been experimented with by numerous artists and scholars (O'Rourke, 2013). Walking cartographers incorporate hand-drawn maps, Global Positioning Systems (GPS), sensory maps, psychogeography, narrative writing, photography, scores, and networked databases to name just a few. Many *WalkingLab* projects have combined walking with a range of mapping techniques including: GPS maps of a city; soundscapes of urban strata; using seeds to map urban permaculture; and line drawings to create inefficient maps of playground spaces. Despite the many creative and inventive techniques used to walk and map place, the prevailing history of mapping is entrenched in imperial and colonial powers who use and create maps to exploit natural resources, claim land, and to legitimize borders. Mapping, argues James Akerman (2017), is "implicated in the formation and maintenance of nation and states" (p. 8). Cree scholar Dallas Hunt and Shaun Stevenson (2017) similarly argue that conventional mapping practices continue to reaffirm dominant conceptualizations of Canada: they write, "[t]he surveying of lands and the production of maps remain an integral mode of solidifying nationalist, and indeed, settler colonialist constructions of Canada's geography" (p. 374). Katherine McKittrick and Clyde Woods (2007) assert that mapping and normalized geographic understandings continue the erasure and segregation of Black subjects. The racialization of space, they argue, is often theorized as essentialized or detached from actual geographic places.

Many artists and social science researchers deploy counter-cartographical approaches to map against dominant power structures, question the assumptions that conventional maps produce, and recognize different spatial knowledge systems. The exclusions and omissions in conventional maps and the impossibility of maps conveying lived experiences, regionalisms, and local knowledges "open up possibilities for resisting geographies of power and for a re-mapping of the landscape on other terms" (Hunt & Stevenson, 2017, p. 375).

This chapter examines three *WalkingLab* projects that re-map – as a form of counter-cartography – erased and neglected histories. In the first section of the chapter we describe the three walking projects. Taking up the ways that maps produce and reinforce geopolitical borders, and the geographies of race, we consider the ways that re-mapping offers possibilities for conceptualizing space that is regional and relational, as opposed to state sanctioned and static. As White settler artist-academics, we problematize the ways that new materialisms and posthumanisms have failed to account for a deeper understanding of the Anthropocene as racialized. In the next section, we consider how walking can re-map archives and disrupt linear conceptualizations of time. Walking as 'anarchiving' attends to the undocumented, affective, and fragmented compositions that tell stories about 'a past that is not past but is the present and an imagined future.' As counter-cartographies and anarchiving practices, the walking projects disrupt dominant narratives of place and futurity, re-mapping Land and 'returning it to the landless.'

Counter-cartography projects

To the Landless, by Métis artist Dylan Miner, borrowed its title from words spoken by anarchist Lucia Gonzáles Parsons (commonly known as Lucy Parsons) at the founding convention of the Industrial Workers of World (IWW). As a woman of African, Mexican, and Indigenous ancestry, Parsons employed feminist intersectional, anti-state, and anti-capitalist activism throughout her life. In her writing and in her organizing, Parsons was often at odds with better-known anarchist Emma Goldman. *To the Landless* asked people to join together on a walk through Chinatown and Kensington Market, in Toronto, and pause in front of Goldman's former house on Spadina Avenue. During the walk participants read from Goldman's and Parsons's writings, and imagined Parsons joining Goldman, who died in Toronto in 1940, for dinner near her house. Unable to separate history from the present and future, Miner asked participants to walk-with and converse-with these two contentious and important activists and thinkers. Conversations incited by the walk focused on the politics of settler-colonialism, capitalism, patriarchy, and immigration.

The Red Line Archive and Labyrinth project, by Walis Johnson, is an ongoing public art project that engages pedestrians in conversations about race, spatial narratives, and the history of the Red Line Map of the 1930s. Redlining began in New York City in 1934 to indicate the risk of real estate development in particular communities. Race was the primary factor in determining where the red line was drawn. Residents in red line neighbourhoods were unable to access housing loans, mortgages, and other financial services. Johnson's family home, which she inherited in 2013, was situated within a red line neighbourhood in Brooklyn. In one iteration of the project, Johnson walked the Red Line Map of 1938 and pulled 'a red cabinet of curiosities.' The red cabinet contained archival material from her family home and other ephemera relating to the red line and the history of the neighbourhood that she finds on her walks.

For the *WalkingLab* iteration of this ongoing project, Johnson collaborated with the Weeksville Heritage Centre in Brooklyn to execute a community walk complicating the narrative of redlining and the way that this policy continues to haunt the landscape today. The Weeksville Heritage Centre is Brooklyn's largest African American cultural institution. It is a multidisciplinary museum dedicated to preserving the history of the 19th century African American community of Weeksville, Brooklyn, one of America's first free Black communities.

Miss Canadiana's Heritage and Cultural Walking Tour: The Grange, by Camille Turner, is a walking tour that examined the Black history of Toronto mapped through Afrofuturist hauntings and places. Miss Canadiana is Turner's performance persona who leads the walking tours. 'Miss Canadiana' wears a red beauty pageant dress, a tiara, and a pageant sash. The performance persona contradicts dominant Canadian myths that Blackness is foreign and that Blackness is not a representative of national beauty. *Miss Canadiana's Heritage and Cultural Walking Tour: The Grange* exposed the intra-connectedness and entanglement between slavery, racialized bodies, colonial historical narratives, and land. The walk explored the complexities of slavery in Canada between 1793, when the act to limit the importation of slaves was passed, which enabled American slaves to cross into Canada and become free while those already enslaved in Canada remained enslaved, and 1833, when slavery was abolished. On the walking tour, Miss Canadiana recounts various narratives and stories, much like one would hear on a conventional historic walking tour. However, Miss Canadiana tells stories of a host of characters, from the Grange area in Toronto, including Peggy Pompadour, a Black woman who was jailed in 1806 for resisting slavery. Mapping Blackness onto the Toronto landscape, the narratives entangle Peggy Pompadour's imprisonment for resisting slavery, and contemporary accounts from Toronto's Black history. Peggy was enslaved by Peter Russell, whose property included a farm on the western edges of the Grange. The Grange takes its name from the Grange home, which is the oldest brick house in the city. The house was built and owned by a powerful and wealthy family, and is now a historic home attached to the Art Gallery of Ontario. The neighbourhood that surrounds the Art Gallery is referred to as the Grange. Black families are recorded as living in that area from 1792.

Borders and labour: re-mapping space

Geopolitical borders are social and physical constructions that paradoxically connect and divide. Borders mark out racialized territories and restrict the movement of people, animals, and pathogens. Current global border fortification projects are fueled by heightened concerns about migration. The reinforcement of borders function to police and protect labour. While some borders were first established to control the movement of cattle and disease, they quickly became racialized sites that restricted human bodies. Borders materialize understandings of purity and safety, yet, as Gloria Anzaldúa (1987) maintains, 'borderlands' enact emotional and physical trauma. As Eve Tuck and Marcia McKenzie (2015) note, borders and border-crossing have been used by social science researchers as a metaphor. However, a figurative use of 'border transgression' fails to account for the lived realities of those who die crossing actual borders each day. Moreover, border-crossing reflects unequal power dynamics where some bodies move freely while others are criminalized. Walking researchers need to similarly question the ways that border concepts get used and materialized in their work.

To delimit borders as a mapping practice exercises mechanisms of power and continues to produce hegemonic worldviews (Hunt & Stevenson, 2017). The formation of the nation state is predicated on geographical understandings, of which maps play a crucial role in creating a stable representation of a landscape. Maps produce a sense of certainty and entitlement to land. As Pamela Edmonds (2017) states, "Canada is spatially produced and narrativized by its forgotten histories" (p. 76).

In North America, the absence of visible borders, such as fences, when settlers arrived, allowed them to believe that the land was unoccupied (*terra nullius*) and, hence, that it was 'free' to claim. "[F]ences, for settlers represented material proclamations, indicating dominion over the land" (Mendoza, 2017, p. 13). Fences demarcate ownership and property and are part of the North American ideology of progress and capitalism. However, in carving up people and place, borders restrict access to vital resources. Dylan Miner (2016) contends that settler colonial borders have impacted and limited ancestral Indigenous practices and fail to recognize Indigenous spatial knowledges. He argues that, from an Indigenous perspective, borders imposed by the state violate ancestral movement across Indigenous territories that were never claimed solely by one Indigenous nation. For example, the Canada-US border impeded his ancestors' ability to live and work in ways that they had previously around the Great Lakes. The border, particularly as it cuts across the Great Lakes region of North America is the subject of many of Miner's art projects. Miner (2012) asks, "What would it mean to develop regionalisms based in Indigenous ontologies and not on modes put in place by settler colonialism" (p. 6)? In thinking-with Land through what he calls alternative cartographies, Miner re-maps personal and collective understandings of the Great Lakes region.

In *To the Landless*, Miner invited participants to collectively walk along Spadina Avenue and through Kensington Market in Toronto. This area is a dense multicultural neighbourhood that has gone through many transitions. Kensington is situated on the traditional lands of the Seneca and Huron-Wendat and Mississaugas of the Credit River, and was settled by Eastern European Jewish immigrants in the early 20th century, and became a neighbourhood of densely packed houses and one of the poorer areas of the city. After WWII, different migrants moved into the area as the Jewish population moved north. Chinatown is located adjacent to Kensington, and the Grange neighbourhood is to the east, on the other side of Spadina Avenue. Kensington is a mix of surplus stores, food shops, and in recent years, trendy cafes and restaurants. Emma Goldman lived in an apartment on Spadina Avenue in 1928. Today, the apartment is on the second floor above a Vietnamese sub shop. Outside on the street is a plaque embossed with her name, while further along the block is a larger plaque for the Labour Lyceum. This was the headquarters of the non-communist trade unions for the Jewish garment district. The plaque contains an image of a notice for a lecture given by Emma Goldman.

Goldman, born in Russia in 1869, moved to New York City in her teens. There she became involved in the anarchist movement as both an activist and a writer. She was known for advocating for birth control and sexual freedom for women, and for her opposition to capitalism. She protested the military draft in WWI and was arrested and jailed. Considered as one of the most dangerous women in the

United States (by the government), she was eventually exiled and deported in the 1920s when the US government feared persons without US citizenship. Goldman spent a year in Toronto but lived out most of her remaining years in Europe, returning to Canada to give lectures frequently. A prolific writer and orator, Goldman is considered one of the most important figures in the anarchist movement. She died in Toronto in 1940.

Along the walk participants read passages from Goldman's texts that had been compiled into a pamphlet by Miner. Property, wrote Goldman,

> condemns millions of people to be mere non-entities, living corpses without originality or power of initiative, human machines of flesh and blood, who pile up mountains of wealth for others and pay for it with a grey, dull and wretched existence for themselves.
>
> (as cited in Miner, 2017, p. 2)

Lucy Parsons was similarly vocal about the perils of capitalism. In her speech to the Founding Convention of the Industrial Workers of the World (IWW) in 1905, she stated that revolution would return the land "to the landless, the tools to the toiler; and the products to the producers" (as cited in Miner, 2017, p. 12). Parsons was born in the southern United States and was of mixed ancestry that included Indigenous, black, and Mexican. Historians have speculated that she was possibly born a slave. She moved to Chicago in her adult years. She was a radical socialist, anarchist, and labour organizer. Like Goldman she was a prolific writer and orator. Her husband Albert Parsons was executed in 1887 for conspiracy in the Haymarket Affair. Albert Parsons was trying to organize a peaceful protest to demand eight-hour workdays, when an anonymous person threw a bomb into the crowd killing police and bystanders. In the aftermath, Parsons, along with other organizers, was arrested. He was found guilty and executed. The Haymarket Affair is seen as the catalyst for the global May Day labour observations. Lucy Parsons was one of the founders of the IWW and similarly campaigned for shorter work days. Parsons died in a house fire in 1942. Parsons and Goldman were often in conflict with each other, in part because their anarchist beliefs stemmed from different generations and different orientations to feminism.

Parson's anarchism and her radical thought was in direct opposition to the White pro-capitalists at the time. The media invoked numerous stereotypes to defame her including calling her a savage, emphasizing her unkempt hair, dark skin, and black eyes. In the press, Parsons was often referred to as 'Negro,' and positioned as a former slave. Lauren Basson (2008) explains that such profiling was in order to "create and legitimize a descriptive distinction between capitalist, American bodies, and foreign, anarchist bodies" (p. 158). The racialization of borders (White American/Black foreigners) made Parsons politically undesirable. Parsons herself denounced any African American ancestry, holding fast to her Indigenous lineage. To be Indigenous, she often claimed, was to be American and as such anarchism was not in opposition to American values, but rather represented 'American' ideology (where the 'true' American was the Indigenous

American). Anarchism, for both Parsons and Goldman, argued for freedom from man-made laws and governments imposed by violence and coercion.

Hunt and Stevenson (2017) suggest that Indigenous maps are "processes through which Indigenous peoples articulate their presence on and right to defend their ancestral lands, territories and resources" (p. 376). However, they also state that counter-cartographical practices, while offering Indigenous peoples alternative and potentially decolonizing geographies, can also maintain dominant mapping practices. In their research into digital forms of re-mapping they note that some forms of technology re-inforce state power through surveillance and capitalism. While cautious that counter-cartographies can re-inscribe settler colonial power structures, they are optimistic about the tensions and frictions that arise in re-mapping practices.

As a counter-cartography, *To the Landless* re-mapped anarchism onto the Toronto landscape. Bringing together Parsons and Goldman in Toronto, Miner re-maps place as regional as opposed to an understanding of place that is marked by official state sanctioned borders. For example, rather than think about Parsons in the United States and Goldman in Canada, the walk activated the two of them together, shifting the arbitrary governmental lines to a different spatial logic based in relations, collective practices, and community organizing.

The walking event took place in the month of May (May 1 being International Worker's Day) and was hosted in conjunction with an exhibition at Gallery 44 and Trinity Square video: *What does one do with such a clairvoyant image?* The walk started at the galleries. The exhibition included a series of photo-based works by Miner, and was curated as a critical response and intervention to 'Canada 150.' 'Canada 150' is a year-long series of events across the country celebrating Canada's 150th 'birthday,' with a total budget of more than 500 million dollars. In contrast to events that celebrated Canada's 'birthday,' numerous counter-events, including art projects, critiqued the celebrations, and Canada's genocidal origins. These critiques included debates about the treatment of Indigenous peoples, residential schools, missing and murdered Indigenous women, and the current social and economic crisis. In imagining Parsons and Goldman in conversation with each other, and in Toronto, the walking event intervened into the 'Canada 150' discourse that commemorates the violently imposed Canadian border and nation state, and which reinforces the narrative of progress and capitalism.

To the Landless's counter-cartography, in the words of Lucy Parsons, imagined an era of labour "when capitalism will be a thing of the past, and the new industrial republic, the commonwealth of labour, shall be in operation" (cited in Miner, 2017, p. 12). Walking and reading fragments of text from Goldman's and Parson's writings, the group paused frequently to discuss place, activism, labour, Indigenous knowledges, and settler colonialism. The collective action of walking, reading, and talking attended to the ways that Indigenous and settler peoples need to engage in "mutual care, to each other and to the land they share" and to re-map and "re-learn" new geographical practices (Hunt & Stevenson, 2017, p. 386).

The counter-cartography performed by *To the Landless* is similarly materialized in the *Red Line* project. As part of her ongoing research-creation events into redlining in New York City, Walis Johnson created a red line labyrinth at the Weeksville Heritage Centre in Brooklyn as her contribution to *WalkingLab*. Marking out in red an intricate combination of paths, Johnson invited participants to walk the red line with her. Black geographies, Katherine Mckittrick (2017) states, are not nouns, but "verbs that are ongoing and never resolved" (p. 99). Articulating a spatial understanding of anti-Blackness and its violence, Mckittrick (2011) argues that Black geographies include the plantation house, the fields, the prisons, the slave ships, and the slave quarters to name just a few. Concerned with the ways that a focus on violence and death perpetuate a pathological repetition of anti-Blackness, Mckittrick states,

> Analytically, there seems no way out, except to name these repetitions – even in their continuities and ruptures – and ask those who are the foci of these analyses, poor black people, to live up to a version of humanness that they are necessarily excluded from.
>
> (in Hudson, 2014, p. 240).

Asking African Americans to assimilate or to simply become included, McKittrick argues, requires Blacks to join the very system that thrives on anti-Blackness. Anti-Blackness is linked to urban infrastructural decay and geographic surveillance. McKittrick (2011) maintains that Black geographies are regarded as dangerous, unruly, and empty, even when they are excessively populated. Black geographies are bound up with the redlining practices and policies, which results in a kind of forced placelessness. As a counter-cartography, McKittrick demands that we turn to artists, writers, and thinkers for whom Blackness "works against the violence that defines it" (in Hudson, 2014, p. 240). Furthermore, while research can focus on the places where Black subjects live focusing on the inequalities of redlining, for example, such studies McKittrick and Woods (2007) state, "can also be read as naturalizing racial difference in place" reducing Black lives to statistics and facts (p. 6).

Johnson's re-mapping project re-claims the community spaces within the red line. *Solvitur ambulando*, Johnson notes, is a Latin term which means 'it is solved by walking.' Like Miner's project, the *Red Line* critically questions the North American narratives of progress and capitalism, which are upheld by racial and economic discriminatory mapping processes such as redlining. Walking, for Miner and Johnson, becomes a thinking-in-movement, a practice that re-maps possible futures. Inviting participants into a conversation as they walk, Johnson considered how walking might create a 'new' geography and record of New York that re-imagines Black people, communities of colour, and the working class at the centre, rather than the margins of society.

The Red Line, as a walking methodology in a more-than-human world foregrounds race. This is to say, it doesn't merely include race, but starts from questions about race, and centres race. Zakiyyah Jackson (2015) and other critical race scholars have argued that the turn to more-than human theories, including new materialisms, have neglected "critiques by black people, particularly those praxes which are irreverent to the normative production of the 'human,' or illegible from within the terms of its logics" (p. 216). Similarly, Tavia Nyong'o (2015) states: we must consider how race "conditions the possibilities of life at or below the threshold of the human" (p. 252).

Jackson (2013) discusses how posthuman scholarship has avoided the critical challenges posed by race, colonialism, and slavery. Furthermore, Diana Leong (2016) asserts that Blackness is the spectre that haunts the Anthropocene. She writes: "The movement for Black Lives has forcefully reminded us that black bodies have historically provided the standards against which the human subject and non-human objects are measured" (p. 12). Nicholas Mirzoeff (2016) argues that the ways in which the Anthropocene has been distinguished as an ecological and geological era is only possible because of the distinction between races. Aligning the genesis of the Anthropocene with capitalism, Mirzoeff contends, ignores the fact that capitalism emerged from transatlantic slavery, imperialist conquest, and settler colonialism. The racialization of the Anthropogenesis, Kathryn Yusoff (2017b) argues, is figured as a production of Blackness as an exclusion. Humanity, she asserts, is racially constituted and how this is in-scripted in geology reinforces global divisions. 'A Black Anthropos,' she argues, would re-centre race, not as a corrective lens, but as an unsettling of how the Anthropocene is currently being narrated. Counter to the whitewashing of the Anthropocene, via capitalism, new materialisms and posthumanisms need to account for colonial displacement through multiple origin stories and their complex intersections. In fact, Yusoff (2017b) contends, the Black Anthropocene has never had the luxury of origins.

As such the insistence on a de-centering of the human needs to recognize the ways that anti-Blackness is constructed in the Anthropocene. For example, Saidiya Hartman (1997) states that too often anti-Blackness is understood as dehumanization, when in fact slavery relied on the abjection and criminalization of the slave's humanness. As Jackson (2015) writes: "Thus, humanization is not an antidote to slavery's violence; rather, slavery is a technology for producing a *kind* of human" (p. 96, italics in original). For example, Jin Haritaworn (2015) states that Environmental Studies as a discipline, often privileges nonhuman animals in more-than-human research and in doing so reflects a desire for an Other who can not "talk back" (p. 212). Responding to new materialisms' and posthumanisms' longing to de-centre humanisms, Haritaworn (2015) argues that what is required are "anticolonial accounts of the world . . . which would naturally be allied to Indigenous sovereignty and self-determination [and] would have the potential to tackle anthropocentrism and dehumanization simultaneously, as relational rather than competing or analogous paradigms" (p. 213). Conceptualizing and understanding the Anthropocene through race, empire, capitalism, slavery, and settler colonialism makes violence, dehumanization, and social inequality central to concerns of environmental studies. *The Red Line* project is one such manifestation of this post-Anthropocene critical work.

Johnson's *Red Line Labyrinth* functions as a spatial enactment of resistance. Walking the red line becomes a transcorporeal materialization revealing the connections between race and place on and through the lived body. While maps are often created as paper (and now digital) records of place, walking as counter-cartography maps more-than just the borders of a place. Walking as a re-mapping involves movement and rhythm of place, sensory materializations of place, and memories that are not simply in the past, but encountered in the present. Walking *The Red Line*, by including transcorporeal practices like walking-with, stories, archives, and alternative ways of being, re-maps a story of survival, futurity, and affirmation.

Anarchives and time

Archival practices, like mapping, have excluded and erased Indigenous and Black bodies. As technologies that served the production of imperialism and settler colonialism, conventional or 'official' archives are cloaked in rational and humanist conceptualizations of the human. Conventional archives function by preserving what they remove from circulation and legitimize through practices of naming. One of the ways that archives are performed is through walking tours. Official and state sanctioned narratives and documents are collected through archival practices and then tours disseminate this knowledge. What information is imparted on a walking tour becomes the legitimate knowledge of a place. This knowledge of place becomes normalized. The practice of incorporating counter-cartography into a walking tour has been used by a number of people and organizations. For example, *First Story* in Toronto hosts a series of walking tours that re-map the Indigenous history of Toronto. On their walking tours, or through the self-guided mobile app, participants encounter Indigenous knowledges and places often erased and neglected on conventional walking tours of the city.

Each of the *WalkingLab* projects discussed in this chapter engage with counter or 'anarchival' practices that rely on fragments of memories, oral stories, songs, marginal ephemera, and affects and emotions. Anarchives, in contrast with official archives, are activities that resist mere documentation and interpretation in favour of affective and material processes of production (Murphie, 2016). Unlike an archive concerned with recording, preservation, and coding practices that aid in the retrieval of data, anarchiving means approaching matter from new perspectives that may be incongruent with conventional archiving practices, in order to activate erased, neglected, and hidden histories. For example, researchers at *SenseLab* have been developing an anarchival practice that generates what they call 'seed banks.' The anarchive, they write, "is invested in the question of how to make felt the infra-perceptible" (*SenseLab*, nd).[1] *WalkingLab* conceives of anarchiving as a practice that stimulates new nodes of production and new compositions. As opposed to a documentation of past activities, anarchives are a "feed-forward mechanism for lives creative process, under continuing variation" (Massumi, 2016, p. 7).

In *To the Landless* participants carried screen-printed pennants. The text on the pennants (three different ones in total) are ambivalent. Miner selected the fragments of text from Parsons' and Goldman's writings, specifically searching for text that could or could not be read as political: *To a Radical Mother*; *Sustaining the Worker*; and *Gesture of Solidarity*. In doing so, Miner points at the ambivalence and the paradox of archival material and the ways that it circulates and flows. Writing about the anarchive, Brian Massumi (2016) notes, that anarchives, need the archive as a starting point. It is the archive that becomes the departure point for the anarchive. Massumi (2016) also states that the anarchive is not contained in the archive (or an archival object) but is the excess or supplement of the archive. The anarchive he writes, "is made of the formative movements going into and coming out of the archive" (p. 7). So, while the pennants used text from Parsons' and Goldman's writing, Miner's fragmented selections and the act of screen-printing them on felt, become spring-boards for anarchiving tendencies. Massumi (2016) argues that the movements of the anarchive are activated between media, gestures, expressions, feelings. These intra-actions reactivate anarchival traces and new ones.

The pennants, likewise, signaled a tension that exists in social justice and solidarity movements. For example, 'gesture of solidarity' "can be mobilized to obscure the very dynamics of colonization" (Gaztambide-Fernández, 2012, p. 43). Such a phrase can be "turned into a commodity to be marketed and sold by both the state and corporations" (p. 44). Walking as a form of protest is similarly complex and contradictory. While its aims are to bring together disparate people it is often co-opted by neoliberalism. Rubén Gaztambide-Fernández (2012), writing about the possibilities of solidarity as decolonization, cautions:

> Most of the time, solidarity hinges on similarities in characteristics, political interests, social needs, or moral obligations. Most relevant to projects of decolonization, yet more rare and complicated to theorize, is a conception of solidarity that hinges on radical differences and that insists on relationships of incommensurable interdependency.
>
> (p. 46)

On the *To the Landless* walk, conversations returned to these tensions and frictions, reflecting on the role contemporary art and group walking plays in solidarity work. Miner and the group of walkers spoke at length about the nature of politics in artistic practices that gesture at political actions. For example, Miner's walk took the form of a walking 'protest,' but didn't function as an 'actual' protest, yet was a 'protest' of a different kind. This is where the work of the anarchive becomes crucial. As a 'feed-forward mechanism,' Miner's walking protest linked the archival traces from Parsons and Goldman, with the walkers' expressions, statements, feelings, and ideas.

For trans, Black, activist Syrus Ware (2017), counter-archives (anarchives) can perform a type of solidarity work. For this to happen though, Ware (2017) argues that counter-archives must *start* with Black and trans lives. This means they can't simply be added to existing dominant archives. Rupturing a progress narrative that is structured via chronological time, Ware (2017) suggests that trans of colour engender a different sense of time, one that challenges how we understand production and assimilation. Starting from the position of a QTBIPOC (Queer Trans Black Indigenous People of Colour) is a counter-archival practice that: problematizes a notion of a past that is not a past; refuses inclusion (new additions to archives) and instead commences with difference; and resists a focus on damage-centred research, where the Black, trans, queer body is fetishized and pathologized (Tuck, 2009; Ware, 2017). Ware (2017) writes that among the many 'things' that constitute a counter-archive are fragments of conversations that emerge on particular street corners in the city of Toronto. These he contends, rupture the ways that conventional queer archives whitewash the archive collection. While the lesbian and gay archives in Toronto are important, the problem is their anti-Black and anti-trans configuring of an archive (Ware, 2017). This is in part because of the kinds of materials that are rendered valuable and hence archivable (Springgay & Truman, 2017c).

In Johnson's *The Red Line* project, archival material collected from her parents' home and the red line neighbourhoods included, among other things: maps, neighbourhood soil samples, the deed to her grandparents' home, a mortgage letter, and photographs. Parading these cobbled together pieces along the streets of Brooklyn in a red cabinet, Johnson's archive is composed of personal artifacts, community conversations and stories, and affects that frictionally assembled between the different participants. Ann Cvetkovich (2003) emphasizes the felt experience of history and how such affects need to be accounted for in archival understandings. In doing so, 'archives of feeling' attend to the ways that affects circulate between the past, present, and future. Archives of feeling are thus shaped from both material objects and affective tonalities, visceral sensations including tears, anger, joy, and numbness. If official archives create value through preservation and naming, then anarchives attend to not only the collection of neglected documents and ephemera, but also the ways that affects circulate and produce archives.

Camille Turner's walking tour intervenes in the logics of official archives. Black history exists in Canada's official archives through the history of the Underground Railroad. This history falsely describes Canada as a country committed to multiculturalism and benevolence (McKittrick, 2007). The dominant narrative of Blackness presents Canada as a safe place that welcomes racialized others. This logic of goodwill, McKittrick (2007) argues, "conceals and/or skews colonial practices, Aboriginal genocides and struggles, and Canada's implication in transatlantic slavery, racism, and racial intolerance" (p. 98). The production of Canada as a White state is indebted to the erasure of Blackness. The erasure of Blackness, Rinaldo Walcott (1997) argues, is ongoing and manifests in "the space and place that bodies, both actual and symbolic, occupy in the nation's imagination" (p. 54).

Turner's walking tours not only re-map this erased and forgotten history onto the Canadian landscape, they also question the mechanisms that enable this ongoing erasure. McKittrick (2007) states that while Canada's mythology has been shaped by the idea of fugitive American slaves finding freedom and refuge in Canada, Black feminism and Black resistance are "unexpected and concealed" (p. 92). Black people arrived in Canada via multiple means, not just as a passage into 'freedom;' and as Turner's walking tour makes explicitly clear, Canada also legalized the enslavement of Black people. In fact, the story of Peggy Pompadour disrupts the tidy Canadian narrative of benevolence and safety.

As an anarchival practice, Turner pieced together fragments that existed of Black history in Toronto. Because there is very little 'official' documentation in the archives, alternative methods, including creating composite fictions, needed to be used. For example, to create the Peggy Pompadour character, that walkers encounter on the tour, Turner used: the newspaper report of Peggy Pompadour running away, text from her bill of sale, historical pictures and information on the jail, the living conditions of the poor in the Grange area at the time, songs passed down from generation to generation, and snippets of conversations with contemporary Black residents of the Grange neighbourhood. Using memory and affect, and elements of science fiction and fantasy, Turner re-imagines a past that is not a past. Turner's walking tour "refuses a unitary, linear, or nationalist celebratory story of Black pride and/or White/Canadian paternalism" (McKittrick, 2007, p. 107). The persona of Miss Canadiana, Peggy Pompadour's story, the sites visited on the walking tour, become departure points for the anarchiving practice that the walking tour enacts.

Mohawk scholar Audra Simpson (2014), in her book *Mohawk Interruptus*, discusses the politics of recognition. Recognition by the official state – through DNA, maps, or by being included in archives – does not undo settler colonial logics. Recognition and representation works via inclusion, where the excluded are initiated into the dominant norm. Recognition is understood as a 'good' practice of multiculturalism. For Simpson (2014), recognition from the state is a form of managing Indigenous peoples. Instead, Simpson posits a politics of refusal as "a wilful distancing from state-driven forms of recognition and sociability in favour of others" (p. 16). While Simpson's research is specifically working within an Indigenous framework, we contend it is useful to read it alongside the work of critical race scholars.

In concert with Simpson's (2007) refusal of recognition, Alexander Weheliye (2014) states that when Blackness is recognized, it is framed in such a way in order to makes it legible and acceptable. Recognition is a process of normalization, which maps Blackness using Euro-Western techniques. Furthermore, Weheliye (2014) argues recognition continues to fetishize Black flesh as inhuman. In composing the character Peggy Pompadour and creating a 'new' oral history of her life – a speculative one – Turner's anarchiving practice resists re-victimizing and commodifying Peggy's story. In shaping the past as a past that is not completed and one that stretches infinitely into a different future, Turner's walk refuses recognition and replaces it with a different map.

Turner's walking tour enacts both a politics of refusal and what Christine Sharpe (2014) calls 'wake work.' Sharpe (2014) uses the concept of the wake to think about Blackness. Her three figures of the wake include: the ceremony that happens after death – as a ritual to enact grief and memory and the passage from life to death; the disturbance in water from a boat or a body – a region of disturbed flow; and wakefulness or consciousness. To live in the wake is to live in the time of slavery and in the afterlife of it, while understanding that it is not over. Wake work is realizing that research happens in the wake. "In the wake, the past that is not past reappears, always, to rupture the present" (Sharpe, 2014, p. 9). In order to produce legible research, we have to adhere to particular kinds of methods, she argues, and those kinds of methods have emerged from taxonomies that configure particular lives as expendable or inhuman. She says we "must become undisciplined" (p. 13). To be in the wake as a methodology is to be in the presence of slavery as something that's not resolved. Wake work is different from reparation. To repair assumes that the past is completed and thus can be resolved. Sharpe (2016) writes:

> In the United States, slavery is imagined as a singular event even as it changed over time and even as its duration expands into supposed emancipation and beyond. But slavery was not singular; it was, rather, a singularity – a weather event or phenomenon likely to occur around a particular time, or date, or set of circumstances. Emancipation did not make free Black life free; it continues to hold us in that singularity. The brutality was not singular; it was the singularity of anti-blackness.
>
> (np)

This singularity, where space and time are infinitely distorted is what Sharpe refers to as pervasive as weather. But while weather and the wake produce anti-Blackness, those in the wake and exposed to weather create their own space-times that rupture and undo these holding patterns. Recognition and reparation enact the forms of solidarity based on sameness, empathy, and knowability. Rather what is needed is solidarity that is in the wake, indeterminate, incommensurable, and unknowable. Walking-with Miss Canadiana and Peggy Pompadour, Emma Goldman and Lucy Parsons, re-mapping and anarchiving asks how these figures and those that walk-with are co-composed in the past, present, and speculative future. What new assemblages and understandings emerge from walking-with? Walking-with becomes a process of anarchiving.

Turner's walk through the Grange, piecing together snippets of ephemera with her imagination, enacts a kind of wake work. As counter-cartographies, her walks revive "the principle of an oral tradition" (Edmonds, 2017, p. 76). Centering Blackness, Turner's walks disrupt linear and progressive conceptualizations of time. If 'the past that is not the past appears in the present' then Turner's walks re-map and anarchive Black worlds and futures. As McKittrick (2017) writes: "[B]lack is in the break, it is fantastic, it is an absented presence . . . it is in between the lines and it is postcolonial; black is . . . afro-pessimist, afro-optimist, afrocentric, afropunk, afrofuturist . . . black is everywhere and everything" (pp. 97–98).

The term Afrofuturism emerged in literary critique as a response to whitewashed futurism of the late 20th century. Much mainstream futurism functions within a Western progress model that perpetuates linear versions of time and universalized futures that continue to abstract the material conditions of race (Nyawalo, 2016). Kodwo Eshun (2003) argues that, in the 20th century, 'avant-gardists' like Walter Benjamin and Frantz Fanon "revolted in the name of the future against a power structure that relied on control and representation of the historical archive" (p. 289). Whereas nowadays the situation has reversed itself: "The powerful employ futurists and draw power from the futures they endorse, thereby condemning the disempowered to live in the past. The present moment is stretching, slipping for some into yesterday, reaching for others into tomorrow" (Eshun, 2003, p. 289). Futurists lure the future that they want, one that keeps them in power, and in doing so they relegate particular bodies (Black bodies) to the past that has never recognized them. In doing so, futurists secure a future for themselves in which Blackness is never a part. In contrast, "Afrofuturism was a way around the racial exclusion encoded in the various media of mainstream Futurism" (Kilgore, 2014, p. 561). Afrofuturism employs an aesthetics of hope as a response to afropessimism and the overrepresentation of Whiteness politically, socially, and culturally. According to Mark Fisher (2013), Afrofuturism "unravels any linear model of the future, disrupting the idea that the future will be a simple supersession of the past. Time in afrofuturism is plastic, stretchable and prophetic" (p. 47). Time becomes out of joint. This is materialized through Turner's anarchive: the narratives, songs, sounds, and places encountered on the walk. This is a time that is looped and haunting, rupturing teleological and linear understandings of time. Afrofuturism as a walking methodology could be described as both a method of recovering histories and futures and as a anarchiving of aesthetic productions that enact such a method. Afrofuturism is not only literary-based but can be a theoretical, material, sonic, performative, mapping, and anarchival practice.

Walking as counter-cartographies

Mapping is a longstanding subject for walking artists and social science researchers (O'Neill, 2017). At stake in the production of maps is their participation in the maintenance and governance of borders and bodies, land dispossession, resource extraction, settler colonialism, spatialized racism, environmental degradation, and gentrification. The turn to matter that has been heralded over the past decade through new materialisms and posthumanisms, while emphasizing the agency and mattering of human and nonhuman entities, has insisted that the crisis of the Anthropocene requires immediate ethical and political interventions. While we agree, the problem – as we have raised in this chapter and throughout the book – is that, while more-than-human theories attend to the agency of nonhuman phenomena, and the ways that humans and nonhumans are entangled in knotted relations, the category of the human has remained intact. Moreover, we assert that more-than-human theories need to account for geographies of race and the mattering of place. In a move beyond the human, research may in fact reintroduce imperial and settler colonial taxonomies, power structures, and systems of knowledge that such research aims to disrupt, particularly in relation to Indigenous sovereignty and race.

The *WalkingLab* projects that we have assembled in this chapter take up walking methodologies in relation to space and time, acknowledging the possibilities and tensions that such work might produce. Counter-cartographies and anarchiving practices might in fact reproduce the very geographies they seek to undo.

However, in attending strategically to re-mapping the past that is not past, these projects offer avenues for imagining a different future. Re-mapping space and time are significant components to a counter-cartographical approach to walking methodologies. Futurity, a theme that we return to again and again, refers to the ways that the future is projected and re-imagined. It also considers how the future is implicated in the past and the present, through different conceptualizations of time. Here time shifts from heteronormative colonial chronos, to vectors, hauntings, spectres, regions, and relations. It also speaks to the ways that any reference to the future makes some futures possible while disavowing others. Walking as counter-cartographies and anarchiving practices enact these understandings of futurity, where the future is not a romanticized ideal, but in constant re-figurations. Futurity, re-mapped in these three walking projects, addresses spatial cartographies and geographies that have been denied to Indigenous and Black peoples through ongoing imperialism and settler colonization. In the words of Lucy Gonzáles Parsons, Black, Indigenous, queer, feminist anarchist, futurity means "the land will belong to the landless" through a mode of activism that remains firmly in the wake, in a politics of refusal, and a counter-cartography that is regional, relational, and collective.

Note

1 *SenseLab* is a laboratory for thought in motion. Based in Montreal, the *SenseLab* brings together an international network of artists and academics working between philosophy, art, and activism. Founded by Erin Manning in 2004, the lab supports projects, events, and publications. http://senselab.ca/wp2/

7 Reflective inversions and narrative cartographies

Disrupting outcomes based models of walking in schools

Walking and education are intimately connected. Walking is often used to move student bodies away from desk-centred learning. Examples include math walks, which are methods for experiencing mathematics in everyday life. Project-based learning sometimes incorporates gallery walks to move students throughout the classroom to view and discuss student work. Perambulation is implemented as an inquiry technique, where students go outside of the classroom to conduct research on neighbourhood features and topographies. Walking is also part of the growing outdoor school movement and features as a physical activity promoted for its health benefits, and as part of green initiatives in schools where it is encouraged as a less carbon-reliant mode of transportation. Outside of school-based learning, walking is incorporated into community arts-based projects, museum and gallery public programming, and as a mode of learning in parks and nature centres.

Recent scientific data from Stanford University links walking with creativity and increased learning outcomes (Oppezzo & Schwartz, 2014). Likewise, researchers focused on risk-taking and outdoor play, have emphasized the importance of movement for childhood development (Brussoni *et al.*, 2015). While these claims might be important reasons to advocate for movement in schools and informal learning environments, the tenuous link between walking and creativity can easily be commodified and normalized by neoliberalism. Furthermore, when the rhetoric of benefits or value is ascribed to walking, educational research becomes trapped in an outcomes-based model.

This chapter deviates from outcomes-based conceptualizations of walking. It focuses on two examples of walking-with research in school contexts. We examine the complex ways that students can engage in walking as a method of inquiry into their world-making. This is the *how* of walking-with as learning.

The first research-creation event takes place in an urban elementary school in the Toronto District School Board (TDSB), Canada; the second, in a state secondary school in Cardiff, Wales. Specific to each of these examples is a focus on walking-with methods in schools and with young people. In the previous chapters, we have examined a number of *WalkingLab* projects, in relation to the extensive history of walking research in the social sciences, and emerging out of complex more-than-human theories. Many of our *WalkingLab* examples have been organized for wide public participation, such as our *Stone Walks on the Bruce Trail*. In this chapter, we demonstrate how similar theoretical orientations to walking-with can happen in school contexts and with students.

The chapter discusses the two research-creation events separately, introducing the research contexts and the complex ways that walking-with emerged. In the concluding section, we discuss the importance of walking-with methodologies in schools. In contrast to an outcomes-based model – where walking contributes to student creativity, attention, and health, which continue to uphold a particular notion of humanism – our two examples, offer the potential for students to critically interrogate humanist assumptions regarding landscape and literacy.

Walking-with the Don River

The Pedagogical Impulse was a research-creation project at the intersections between social practice art, knowledge production, pedagogy, and 'school.' As a site for artistic-research in art and education, the project initiated a number of experimental, critical, and collaborative projects including a series of artist-residencies in schools and community spaces in Toronto, Canada (Springgay, 2013b; Truman & Springgay, 2015). Documentation for the projects can be found at www.thepedagogicalimpulse.com (Rotas & Springgay, 2014; Springgay, 2014; Springgay, 2015; Zaliwska & Springgay, 2015). The residency *Upside-Down and Backwards*, with artists Hannah Jickling and Helen Reed explored artists' investigations into the Canadian landscape, through several field-trips and in-class research projects. The artist-residency took place in a large elementary school in downtown Toronto, with a grade three and grade six class. The school is located in a densely packed neighbourhood of high-rise buildings and concrete courtyards, and is in walking distance to the Don River, an important water-way through the city. The school population was predominantly composed of new Canadian families, many of whom had been in Toronto for less than five years, and many who identified as racially and ethnically non-White. The artists worked with the teachers and the students to develop a series of projects that asked questions about entanglements between nature and culture, and intervened into the sentimental colonial nostalgia for landscape painting that persists in the Ontario elementary curriculum. The residency resulted in a series of inversions, reflections, and refractions between nature and culture. The classes created *Endless Paintings* on the banks of the Don River, hiked with *Rearview Walking Sticks*, and created landscape reflection portraits.

While the school community is adjacent to the Don River, and easily accessible via different walking paths and routes, most of the students and their families did not make use of these parklands on a regular basis. The teachers' initial propositions to the research-team were to 'do something' on the banks of the Don, but without falling into the trap of the Canadian ideal of immigrants experiencing the Canadian 'natural' landscape. They noted that recent standardized tests had included questions about canoeing in Algonquin Park,[1] a concept both unfamiliar to their students, and out of place in the context of their urban school. The canoe, in the context of the artist-residency, first came to the attention of the teachers in an initial presentation to the school by the artists and the research team. The artists presented previous work they had done queering the canoe including: their col- laborative work of making a canoe into a studio (Canoedio); their paddling class- rooms at Portland State University; and Jickling's paper maché pumpkin canoe, which she paddled on the Yukon River. The teachers, who were interested in dis- rupting normalized and nationalistic environmental education narratives, recog- nized the canoe as a vehicle by which Whiteness claims Indigenous knowledges (Baldwin, 2009a; Erickson, 2013), but simultaneously found Jickling and Reed's canoe projects a unique departure for this otherwise iconic Canadian symbol.

The artist-residency unfolded over a month-long period with Jickling and Reed working in the grade three and grade six classrooms separately for a half-day each. For some of the culminating projects, the two classes came together. Micro- interventions took place each class period and the students incorporated walking into their daily research. Classroom research with the students included examin- ing contemporary artists' projects that critique or offer different understandings of landscape than those of the Group of Seven.[2]

Heroic images of voyageurs[3] and the Group of Seven's pristine landscapes are often considered mapped directly onto a Canadian sense of place and identity. Jickling and Reed introduced the students to contemporary art that looked criti- cally at the Canadian landscape and offered counter-images. These included: Jin- Me Yoon's photographs that place her Korean community, family and self into a landscape painting by Group of Seven member Lawren Harris; artists Elinor Whidden, Terrance Houle, Kainai Nation, and Trevor Freeman who take the icon of the canoe that appears uncritically in Canadian textbooks, literature, and visual culture and place it in landscapes very different from those swept by the great northern winds; and Cree artist Kent Monkman's paintings that re-enact iconic landscape paintings, but tell the story of Indigenous genocide. The curricula also included queer work by Michael Morris and Vincent Trasov, specifically their *Colour Research*, and Ian Baxter's reflective souvenirs, which breach the repre- sentational surface between the self and the natural, allowing the artist and viewer to see themselves within and complicit with nature.[4] These in-school lessons alongside walking-with research projects around the school, shaped the basis for the larger projects.

Conventional curricular approaches to landscape include sketching and paint- ing *plein air*, meaning 'outside.' These works are often then used for larger proj- ects back in the classroom space. Jickling and Reed introduced the students to a number of different ways to approach painting and landscape, and together the students and the artists created a project they called *Endless Paintings*, after work by Michael Morris and Vincent Trasov. In the classroom, students painted a series of wooden panels measuring approximately three feet by six inches. Each student painted one panel using techniques from colour theory – starting with one colour (e.g. red) – and moving through different tints by adding white paint. Each panel had eight, evenly divided sections, with one section for the colour hue, and seven for the gradient tints. The wooden panels where then mounted on wooden stakes. On the day of the *Endless Paintings* intervention, the class walked to a section of the Don River near their school. On the river, they were greeted by the artists, who arrived in a canoe, carrying the painted wooden colour bars.[5] In small groups the students spent the morning walking the banks of the river, with their bars, and a digital camera. Their task was to arrange the bars in the landscape – on the sandy shore line and in the water – and to photo-document the different configurations. A mid-day snack was provided to the students, which included juice boxes that the artists had covered in similarly tinted paper. Each of the students' bars had been photographed and reproduced on paper that was then adhered to the juice boxes, so that the boxes, much like the wooden bars, had hue to tint images. The students were invited to similarly compose the juice boxes (juice bars) on the river bank and take pictures. As a final disturbance into landscape, all of the students worked with Jickling and Reed to compose their bars into a giant rainbow facing a bridge that spanned the river. The result was a rainbow reflection on the Don, which could be seen from the bridge. Earlier in their classroom-based lessons, Jickling and Reed had shown the students a historical landscape painting that they uncovered in the Toronto archives: the painting looks north along the Don from the same vantage point of this bridge.

In another culminating walking-with project, the classes walked to a different section of the Don River; to the now gentrified Brickworks Park.[6] Here the students walked-with Elinor Whidden's *Rearview Walking Sticks* (on-loan by the artist). The *Rearview Walking Sticks* are made from found large tree branches and discarded rearview car mirrors. As a walker uses the walking stick, the rearview mirror enables them to see behind them on the path. The sticks suggest usefulness, but are ultimately ridiculous or burdensome.

In addition, students used walking-with round mirrors the size of an average child's head and digital cameras to stage a series of reflections, complicating the gentrified parkland. Students placed the mirror in front of their faces and a partner photographed their portrait, but with a reflection of land, sky, or park object (e.g. a brick wall) in the mirror. The results produced a series of student portraits, in which their faces become entangled, following what Haraway (2016) calls 'natureculutures.' Natureculutures insists on the co-imbrication of human and nonhuman world-making.

Juice boxes were covered in reflective mirror paper, and the students used these mirrors to create additional walking-reflection assemblages. As the students spent the day walking the Don and creating reflective resistances into the landscape, small groups of students could walk to the top of the highest point at the Brickworks, on a rotating basis, to look out through a telescope the artists had set up. The telescope was focused on an upper balcony of one of the apartments that surrounds the school (south of the Brickworks), and where the students live. On the balcony, a student had arranged a series of the earlier wooden colour bars, and the students had the opportunity to bring their own living space into focus with the otherwise distant parkland of the Brickworks.

Reflective interferences

Walking-with, in the context of this residency, functioned propositionally and enabled the students, teachers, and artists to enter into a series of speculative middles and (in)tensions about naturecultures, landscape and landscape art, and environmental and place-based education. In Canada – in public art galleries and museums, and in the school curricula – landscape is approached through dominant national narratives of wilderness, remoteness, and empty space (Baldwin, 2009b; 2010). Landscape, writes Bruce Braun (2003), is constructed as White space.

Landscape art conventionally functions to bring students into contact with 'nature.' In schools this is typically done by looking at landscape art in the classroom, field trips to galleries, and by re-creating landscape art, often in a similar style as the celebrated and quintessential national artists. Environmental education, of which art education plays a role, while becoming more wide-spread in Canadian elementary schools, relies on post-racial contexts, which mask the ongoing violence of settler colonialism (McLean, 2013). In doing so, landscape is presented as innocent. Sheelagh McLean (2013) contends that outdoor education programs, which are one form of environmental education, are motivated by the ideals of reconnecting students with landscape and nature, often to enjoy its beauty and untainted aesthetics. Students are sometimes presented with environmental problems, such as waste, climate change, and de-forestation, but these dominant narratives silence how capitalism, White supremacy, and settler colonialism are part of environmental degradation. Walking is often positioned as both a way of connecting with landscape, and as a more environmentally sustainable solution, but fails to consider its role in White settlers' claim to land. Similarly, landscape or 'nature' art becomes a stand-in for environmental engagement. These pedagogical methods continue to situate children outside of nature, and view nature as inanimate (Malone, 2016). New Canadian students and their families don't often see themselves reflected in Canadian vistas and landscape art, and as such the dominant discourses that separate nature and culture persist. For example, when the students were shown the painting of the Don River, they couldn't conceptualize that this was a place only a 20-minute walk from their homes. In fact, some of the students could see the Don River from their balconies, but to them, this landscape painting did not reflect their understanding of landscape or Toronto.

Karen Malone (2016) writes that current Anthropocentric beliefs postulate that humans are not nature, that humans used to be better connected to nature, and that humans can dominate nature. She notes that current educational environmental reforms are predicated on these Anthropocentric beliefs. Furthermore, Malone critiques the settler colonial approach to education that advocates for nature-based learning that continues to privilege Whiteness, heteronormativity, and ableist understandings of 'the natural world.' Families and communities who don't engage with particular forms of nature-based learning are seen to be deficit "for denying their children from having this restorative, nature-rich childhood" (p. 44). We add that such problematic understandings of nature and landscape continue to promote particular versions of citizenship, nationalism, and belonging where some bodies are already marked as inhuman, unnatural, and out of place in nature (Chen, 2012; Kafer, 2013; Jackson, 2015; Thobani, 2007). McLean (2013) contends, that while place-based environmental curricula purport decolonization, they often reproduce structures of Whiteness. She writes: "[N]ature is constructed as a cleansing system, where White bodies can escape the negative consequences of urban industrialism and reclaim identities of innocence" (p. 360). This was reflected in the students' journal writings, where landscape was defined as something outside of the urban place of Toronto, not something that they had experienced, and often defined as 'Canadian.' Debbie Sonu and Nathan Snaza (2016) argue that critical environmental and place-based learning "would instead investigate the complexity of an ecocrisis in relation to the struggle for humanization, problematizing, then politicizing" (p. 263). The students' investigations into the locality of the Don River problematized dominant narratives of landscape and nature, inquiring into their own intra-actions within place. Sandra Styres, Celia Haig-Brown, and Melissa Blimkie (2013), in their work on Land as pedagogy and as first teacher, argue that place-based education needs to consider how

> each learner is grounded, shaped, and informed by the Land and how pedagogical practices based in deepening understandings of Land can be (re) claimed, (re)constructed, and (re)enacted within the cultural and linguistic diversity inside and outside urban classrooms, informal learning environments, and communities.
>
> (p. 40)

While *Upside Down and Backwards*, did not focus on Indigenous knowledges of Land, the walking research emphasized contemporary Indigenous artists' works that rupture and contest dominant images of landscape and national identity.

Margaret Somerville and Monica Green (2015) maintain that posthuman place-based learning and environmental education research require an attention to *intimacy*, to counter the idea of nature as distinct from culture. Research methods, they contend, need to 'start where we are' and must include the social, material, and discursive constructions of place. In *Upside-Down and Backwards*, the teachers and artists started from the proposition of intimacy. This conceptualization of intimacy is not a human-centric model of care, where students were asked to get to *know* their local environment experientially, or how to make better sustainable choices regarding the environment. Somerville and Green's (2015) posthuman intimacy emphasizes affective, intensive moments of encounter, where something unknown, indeterminate, and unprepared for takes place. If, as McLean (2013) argues, that environmental education lacks a critical race analysis, while essentializing nature as White space, innocent, and empty, then how might walking-with create different spaces for racialized students to insert themselves into landscape, and in doing so interrupt dominant ideologies associated with nature? As opposed to an understanding of intimacy as innocent and inclusive, walking-with becomes an intimate practice that obstructs and contests the dominant Anthropocentric narratives. Intimacy becomes acts that inhere, intervene, and make visible students' entanglements within landscape.

The students engaged with different walking propositions during the month-long artist-residency. On one hand, walking was a means by which students accessed the Don River. Walking to the river, the students first began to experience the intimacy of place, as the walks meandered through familiar paths and neighbourhoods. Some of the walks to the river were twenty minutes long, while others upwards of forty minutes. Typically, nature-based learning, as explained by Malone (2016), asserts that nature is something distinct from culture, urbanization, and humans. Landscape, in the Canadian context, is often associated with the wilds of Algonquin Park, and not the Don River. In walking-with the Don the students moved with the intimate contours of landscape.

The students also used walking-with and different research-creation methods on the banks of the river and amongst the wetlands. Cameras, colour bars, and mirrors became part of their walking inquiry into landscape. Starting with a series of questions about landscape and identity, the students created different research-creation interventions that inserted themselves into their regional and local landscape.

The *Rearview Walking Sticks* offered another method for walking inquiry. The walking stick symbolizes walking on rugged terrain where additional support is necessary. The *Rearview Walking Sticks* functioned in a similar way, but were also absurd. Using walking sticks to walk in a restored wetland, on human-made wooden boardwalks, and well-groomed gravel paths seemed out of place, suggesting an inappropriate or unruly understanding of walking behaviour. Jack Halberstam (2011) argues that success, mastery, and heteronormativity require counter approaches that need to "embrace the absurd, the silly and the hopelessly goofy" (p. 187). Halberstam contends that, in education, seriousness, rigorousness, and disciplinary training confirms what is already known in advance. The walking sticks were out of place – unnecessary in a gentrified parkland – yet, understood as illogical, they disrupted the assumption that there is a need to know how to behave, to know in advance how to walk in landscapes. This we contend, is another form of *Queering the Trail*.

The sticks, with their mounted car mirrors, pointed at both walking and motorized mobility. In addition to the absurdity of these sticks used to walk on boardwalks, the mirrors were useless and obstructed students' sight. As navigation devices, looking behind you while walking forward, complicates issues of safety and orienteering. The juice boxes served as another ridiculous tension in the projects, pointing at the problems of juice boxes and straws in the abundant accumulation of school garbage, while simultaneously being used to create a myriad of assembled reflections.

These absurdities were punctured by the students' reflections caught in the in-between space of the mirrors – both in the walking stick mirrors and in the juice box mirrors. Not one student and one reflection, but a multitude of diffracted bodies interrupting the landscape and walking. In contrast to dominant images of landscape as wild and empty, *Upside-Down and Backwards* swarmed with more than 70 children's bodies, moving, walking, dancing, talking, laughing and sometimes screaming. The students' portraits and their walking-with experiments explore land and body, nature and culture, not as severed, but as entangled with colonization, immigration, urbanization, and pollution.

Building on the work of feminist new materialist and posthuman scholars on the issue of timescales, the reflective walking-with projects enact what Kathryn

Yusoff (2017a) calls a geoaesthetics, a form of "experimenting with what life *can* or *might be* in both its virtual and future anterior modes" (np). The problem with the Anthropocene, she argues, is that it presents time as inhuman – as both before and after us – or as outside of ourselves. The conflicting arguments over the dating of the Anthropocene, or what she calls Anthropogenesis, continues to uphold 'a' particular story of 'Man' and as such who counts as human. In contrast, what we need, she argues, "is the imagination of a hundred million Anthropocenes that adequately map the differentiated power geometries of geology and its uneven mobilization through different geosocial formations" (2017a, np). Walking-with *Rearview Walking Sticks* becomes one technique for thinking beyond the time of origin stories with beginnings and endings to an affective understanding of temporality. Yusoff (2017a) writes, time is a "material cut into bodies: real, actual, specific, vulnerable, bodies; bodies of those that do not get to count as fully human in the current biopolitical order; bodies of earth, bodies of nonhuman organisms, social and geologic bodies that *matter*" (np, italics in citation). Geoaesthetics are not representations of more-than-human worlds, but experimentations that open spaces of resistance and bewilderment: *Endless Paintings*, infinite reflections, indeterminate landscapes teeming with human and nonhuman bodies. Snaza and Sonu (2016) argue that a posthuman ethics, particularly one that is accountable to naturecultures, is one in which the capacity to act recognizes this capacity in all matter. This affective force, they write, requires an "ethical responsiveness" that is creative, open, and "ontologically located" (p. 275).

Working against the history of Canadian landscape, which is temporal, spatial, and racial, the walking-with events contest the imagined images of citizenship and identity. The work contributes to critical discourses and contemporary art practices on race, ethnicity, colonialism, and land. Positioning the project in larger contemporary art discussions/practices that disrupt neutrality and re-imagine marginalized histories, Jickling and Reed and the students resisted the racialized dispossessions of belonging, creating new spacetimes and landscapes.

Narrative cartographies: more-than-representational inquiries into school space

Dérive through these Charter'd Halls[7] was a four-month in-school research-creation event that Sarah Truman conducted with grade nine English students at a secondary school in Cardiff Wales, UK (Truman, 2017). The secondary school is situated in a leafy middle-class neighbourhood, but draws from a large catchment area in the urban centre, where many students are first generation immigrants and are ethnically diverse. The focus of the project was to explore the relationship between walking, writing, and youth cultural production as emergent literacy practices. The study included eighteen students from five different English classes. The students in the project voluntarily signed up to participate and were taken out of their regular English classes twice a week, for an hour, to walk-read-write collectively. They commandeered the picnic tables outside of the school, as a meeting place. Their walking-reading-writing experiments took place outside the school, in the surrounding neighbourhood, and some drifted into the school halls.

The research-creation events critically examined the English curriculum that focuses on a particular Euro-Western canon of literature, in particular, the students analyzed the relationship between walking and writing. There is a long history of walking as a method of gathering inspiration for philosophy and writing practices in Western Europe: The peripatetic school meandering beneath the columns (*peripatoi* meaning colonnades, or covered walkways) to learn philosophy under the tutelage of Aristotle; the poets Charles Baudelaire and Arthur Rimbaud, and even the piano player Erik Satie was known for his walking and creative practices (Gros, 2014). The walking-curricula included works by Virginia Woolf, who describes an evocative winter stroll in search of a pencil in *Street Haunting*, and W.G. Sebald's *The Rings of Saturn* that draws from memories of a walking tour of the Suffolk coast where the physicality of the main character's own walk serves as the structure of the narrative that is then entangled in history and other curious memories that arise. The students also examined work by non-Western writers including: Li Bai and Du Fu who wandered the countryside in 8th century China composing poetry, and Ikkyu who wandered Japan in the 15th century. These examples draw on not only writers who walk for inspiration, but who write about walking. Michel de Certeau's (1984) work on 'writing the city' was also read by the students. According to de Certeau (1984), walkers use "turns of phrase," and "write" the city, through their "itinerant, progressive" movements (p. 134). These conventional and canonical works were critically interrogated alongside the work of Harryette Mullen, and the students' own practices of reading, writing, and walking. The students examined the relations between walking as a method for generating content, as a narrative device, or a literary theme. They also critically challenged recent research by social scientists and educators who extol the virtues of walking as an aesthetic practice, a method for inciting creativity, and form of social engagement or public pedagogy.

The students would meet each class period at the picnic tables, where Truman would introduce them to the day's proposition. There would be readings that the students would do, while walking, that related to the prompts, and the activation of the proposition would involve walking-reading-writing. The picnic tables served as an anchoring place, but much of the lesson would be in motion. Most of the walking-with was enacted as a group. Sometimes the students walked in small groups or pairs, but never alone in the context of the classroom. Out-of-school assignments might require the students walk alone (as in to and from school) but the focus of the research-creation in-school study was to walk-with, thereby further troubling the genealogy of walking as individual and autonomous.

Propositions included: exploring rhythm and movement in literature through walking-writing, creating video-poems of place, writing speculative versions of the city, describing more-than-human entanglements through Tanka poetry, and highlighting social injustices experienced by walking through 'publishing' their writings on telephone poles for strangers to read. Rather than structuring the project around an assessment framework of literacy practices, the research-creation events focused on the ethical-political concerns that emerged through the students' walking-reading-writing (Truman, 2017). For the purpose of this chapter, we will focus on one of the walking-with propositions: the dérive as a way of walking-thinking-mapping the relations that make up 'school.'

As a proposition for the project, the students walked-with Dee Heddon and Cathy Turner's (2010) notion of *Toponarratives*, which they describe as a "collaborative, partial story of place constructed by at least two walkers" (pp. 2010; 2015). Students learned about the dérive and its relationship to Situationist International's psychogeography (see Chapter 3 for a critical approach to these methods). James Corner (1999) states that drifting allows for "mapping alternative itineraries and subverting dominant readings and authoritarian regimes" (p. 231). Many walking scholars and artists have used versions of the dérive to map space, including Tina Richardson (2014), who discusses how she and student psychogeographers at the University of Leeds emotionally mapped their campus.

The students were intrigued by the notion that within a dérive, the idea is to drop usual 'relations' and set out to explore 'appealing' and 'repelling' places as well as 'switching stations.' Switching stations are what the Situationists called the compulsion to switch directions. The students were eager to try this out in school, although, as one student noted, the places of repulsion may outweigh the places of attraction. Several students commented that while conducting a drift in school may be possible, deliberately walking in some places in the city and at certain times of the day, may be dangerous, particularly for racialized and gendered bodies (Truman, 2017).

Morag Rose (2015) states that the dérive should be used as a "tool for questioning, for opening dialogue, for exploring space: a tactic, *not* a solution" (pp. 151–152, italics added). For the dérive, no one student chose the directions taken by the group. Rather, the class moved as a relational mass and attended to the *how* of place through movement and language. As Springgay (2008) proposes, drifting provokes an intimacy where knowledge of place is not something grasped from a distance but emerges through a proximity facilitated by walking. But as the students noted in their writing, conversations, and journal writings, intimacy does not always produce comfort, care, or convivial relations. The intimacy of a dérive is a frictional encounter that rubs against the city, the school, and the neighbourhood, producing intensive affects, sometimes violent, always fraught with power, and never neutral.

The students' dérives, which occurred over a number of classes, resulted in the creation of a series of narrative cartographies. Unlike Richardson's maps, which are composed of line drawings, or Jeremy Wood's GPS maps that he created for *WalkingLab*, the students used a number of literary devices such as listing, hyperbole, alliteration, rhyme, and synaesthesia to create narrative cartographies of the school. The literary maps function as more-than-representational cartographies, through marking out affective and subjective understandings of place, as opposed to actual topological features. The students' maps are created using words, as opposed to line drawings. Additionally, their maps can't be used to physically locate oneself within the school. Rather, their narrative cartographies map affective expressions of schooling. Mapping is a common practice in school curricula across a range of subjects. Typically, such pedagogical exercises map the topology of school space, or students' routes to and from school. Such maps are descriptive and representational.

While traditional maps chart and graph the topology of a place, codifying, naturalizing, and stratifying it, contemporary mapping practices, particularly ones affiliated with walking, consider mapping as indeterminate, and unfolding in spacetime (Springgay, 2005). Deleuze (1998), writing about the diagram, distinguishes maps as experimental and expressive. Maps, he contends are not representational, but productive. Maps extend from one map to the next, assembling through rhizomatic links and passages, and as these multiple maps map each other, new maps are produced. In *A Thousand Plateaus*, Deleuze and Guattari (1987) distinguish between the tracing and the map. Tracings are the lines drawn between two points on a map. They are exact and function in a coded or stratified manner. Tracing could be said to constitute relative movement that we discussed in Chapter 4. Maps, on the other hand, are experimental and produce connections between multiple things. Maps are open and can be constantly modified. The students' narrative cartographies, as we'll discuss in the next section, exemplify this understanding of mapping.

More-than-linguistic rhetorics

Walking-with, in the context of this in-school research-creation event, functioned propositionally and enabled the students to enter into a series of speculative middles and (in)tensions about schooling and place. In particular, the students examined how certain bodies, through the intersectionality of gender, race, ethnicity, are already marked as being out of place, and as such how walking and movement are constrained, disciplined, and codified. The students' narrative cartographies point at the multiple tensions of walking-with inside and outside of school space.

One of the literary devices used to create the narrative maps was synaesthesia. Synaesthesia is a literary device wherein the writer uses words associated with one sense to describe another (see Chapter 2). The students' synaesthesia dérive was a practice of de-territorialization of language and place. The deliberate mixing of sensory descriptions disrupted the habitual use of language to describe smell, taste, touch, sight and sound and conveyed the affective responses of the students in complex ways. For example, one student scribbled on their map: *The cleanest air ever breathed flows in currents carried by the turquoise tapping on the keyboard. The dustless musk of perfect white spray-tanned on every wall.* Another example states: *Salted sweat grunted out of limbs.* And a third: *The air takes on a different taste, sweet and hazy. Splinters of the soft brown shades linger humid on my eyelids.*

Other literary devices included listing. The use of listing as a literary device links seemingly disparate agents into a tense unity. Although lists act using asyndeton (the removal of ands), an invisible *and* also haunts them. As narrative cartographical practices, the lists not only function to connect words and phrases in the list, but other literary devices that were simultaneously marked on the students' maps. One such list read:

Thunder of feet
Rough Walls
High climb
Food falls
Spider webs
Peeky holes
Cold air
Bell tolls

This list was used to map a stairwell in the school's interior.

Lists function similar to Deleuze and Guattari's (1983) partial objects, which infer gaps and assemblages. Partial objects are "pieces of a puzzle belonging not to any one puzzle but to many" (Deleuze & Guattari, 1983, p. 43). The lists do not represent a unified or totalizing whole, but rather create "aberrant paths of communication between noncommunicating vessels, transverse unities between elements that retain all their differences within their own particular boundaries" (p. 43). The synaesthetic maps and the lists reveal the ways that students' understand institutional space and its affect on student bodies and learning. Elizabeth de Freitas' (2012) writes that diagrams (maps) function as a "breaching experiment . . . inviting the reader to break with the usual diagram conventions and imagine a new diagramming practice that might better address the irregular and asymmetric tangles of interaction" (p. 589).

Another walking and mapping technique included the re-naming of school spaces. For example, the office is named 'swivel chair blues' and the cafeteria is called 'the gorge.' Other examples include: 'Blue Place for lonely people' where the 'cogs of Brains Working hard,' was in the final map changed to 'Brains *Washing* hard.' Another student re-named the examination room 'Data Source,' with 'No-exit.' These humorous descriptions evoke what Halberstam (2011) calls the "toxic perversity of contemporary life" (p. 3), where success and progress continue to marginalize students labeled as at risk, urban, and outside of mainstream culture. Chairs, cafeteria, stairwells – the objects that often fall outside the perceptual field of education in favour of curricular documents, standardized, texts, assessment reports – move into the centre and link up with other connective devices on the maps. As Sara Ahmed (2010) notes, "to experience an object as being affective or sensational is to be directed not only toward an object, but to 'whatever' is around that object, which includes what is behind the object, the conditions of its arrival" (p. 33).

The students' narrative cartographies attend to more-than-human elements encountered during the dérive, and what Truman (2017) calls "more-than-linguistic *rhetorics*" (p. 151). Rhetoric generally refers to oral or written skills of persuasion. Within this conceptualization, there is generally an agent (human speaker or writer) who deploys rhetoric convincingly, while the media activated (the rhetoric) is inert until invigorated by a speaker and impressed upon a listener-reader. A new materialist account of rhetoric would consider not just the agency of the speaker-writer, and the agency of the listener-speaker based around a linguistic code, but also the emergence of persuasive 'rhetoric(s)' in other forms of matter. These more-than-human rhetorics emerged on the walks: the rotten banana covered in dust on the window ledge in the stairwell; the angle of light and insect chatter on the school field; the oozing toilets in the boys' bathroom; and the mirrored windows into the examination hall, all enacted an affective agency that was persuasive in the cartographical process. This is what Halberstam (2011) calls "'sideways' relations, relations that grow along parallel lines rather than upward and onward" (p. 74). Kathryn Bond Stockton (2009) offers sideways as movement that is horizontal, rather than vertical. Sideways is a transmaterial movement that creates connections and forces between things not relegated to heteronormative reproduction. More-than-linguistic rhetorics resist the steady progress of success and intervene in the common literacy practice of benchmarks, outcomes, and proficiency. Language, Truman (2016a) writes, becomes "part of a horizontal ontology emerging alongside other social-material forces, instead of merely a medium for representing them" (p. 137).

While the field of literacy studies in education has expanded to include math literacy, environmental literacies, emotional literacies, and multi-literacies, the problem remains that such variations actually restrict literacy practices (Simon, 2011). Aparna Mishra Tarc (2015) argues that including different media in literacy education is not the point, but rather what is needed is a re-reading of what it means to be literate. She contends that we cannot "continue to practice literacy without thinking about the dominant forms of life it produces" (p. 130). Literacy "in its multiplicities," writes Truman (2017) "continues to function within a hierarchy where some kinds of literacies matter more and are superior to others" (p. 113). Like landscape, which continues to demarcate nature as White and neutral, and as such marking racialized students as outside of nature, literacy functions as a White civilizing process, that neutralizes, sanitizes, and commodifies language. Literacy, both historically and as it is performed currently, is built around a White supremacist-monoculture (Tuck & Gaztambide-Fernández, 2013). To be literate means to know in advance what literacy is, and how to perform literate acts.

The students dérives as narrative cartographies mapped students' understandings of how language functions to control and dehumanize students. Walking-with became a method for exploring inside and outside of school place collectively, to consider the ways that language is already pre-supposed and pre-determined in advance. As the students assembled their maps on large paper, using poems, lists, descriptions, and other literary devices, the maps enabled new connections and different ontologies to become possible. If maps function as "less of an organization of bodies than a cartography of incipient tendencies, of force of form" (Manning, 2013, p. 81), then the students' walking-with and mapping has the potential to open up different configurations of literacy.

Walking-with, as a narrative cartographical practice, shifts literacy from its concern about particular 'coded' meanings toward "affective intensities and their effects produced across texts, bodies, and interactions" (Leander & Boldt, 2013, p. 38). The students' maps create intimate diagrams of school places that record not a representation of place, but their entangled relations of learning, institutions, and literary practices.

Implications for walking methodologies in education

In our highly technologized era, student mobility is often tied to cars, buses, and trains. Likewise, students are highly sophisticated users and consumers of digital technologies and their urban space (including schools) is mediated by screen culture. To counter what is perceived to be the negative effects of digital technologies on young peoples' lives, educators turn to walking as a slow, antiquated, and embodied way of moving through space. Walking becomes a way to reconnect with place and people, it is 'anti-technology,' and valued because of perceived (albeit pathologized) understandings of health and environmental consciousness. These logics function to inscribe a before and after technology, where walking is esteemed because of its neutrality, purity, and accessibility. However, such arguments neglect to consider how different bodies and subjectivities are materialized through walking, and simultaneously the ways that walking disavows different bodies based on gender, race, class, and ability. In Truman's in-school project, the intersectionality of gender, race, and ethnicity was discussed by the students as limiting rather than enabling factors in where they could or could not walk, including routes to and from school. When walking is valued for its health benefits or used to promote 'green' initiatives in schools, such as 'Walk to School Wednesdays,' the legacies of walking as White, male, autonomous, and as part of ongoing settler colonialism remain intact. Furthermore, to infer that students' lives require 'disconnection' so that they can become more meaningful, continues to pathologize young bodies as deviant and in constant need of regulation and control. Walking rationalized through discourses of 'disconnection' and 'reconnection' only serve as a punitive measure. In addition, reconnection, as we discussed in the *Upside-Down and Backwards* project, is part of the production of White subjectivity, where some bodies have never been connected.

If walking is going to make an impact in schools, it cannot be conceived through the logic of anti-technology. Walking must not remain trapped in images of a life 'before' technology, but rather conceived of as part of the fabric of contemporary mobility. Walking-with needs to be understood as a practice that enables critical inquiry. Walking is neither simple, slow, nor benign. Walking-with is complex, unruly, and political.

Walking-with as a method of research in schools enables students, teachers, artists, and researchers to move within school spaces and outside of the classroom to ask questions about the environment in which we learn and live. Walking is valued because it offers an immersed and emplaced approach to research and learning, where students' bodies become entangled with the senses and space. Yet, place, as we discussed in Chapter 1, can become a backdrop to research, a mere description of context, and rarely takes into consideration the ongoing dispossession of

Indigenous peoples, people of colour, and ethnic minorities. Walking in diverse locations with students needs to be more-than an activity that moves them outside of the confines of institutional spaces. Sonu and Snaza (2016), commenting on different types of environmental and ecological activities in schools, remind us that "without interrogating the implicit and fundamental assumptions about the human subject itself, namely its dis-embeddedness from both nature and nonhuman materiality, we run the risk of enforcing a momentary ethics temporarily satisfied through contained activity and manipulation" (p. 264). Whether it's environmental education, landscape and arts curricula, or literacy in its various forms, place must become situated, relational, and intimate.

Intimacy, however, is a slippery word. It is often associated with concepts like proximity, warmth, innocence, and familiarity. Yet, intimacy can be asymmetrical, violent, controlling, and alienating. What intimacy looks like, feels like, and how it is performed, is context- and subject-specific. Intimacy is selective and as such it is exclusionary. As a frictional concept, what intimacy shows, in both of the in-school examples, is how it can become a mechanism of control and governance. What the in-school walking-with events underscore is how intimacy is always entangled with politics.

To intimate is to communicate indirectly, to hint, or to imply. Both intimacy and to intimate have roots in the word *intimus* (inmost), suggesting an interiority, an intrinsic quality, and a familiarity. The Whiteness of nature and nation is intrinsic to landscape art. Literacy hierarchies and taxonomies are similarly invested in intimations. So how might walking-with unsettle innocent and intrinsic understandings of intimacy?

Walking-with can be a significant and important method for working with students in educational contexts, if it does not become instrumentalized as an anti-technology and as an uncritical mode of being in place. Walking-with is an ethical and political response-ability that intimately understands that any *step* towards a different world is always imbricated in a particular conceptualization of the human, one that continues to re-inscribe a separation between nature and culture, human and nonhuman, landscape and Other. As the *Rearview Walking Sticks* and the narrative cartographical maps instantiate, walking-with materializes horizontal and sideways ontologies where spacetimes reflect, invert, and bend.

Notes

1 Algonquin Park is a Provincial Park approximately three hours north of Toronto. Located between Georgian Bay and the Ottawa River, the park has over 2,400 lakes. As the oldest Provincial Park in Canada, it is a popular destination for camping, canoeing, and cottagers.
2 The Group of Seven were a Canadian group of landscape painters from the 1920s. Their iconic images of windswept White Pines, isolated karst rocks, and water-ways still permeate the Canadian National identity.
3 Voyageurs were French Canadians who traded furs in the early 18th and 19th centuries and canoed over long distances. Images of them in canoes, trading with Indigenous peoples, position them as heroic and strong, and are associated with dominant ideologies of Canada as 'untamed' wilderness.

4 Some of the artist-residency themes were compiled into Image Banks to be used as resources for lesson plans. The one on landscape can be found at: https://thepedagogi-calimpulse.com/land-and-place/

5 The initial desire had been to have students canoe and walk in this project. However, because of TDSB rules about elementary students in or on water, the students were not allowed on the river in canoes. Instead, the artists arrived by canoe, and the canoe sat on the shore. The students enjoyed 'queering' this Canadian symbol, arranging their colour bars within it, and using the colour bars as paddles in the sand.

6 The Evergreen Brickworks Park (commonly referred to as the Brickworks) is a corporate landscape urbanism project that has re-purposed an old brick factory in Toronto into a space with hiking and biking trails, a weekly farmers market, an upscale café, restaurant, and 'green' shop and garden centre. The park supports a children's garden and programming, and in the winter, there is a public skating rink. Buildings on the site can be rented for corporate events and weddings. Evergreen is a Canadian charity dedicated to restoring watersheds and support urban biodiversity.

7 William Blake's poem *London* describes to the city of London as 'charter'd' – suggesting control, surveillance, and constraint.

8 A walking-writing practice
Queering the trail

We trudge single file into the screaming snow. Piercing flakes force our heads downward into the cover of our coats. Our footfalls timid on the black ice. The sharp smell of cold stings our noses and slices through to the back of our throats. We scurry, slip, and slide. The squall subsides and we're enveloped in a muted landscape of blue. Shadows from bare tree branches penetrate deep into the snowbanks. Streetlights become salmon infused halos. The air crackles and hums. The squall is already a body-memory. Enveloped in the purple blue haze of a Toronto winter's evening, we walk for hours.

The final chapter of *Walking Methodologies in a More-Than Human World* serves two purposes. First, it responds to on-going questions that have been asked of us, at conferences and by colleagues and students, regarding our collaborative walking-writing practice. Second, but intimately connected to the first point, the chapter functions as a kind of summation, drawing together pivotal concepts that structure the book and our walking-writing practice such as: *land and geos*, *affect*, *transmaterial*, and *movement*.

The chapter is presented as a series of walks. We use the propositional form for this chapter because propositions are not directions or procedures for writing (see Chapter 5). Propositions act as hybrids between potentiality and actuality: they propose what could be (Truman & Springgay, 2016). According to Whitehead (1978), a proposition is a "new kind of entity. Such entities are the tales that perhaps might be told about particular actualities" (p. 256). As a propositional form, we invite readers to engage with each section as a walk. We propose a walk you might take while reading the section. These are merely suggestions and we encourage you to propose your own walks too. We use the propositional walk form to: examine the entanglements of walking and writing; explore our walking-writing as speculative concept generation; consider the affective surfaces that arrive in the walking-writing process; interrogate a feminist politics of collaboration; and consider how rhythm and time's queer touching instantiates an ethics that is accountable to the infinite encounters of which we are all a part.

Each walk should not be taken as a formula. This is not a how-to manual. Rather, the purpose of the walk is to think-in-movement as "techniques of relation," which Manning and Massumi (2014) evoke as a catalyzing and modulating gesture (p. 91). Walking-writing is a practice of invention, where the movement of thought is *more-than* a moment of walking, thinking, or inscribing.

In the first walk, *queering*, we introduce different walkers who investigate walking as a thinking-making-doing, and as a political praxis. While there are numerous books and resources on walking that feature walking-writers, artists, and researchers, there are fewer comprehensive sources focused on women walkers, racialized and Indigenous walkers, queer and trans walkers, and differently abled walkers. Amy Sharrocks and Clare Qualmann (2017) organized a series of events and a study guide that includes a directory of women walking artists and a detailed bibliography. The *Walking Women* events and study guide are indebted to the ongoing scholarship of Dee Heddon and Cathy Turner on walking women, and Dee Heddon's and Misha Myers' the *Walking Library Project* (Heddon and Myers, 2014; 2017). The Walking Library is a project where the artists-scholars and the people they walk with, carry a library in a large backpack. The project investigates how collective reading and writing in situ affect the experience of place. The project also seeks to make visible women walkers and women who write about walking. Sharrocks, Qualmann, Heddon, Turner, and Myers all note the lack of visibility of walking women from the canon of walking research. *Walking Methodologies in a More-than-Human World* expands on their *Walking Women* resources to include a diversity of walkers that are excluded from the literature on walking.

In the first walk *queering*, we introduce walks by women, Indigenous walkers, people of colour walkers, and queer and trans walking artists, whose methods of walking defamiliarize the historical tropes of the lone walker drawing inspiration from the landscape. Some of these artists' projects link walking and writing, while others illustrate a thinking-in-movement.

The next five walks are walking-writing propositions that shape our collaborative practice. These are: *differentiation*; *surfacing*; *activation devices*; *with*; and *touch*. The final, seventh walk, *contours*, re-visits key concepts in the book and reflects on the implications of walking methodologies in a more-than-human world.

Walking-writing is a thinking-in-movement. Walking-writing is a practice of concept formation. We do not conceptualize walking in one register and writing in another, any more than we understand our research-creation walking events as pre-writing. Walking activates the creation of concepts. To walk is to move-with thought. In addition, we understand writing as something more-than what exists on a page or in a book. Walking-writing is experimental and speculative. Walking-writing surfaces. It is viscous and intense. Walking-writing is collaborative.

Walk one: queering the Euro-Western walking tradition

Read this section then go on a walk. Queer the trail. Defamiliarize Euro-Western traditions and other heteronormative, solo perambulations that link walking with unfettered inspiration.

Artists and writers experiment with different methods of walking and writing including poetic structures, the body, and land. For example, African American poet Harryette Mullen's (2014) book *Urban Tumbleweed* documents her daily walking practice through 366 Tanka poems written for each day in a year, plus one. Tanka is a traditional form of Japanese verse, and Mullen incorporates this sparse poetry with her walks in Los Angeles through diverse neighbourhoods, exposing the ephemeral, lived experience of her daily practice. Barbara Lounder's *Writing/Walking Sticks* is a set of 26 custom-made walking sticks, each one fitted with a small self-inking stamp on the bottom. Each stamp bears a different letter of the English alphabet and leaves a water-soluble inked impression on the ground. Vanessa Dion Fletcher investigates her relationship between language and land, specifically her Potawatomi and Lenape ancestry, in her walking projects. In *Writing Landscape*, Dion Fletcher walks repeatedly on the land as a form of bodily writing.

Blue Prints for a Long Walk is a project by Anishnaabe artist Lisa Myers whose walking practice maps invisible lines of family history, settler colonialism, and cultural memory. The project traces a 250-kilometre path along the northern shore of Lake Huron, Ontario, between Sault Ste. Marie and the town of Espanola. This path, often forged along railway lines, marks the route her grandfather took home when he ran away from a residential school, and subsisted for days on wild blueberries that grew along the track. In addition to walking, she created 54 postcard-sized etchings of railway ties and screen-prints made out of blueberry pigments. These postcards map out a section of Myers's walk topologically, through its waterways and the path of the Canadian Pacific Railway. Walking becomes a means to interrogate and animate a personal and collective history that is shaped by land, rhythm, and the sensuous textures and tastes of blueberries.

Trans Black artist and activist Syrus Ware's practice takes on many different forms. As part of the *New Field* project organized by *Public Studio* and in partnership with *WalkingLab*, Ware collaborated with youth from the Lawrence Heights area in Toronto. *Future Rememberings* – a daylong walk on the Bruce Trail – incorporated wild foraging and off the grid sustainable living to inquire into environmental and socio-political crises. The walk, which took the form of an ecology and mobile drawing class, speculatively and experimentally imagined collective futures.

Latai Taumoepeau uses walking and performance to examine issues of climate change in the Pacific region. In her piece *Ocean Island Mine*, she moves a 500 kilogram block of ice using a shovel and by walking over a short distance repetitively. The work excavates the 'solid white' rock into invisibility. In *Stitching up the Sea*, she walks, wearing brick sandals on her feet on broken glass. Using a Tongan mallet (which is typically used to beat plant fibres into pulp) to smash glass waste material, the durational walking performance, activates Indigenous knowledges and identities alongside larger questions regarding climate change.

In yet another example, queer Black writer Rahawa Haile walked the Appalachian Trail from Georgia to Maine and wrote about her long-distance solo-hike.

As the only Black woman to walk the trail solo end to end, Haile's project examined the relationship between walking, race, and belonging. On the walk, she carried books by Black authors, which she left in trail shelters along the way.

In academic scholarship and popular literature, walking is extolled and prized because: it benefits health; inspires creativity; attunes the walker with landscape; and is a tactic for re-writing the city. While these fraught inheritances nudge at our practice, *WalkingLab* has intentionally sought out collaborations with women walkers, Indigenous walkers, queer and trans walkers, differently abled walkers, and people of colour to *Queer the Trail*. This is the ethical-political thrust of our walking-writing practice.

Walk two: differentiation

Pick a destination. Walk to this destination. This could be an errand stroll. You might walk to a store. Or you might pick a destination, such as a creek. Where you go doesn't matter, but it's the kind of walk where you have an intention. Take a different path than you might normally walk. Walk slowly.

We've been writing for what seems like days. Teacups perch precariously on stacked books on the dining table. Trails of cracker crumbs coated in tahini and miso gravy weave their way through papers that contain hand-written notes, diagrams, and doodles. Our laptops sit side by side. We write side by side. When we take notes from other scholarly texts or start thinking about ideas, one of us types, the other paces and talks. We shift roles frequently. We interrupt each other. *We argue!* When we write the sentences and paragraphs that shape our computer-generated texts, we sit next to each other. One laptop composes the text, the other has our notes open for references. We still scribble ideas and maps and thinking-doodles on scraps of paper. Both of us like pencils. Sarah likes mechanical pencils. Stephanie isn't as particular, just as long as the pencil is sharp. Occasionally we use Google Docs and write over Skype.

We arrive at a concept, a theory, a word, or an incomplete idea. We need to move. We propose a walk. We need nutritional yeast. We walk to the store, walking-thinking the concept as we move. We walk around the block. We walk the road at the cottage, to the end and return. We go to the bank. These are strolls with a destination. They are short walks. They get us away from our laptops. They move us away from tables and chairs. They are practical. However, these walks are not 'breaks' from writing. We write as we walk. *We walk a concept*. Or as Erin Manning would say: "Take the thought for a walk" (cited in Truman, 2016b, p. 104). Move thought. Think-in-movement. Writing doesn't begin at the moment of inscription. As you amble to your destination you are still writing. You are writing in movement.

Walking-writing generates speculative middles. Speculative middles, as we discuss in Chapter 5, are propositional, excessive, indeterminate, and frictional. Manning and Massumi (2014), use Deleuze and Guattari's (1983) concept of a "disjunctive synthesis" to describe the middle (p. 33). This is a paradoxical state, (in)tension, where the composition of things coming together produce something else. Walking-writing intentionally activates a disjunctive synthesis. Walking-writing is a practice of muddling things, of making problems, and agitating thought. In the speculative middle, one does not resolve or clarify an idea, rather walking-writing complicates, stirs, and unsettles thought. In fact, sometimes nothing comes out of a speculative middle. Sometimes it's about failure and a letting go.

On one such walk 'around the block' we problematized the use of methods in qualitative research. Thinking-with our own practices of research-creation we struggled to find language to describe the middle, muddling, excessive milieu. Our walking-writing gesticulated, we raised our voices. Walking-writing allows us to engage with different registers. There is an affective intensity through the mobility of thought. The speculative middle is actualized, we are in it, but simultaneously it's differentially linked to all kinds of speculations of what could be. Walking-writing actualizes at the very same time as producing the virtual, which in turn makes new actualities become possible. As a differential, it keeps propelling itself, but in difference.

Walk three: surfaces

Go for a long walk. Time, distance and direction are dependent on your own abilities and needs. It's not important where you walk, but that you spend time walking. This is a walk that surfaces.

One of the places we frequently walk-write is the road behind Sarah's parents' cottage on Georgian Bay in Wahta Mohawk Territory. The road is hardened gravel and winds and twists its way through boreal forest and sharp cuts of the Canadian Shield. Twelve Mile Bay flows on one side of the road, while on the other is 'undeveloped' Crown Land. Pine trees and moss scent the air; raspberries ripen on bushes. The sound of mosquitos swarm around our ears. For cottagers, this is land of privilege and luxury. Family holidays and writing retreats. Across the bay is the Moose Deer Point First Nation.

Kathleen Stewart (2013) describes place through terms like atmosphere, surface, and event. Surfaces are ambient and affective. Surfaces do not refer to a specific location or form but the tonality, the expressiveness, and undulation of body-space. Surfaces vibrate, flow, and move. Surfaces are not without duration. Surfaces are not the site upon which walking-writing takes place, but full of "drama, intensity, an energetics of tension and release" (Stewart, 2013, p. 276). Surfaces are affective, their intensities pass between bodies and "spread out across a vast atmospheric field" (p. 276). In a walk that surfaces, you are not traveling to the store to buy something. Unlike the errand stroll, where the intensity lies in pushing thought to an edge, surface walks are visceral, bodied, and shimmer.

Surfacing is writing. Surfacing writes the body. Surfacing is "tentative, ephemeral, incidental though powerfully felt. Something atmospheric distributed across a geography of elements that swell" (Stewart, 2013, p. 276). Surface walks foreground bodily intensity. On these walks we might get thirsty, sweaty, or need to pee. In the winter, coldness seeps in. We feel the walk in our calves and on the soles of our feet. The pace of walking undulates. There is an irregular rhythm of speeding up and slowing down. Surfaces pause. Surfaces lose their way. They disorient and defamiliarize.

On such walks, conversations drift between theory, stories, observations and are also punctured by long periods of silence. The intensity is shaped by duration, pace, and the topology of place. Speculative middles happen, but these walks don't necessarily begin with a particular thought or concept that needs to be pushed to the edge. Ideas are not concretized. They *quiver*. It's all about surfaces. These surfaces are atmospheric. Surfaces as affective walking-writing. Surfaces are not the subject of the walking-writing. Sarah Cefai (2016) states that "the rhythm of a place enters us, enters the process of writing" (p. 14). This is a rhythm that surfaces. It shimmers or folds like a wave.

Walk four: activation device

Go on a walk and bring some kind of activation device. This could be a camera, sound recorder, some wool to felt, paper to write poems, postcards, a geothermal measuring device, mirrors, or walk scores. Use the device on the walk, not to record or capture your experience of the walk, but to alter the function of the walk.

The activation device experiments with the walk and enables new ways of thinking-making-doing. Much like the speculative middle, the activation device pushes walking-writing to an edge. It forces something new to occur. The activation device is not intended to extract or collect information, but to insert itself within the walking-writing practice as a thinking-making-doing.

One possible activation device is an altered gait walk.[1] On such a walk, participants modify habits of walking through various modalities. For example, carrying a giant bouquet of helium balloons, walking backwards using a handheld mirror, carrying a bucket of water that reflects the sky, wearing high heeled shoes, wearing a roller skate on one foot, or filling your pockets with rocks. Some of these are captured on the *WalkingLab* website. For other examples, see Chapter 5 where we discuss pinhole photography, walk scores, and the dérive, and Chapter 2 where we introduce synaesthetic methods.

Stephanie frequently hand felts wool around rocks as a 'writing' practice. Posing the question 'How to write as felt?' she interrogates the process of making felt with wool (felt as force and intensity), as affective feelings (felt as affect), and as a felt event (felt as transmaterial) (Springgay, forthcoming). She invokes these various *matterings* of felt in order to generate a practice of writing that engenders bodily difference that is affective, moving, and wooly. She is particularly interested in thinking about felt's engagement with touch, for felt invites, if not demands touch. Felt is a dense material of permanently interlocking fibers. It is a non-woven fabric made using natural fibers, a binding agent, and a process of agitating the fibers such as rubbing. Gilles Deleuze and Felix Guattari (1987) use different textile processes to flesh out the concepts of striated and smooth space. Because weaving has a warp (threads set against the loom) and weft (threads that move in between the warp) it creates a striated space that is delimited. Felting and some needlework like crochet and embroidery on the other hand create, what they call smooth space. This is space that vectors out, spreads, and surfaces.

Deleuze and Guattari (1987) call felt an "anti-fabric," made by the agitation or entanglement of fibers (p. 475). It has no warp and weft, and "is in no way homogeneous: it is nevertheless smooth, and contrasts point by point with the space of fabric" (p. 475). Felt spreads out infinitely. Felt is irreversible. Once wool is felted it cannot be undone and the fibers returned to their original state. "Felt comes into existence, comes to matter, as a result of an unpredictable interaction of tendencies (of the fibers, of the manner and the conditions in which they are worked)" (Thompson, 2011, p. 23). Felting rocks while walking Stephanie describes as a touching encounter composed between human and nonhuman matter. Felting is a practice of writing as a *thinking-making-doing*. Felt, writes Jeanne Vaccaro (2010) "cannot be known mathematically, like textiles – calculated, quantified, or mapped on a horizontal-vertical grid. It is the result of the destruction of a grid. There is no pattern to follow" (p. 253). As felt emerges it builds into itself the possibility of improvisation; a rhythm without measure. Felting invokes the intimacy of touch (Springgay, 2008). To felt, scales of wool touch and entangle, and fingers and hands wrap around each other and the wet wooly mass. To felt demands friction, and friction is indebted to touch. To touch is the opening of one body to another; it is an interval, an event.

These examples, as we keep re-iterating, are not methods of data collection or documentation. They rupture and queer the walk, they slow us down and change our gait, they problematize what it means to walk, they agitate and provoke. Activation devices are not required for every walk, but they might be necessary. They propel us into a speculative middle and churn our thinking. They surface. They function propositionally because we don't have a clear procedure of how they will activate the walk beforehand. They are prompts for further walking-writing, as opposed to a representation of the walk. Manning and Massumi (2014), writing about thinking-making-doing at *SenseLab*, comment that terms like improvisation, emergence, and invention and a general sense of just letting things flow, lack rigor and focus, and risk being used in a cursorily manner. We extend their arguments, to add, that activation devices can't sit outside of the walking-writing event. By this we mean they can't simply be creative activities, such as collaging data transcripts, that bear no weight on the walking-writing event inside the event. Activation devices need to mobilize thought, stimulate differentiation, and act as tensiles – capable of being stretched, but also in frictional tension.

Walk five: 'with'

This walk requires a group of humans and/or nonhumans. The group can be of any size. The group composes only one aspect of 'with.' 'With' is about co-composition rather than inclusive collaboration. Bring a notebook and a pencil. A blanket or a ground cover is recommended but not necessary. Walk until you find a comfortable place to sit and write together.

Astrida Neimanis (2012) writes that transcorporeality, intra-action, relationality, companion species and other concepts that inform new materialisms and posthumanisms all engender a form of 'with.' She wonders, though, why the concept collaboration is rarely mentioned in the pivotal feminist texts that mark this burgeoning field. Perhaps, she argues, there is a danger in idealizing the sentimentality of collaboration. We need, she contends, to differentiate different kinds of collaboration, to ask questions about the consequences of relating. "Collaboration," she writes, "is sweaty work replete with tense negotiations" (p. 218).

WalkingLab organizes *Itinerant Reading Salons*, where we gather groups of people together to walk and read. Sometimes readings are shared before the walk and we use the walk to discuss the readings closely. We might select a quote or a 'minor concept' that we work as we walk (Manning & Massumi, 2014). In other instances, we bring the readings on the walks and pause along our journey to read out loud together. Reading out loud changes the pace of reading, its tempo and shape, much like a walk alters our movements, rhythms, and pace.

One such 'with' walk took place on the Mornington Peninsula, Victoria, Australia, with *WalkingLab* collaborators Mindy Blaise and Linda Knight. Our weeklong *Itinerant Reading Salon* began propositionally with the question: "What if we stand speculative for a moment before the speculative turn and check our feminist itinerary again?" (Åsberg, Thiele, and van der Tuin, 2015, p. 164). Having attended a number of academic conferences, where the new materialisms and posthumanism proliferated, but without any critical regard for its feminist genealogy, we felt the need to re-visit some of the feminist contributions to the field and to ask questions about 'with': inheritance, relations, response-ability, friction, and situatedness.

We read together. Out loud. We took notes individually in our notebooks, and we scrawled concepts, questions, and ideas on chart paper and in the sand. We walked along the beach and over volcanic rock. We sheltered ourselves from the sea wind in a bower of Moonah trees to write. One of our writing propositions was 'tentacles.' We wrote for 30 minutes. Then each of us read aloud to one another. We followed this by asking further questions from which another writing proposition emerged. We wrote again. We continued until we reached a point where the wind and flies were no longer bearable. We walked back to our accommodation. More questions emerged as we cooked together and continued reading out loud, writing together and apart. 'With' "demands work, speculative invention, and ontological risks. . . [and] [n]o one knows how to do that in advance of coming together in composition" (Haraway, 2008a, p. 83).

When walking-writing, the 'with' has to be held (in)tension all the time. It's not just that four feminist academics were working together, but that we were thinking, problematizing, and speculating on 'with-ness,' response-ability, matters of concern, and situatedness as ongoing propositions. This 'with' can also be extended to include a politics of citation. Citational practices, argues Sara Ahmed (2013), structure a selective history of disciplines. She writes that these structures are "screening techniques" where "certain bodies take up spaces by screening out the existence of others" (np). The academic collective *Feminist Educators*

Against Sexism (#FEAS), organized by Mindy Blaise, Linda Knight, and Emily Gray propose a 'Cite Club.'[2] FEAS has established an e-mail group where members share their work and cite one another when possible. Cite Club addresses the call by Eve Tuck, K. Wayne Yang and Rubén Gaztambide-Fernández (2015) to "consider what you might want to change about your academic citation practices. Who do you choose to link and re-circulate in your work? Who gets erased? Who should you stop citing?" (np). 'With' requires that we walk-write-think-cite as a political practice of co-composition.

Walk six: touch

Go on a walk. Feel your feet on the earth. Touch the breeze. Attend to impressions. Caress the thoughts that weigh on you as you amble. Feel the haptic; the corporeal. Walk in a graveyard if you can find one.

We enter the mossy Victorian gates into a grove of tall trees. City traffic becomes muted and our footfalls crackle on the gravel path. Petals lilt off the branches, grass winnows, and crumbling tombs mark our passage into the heart of the cemetery. As walkers, we return to cemeteries because of their affects and surfaces, because they are places of thresholds, where edges touch incommensurably.

Walking-writing invokes the intimacy and rhythm of touch (Springgay, 2008). Touch involves the physical contact of skin on matter. Touch conjures the immediate, proximinal, and bodily. When we touch, Manning (2007) explains, "we reach toward that which is in-formation or trans-formation . . . altering us" (p. 85). Touch threatens boundaries opening up different corporeal ontologies.

Walking-writing evokes what Barad (2012) refers to as a queer self-touching. When we touch ourselves, she states, we encounter an uncanny sense of the stranger or otherness within the self. Using quantum theory to shape a theory of self-touching, Barad explains how a particle touches itself creating an infinite set of future possible virtual particles. The infinite set of possibilities of interaction entails a particle touching itself, and then that touching subsequently touching *touch* itself. She writes: "Every level of touch, then, is itself touched by all possible others" (p. 212). This radically queers any notion of difference and identity. Self-touching, she argues, "is an encounter with the infinite alterity of the self" (p. 213). In touching,

> each individual always already includes all possible intra-actions with "itself" through all the virtual Others, including those that are noncontemporaneous with "itself." That is, every finite being is always already threaded through with an infinite alterity diffracted through being and time.
>
> (Barad, 2012, p. 213)

This self-touching, Barad states, is a queer perversion of being and time. If there are infinite possibilities of touching, then all matter is composed of infinite variations and multiplicities. Queering touch emphasizes difference as multiplicities as opposed to difference 'from.' This is another way of saying that matter emerges from entangled intra-actions and relatings, and that matter itself is "always already touched by and touching infinite configurations of possible others, other beings and time" (Barad, 2012, p. 215). Walking-writing the cemetery means we need to think about touching encounters beyond the actualized ones concretized through our feet touching the ground. Walking-writing needs to extend beyond an embodied and sensuous description of how a body encounters a place in the present, to consider the queer self-touching perversions of which we are all a part.

If matter touches, then this has profound effects on our place in the world. As Barad (2012) contends, touch has an immense impact on how we become response-able. Touch queers and perverts individual identity. Touch, for Barad, doesn't require that we foreground inclusions. It's not about admitting what is excluded but about thinking the thresholds of the touching encounter, the thresholds of limits of what is included and excluded. Touching then is an "ethics committed to the rupture of indifference" (Barad, 2012, p. 216). This isn't an ethics that determines who gets to belong or participate, but an ethics that queers and undoes the limits of what counts as human or otherwise in the first place. Self-touching means thinking about alterity – our touching indifference – within ourselves. It requires an ethics response-able to the inhuman within us. Walking-writing recognizes the radical indeterminacy and openness, the ongoing inventive intra-actions of difference that make up the world. For example, Mel Chen (2012) writes about walking a city street and ingesting the bodies of self and other: skin particles, perfume, body odor, and hair follicles. To walk incites a touching encounter.

Eva Hayward (2010) evokes another discussion of queer transmaterial touching through their haptic concept fingeryeyes. Fingeryeyes enable tentactular multispecies encounters, which are "impressions, thresholds of emergence" (p. 580). Invoking the terms pervert and invert, as queer transmaterial touchings, Hayward muses on bodies' pliability and modification. Tentacular touchings are an ethics that is "about responsibility and accountability for the lively relationalities of becoming of which we are a part" (Barad, 2007, p. 303). From a methodological point of view, touch dislodges the reliance on occularcentrism so prevalent in qualitative research, to consider how transmaterial bodily practices re-configure how we come to know. To pervert means to twist, warp, and misinterpret. Perversion arrives in the form of *Queering the Trail*.

Cemeteries conjure up a pastness that is indebted to enduring clock or chronological time. Gravestone markers etched with beginning and end dates tick out a metered understanding of life. Queer self-touching evokes other approaches to time, that teem and unfold in the microcosms that proliferate as multiple touching encounters. This is a time that is imperceptible, absolute, and decisional.

Scholars like Eleni Ikoniadou (2014), Lisa Blackman (2012), and Patricia Clough (2010), who write about affective dimensions of media, note that what affect does to mediation is to push rhythm beyond a metric conceptualization towards rhythm "as an assemblage of tensions traversing all participating bodies-living or inanimate" (Ikoniadou, 2014, p. 152). Affect as force and intensity surfaces rhythmically, where rhythm is sensation, not metric chronological time. For Deleuze (1994), rhythm exceeds the cognitive and the rational through affective force. Clough (2010) calls this "rhythm affect," where time pulses with vibrations, "with rhythms ready for propagation or infection" (p. 228). Walking-writing understood as an affective and rhythmic practice displaces linear time. Self-touching perverts time. Inverts it. Time is contemporaneous and tentacular – spreading out pastness, presentness, and futurity all at once. As Ikoniadou (2014) writes: "Understood in this way, rhythm no longer belongs to a body as a quality or asset and it is not attached to anything other than itself. Rhythm may not emerge tied to a plane of action or to something else outside it, allowing instead for an (inter)action between different planes, or bodies" (p. 154). Walking-writing lends to both a metric and an affective understanding of time. As metric, we might think of patterns and tempos marked out as feet touch the ground. But this is only one aspect of walking and time. This linear time normalizes bodies and space. Time progresses from one individual moment to the next shaping the past and the future. This is an orderly and sequential understanding of time. It also marks out an interior and an exterior understanding of bodies and place. But affect, surfacing, and vibration require time be conceived differently. This is time as indeterminate, instable, and intensive.

Walking-writing, like other affective mediations, are modes of expression that enable the insensible, incommensurate, indeterminate to be felt. Walking-writing offers the possibility of touching materiality. This opens us to a transmaterial ethics. As we have written throughout the book, ethics is not about including the inhuman, or bringing it into the centre. Rather ethics is a recognition of

> the inhuman, the insensible, the irrational, the unfathomable, and the incalculable that will help us face the depths of what responsibility entails. A cacophony of whispered screams, gasps, and cries, an infinite multitude of indeterminate beings diffracted through different spacetimes, the nothingness, is always already within us, or rather, it lives through us.
>
> (Barad, 2012, p. 218)

We emerge from one graveyard and find ourselves in another city and another threshold. This time we descend 130 steps into the Paris Catacombs. The rock layers of the catacombs travel back in time 45 million years, and the deep cavernous tunnels of limestone date from the Lutetian geological stage. The name Lutetian comes from the Latin name for Paris. The catacombs were created in the 18th century in abandoned underground quarries. These quarries which extracted limestone, marl and gravel, beauchamp sand and other materials were dug out from beneath the city to build the city above ground. Small plaques dot the walls of the tunnels, indicating street names and other directional signs from above ground.

In the 18th century the tunnels were filled with remains from the largest Parisian cemetery, 'The Saints-Innocents.' The catacombs are what Kathryn Yusoff (2017b) calls 'earth archives' – deep histories of nature-culture entanglements. Here Yusoff is using the term archive to note not only the layers of geo-strata, but to emphasize the ways that the human and geology are imbricated in one another.

The geosocial catacombs attest to the complicated histories of stone that have constituted different becomings. The deep time of geo-strata is intertwined with piles of bones, destabilizing chronological time. Time in the catacombs becomes synchronous. It spreads out like a wave enmeshing walkers' bodies with stones, dust, and geo debris. Queer time, where time becomes affective, variant, and indifferent.

The *Stone Walks* that *WalkingLab* organizes and performs in various locations considers stones from the perspective of inhuman animacy and the geo-social (Springgay & Truman, 2017c). Our walking-writing practice emphasizes the animacy of stone, thereby unhinging affect as solely a human quality. The animacy of stone, Jeffrey Cohen (2015) suggests, is significant in shaping an ethics that is not human-centric but an ethics that ruptures "ontological solitudes, defying exclusive taxonomies, undermining closed systems" (p. 228). This shifts ethics from a moralizing discourse directed by humans towards inhuman others, to a response-ability that is shaped by relations, entanglements, and intra-connected touchings.

Walk seven: contours

Contour walks follow edges. Contours edge. Edges are the limits, the thresholds, marking passages between things. To edge means to move gradually, carefully, or cautiously. Take a walk that contours.

Contours can be lines, outlines of a form or a body. Contours edge things. As a verb, contours make and shape things. Contours are processual. Contours germinate and assemble. Walking-writing contours thinking-in-movement. As a practice of edging, contours are thresholds – an in-between space. Thresholds are full of potentiality. They seed things.

The contours that edge walking-with – *Land and geos, affect, transmaterial,* and *movement* – have been shaped and assembled through our walking-writing and the many *WalkingLab* events and projects that are the basis for our scholarship in this book. Part of our contouring has been to hold in tension the history and inheritances of walking and walking methods. Who walks, how they walk, and where requires constant queering.

We are indebted to the rich and extensive body of scholarship on walking methodologies across a range of disciplines in the social sciences and humanities. Particularly those artists and scholars that have collaborated with us at *WalkingLab* pushing our walking-with to a threshold.

Walking Methodologies in a More-Than-Human World extends critical and diverse walking methodologies and proposes: i) walking-with Land and geos as crucial aspects of critical place-making; ii) understanding hapticality and affect as differential components of sensory inquiry including the ways that affecting subjectivities attend to the affective forces of race; and iii) enlarging an understanding of individual embodiment through transmateriality and theories of trans movement that proliferate as difference. Furthermore, the more-than-human theories of Land and geos, affect and transmateriality have generated different ways to think about: iv) participation as immanent movement; v) the need for qualitative research methods beyond proceduralism; vi) walking as counter cartographies and anarchiving practices that emphasize relational and regional ways of re-mapping space; and vii) walking-with as critical practices that de-centre humanisms in landscape and literacy in-school contexts.

Shifting the focus from walking as a method to move from one point to another, towards an emphasis on walking as an entangled, transmaterial, affective practice of experimentation, our research considers the ethical and political dimensions of ambulatory research. Frictionally theorizing walking scholarship with feminist new materialisms, posthumanisms, queer and trans theories, critical race theory, Indigenous scholarship, and critical disability studies offers vital interventions into walking's potential as a research methodology. Our queer orientation to walking methodologies is significant because it emphasizes the speculative and experimental potential of walking as research, while simultaneously attending to the complexities of subjectivities, mobilities, and situatedness. *Queering the Trail*, as concept for critical walking methodologies disrupts the all too common tropes of walkers drifting through the city or rambling along a country path, and the normative narratives that inscribe walking as inherently healthy and meditative.

Walking can be overlooked in qualitative research because of its ablest Euro-Western history or because it is assumed to be uncritical. Likewise, with the increasing advancement and turn to digital technologies, walking is marginalized because of its pedestrian and everyday nature. Conversely, walking can be romanticized as a method to counter technology, and conceptualized as a practice of 'returning' to something 'more-human and more-embodied.' The theories and experimentations that compose this book attest to walking's capacity to interrupt these assumptions. *Walking Methodologies in a More-than-Human World* demonstrates that walking is an important methodology and method for thinking ethically and politically about bodies, movement, and place. Walking-with becomes a practice of thinking-making-doing that attends to transmaterial knottings between all matter.

The sun is contouring and edging its way out from behind a low-lying cloud, and the mountains on the fjord shift into dark purple and green focus. We conclude with this walking proposition:

Take your research for a walk. How will you respond by walking-with?

Notes

1 The altered gait concept is borrowed from artist Donna Akrey.
2 Feminist Educators against Sexism (FEAS) seeks to challenge and eradicate sexism and gender inequality in the academy. www.genderandeducation.com/issues/introducing-feas-cite-club/

References

Adams, V., Murphy, M., & Clark, A. (2009). Anticipation: Technoscience, life, affect, temporality. *Subjectivities, 28*(1), 246–265.

Adese, J. (2012). Colluding with the enemy?: Nationalism and Depictions of 'Aboriginality' in Canadian Olympic Moments. *American Indian Quarterly, 36*(4), 479–502.

Ahmed, S. (2004). *The cultural politics of emotion*. New York, NY: Routledge.

Ahmed, S. (2006). *Queer phenomenology: Orientations, objects, others*. Durham, NC: Duke University Press.

Ahmed, S. (2008). Open forum imaginary prohibitions: Some preliminary remarks on the founding gestures of the 'new materialism.' *European Journal of Women's Studies, 15*(1), 23–39.

Ahmed, S. (2010). Happy Objects. In M. Gregg & G. J. Seigworth (Eds.), *The affect theory reader* (pp. 29–51). Durham, NC: Duke University Press.

Ahmed, S. (2013, September 13). *Making feminist points* [Web log comment]. Retrieved from https://feministkilljoys.com/2013/09/11/making-feminist-points/

Ahmed, S. (2015). *Feminist Killjoys* [blog]. Retrieved from https://feministkilljoys.com

Akerman, J. R. (2017). Introduction. In J. R. Akerman (Ed.), *Decolonizing the map: Cartography from colony to nation* (pp. 1–9). Chicago, IL: Chicago University Press.

Alaimo, S. (2010). *Bodily natures: Science, environment, and the material self*. Bloomington: Indiana University Press.

Alaimo, S. (2016). *Exposed*. Minneapolis, MI: University of Minnesota Press.

Anderson, J. (2004). Talking whilst walking: A geographical archeology of knowledge. *Royal Geography Society, 36*(3), 254–261.

Anzaldúa, G. (1987). *Borderlands/La Frontera*. New York, NY: Aunt Lute Books.

Aoki, J., & Yoshimizu, A. (2015). Walking histories, un/making places: Walking tours as ethnography of place. *Space and Culture, 18*(3), 273–284.

Åsberg, C., Thiele, K., & van der Tuin, I. (2015). Speculative before the turn: Reintroducing feminist materialist performativity. *Cultural Studies Review, 21*(2), 145–72.

Baldwin, A. (2009a). The white geography of Lawren Stewart Harris: Whiteness and the performative coupling of wilderness and multiculturalism in Canada. *Environment and Planning, 41*(3), 529–544.

Baldwin, A. (2009b). Ethnoscaping Canada's boreal forest: Liberal whiteness and its disaffiliation from colonial space. *The Canadian Geographer, 53*(4), 427–443.

Baldwin, A. (2010). Wilderness and tolerance in Flora MacDonald Denison: Towards a biopolitics of whiteness. *Social and Cultural Geographies, 11*(8), 883–901.

Banerjee, B., & Blaise, M. (2013). There's something in the air: Becoming-with research practices. *Cultural Studies ↔ Critical Methodologies, 13*(4), 240–245.

Barad, K. (2003). Posthumanist performativity: Toward an understanding of how matter comes to matter. *Signs: Journal of Women in Culture and Society, 28*(3), 801–831.

Barad, K. (2007). *Meeting the universe halfway: Quantum physics and the entanglement of matter and meaning*. Durham, NC: Duke University Press.

Barad, K. (2011). Nature's queer performativity. *Qui Parle: Critical Humanities and Social Sciences, 19*(2), 121–158.

Barad, K. (2012). On touching – the inhuman that therefore i am (v1.1). First published in *Differences: A Journal of Feminist Cultural Studies, 23*(3), 206–223. Corrected and reprinted version retrieved from https://planetarities.sites.ucsc.edu/wp-content/uploads/sites/400/2015/01/barad-on-touching.pdf

Barad, K. (2015). Transmaterialities: Trans*/matter/realities and queer political imaginings. *TSQ: Transgender Studies Quarterly, 2*(2), 387–422.

Barrett, E., & Bolt, B. (Eds.). (2013). *Carnal knowledge: Towards a 'new materialisms' through the arts*. London, UK: I.B. Tauris.

Basson, L. (2008). *White enough to be American?: Race mixing, Indigenous people, and the boundaries of state and nation*. Chapel Hill: The University of North Carolina Press.

Bates, C., & Rhys-Taylor, A. (Eds.). (2017). *Walking through social research*. London, UK: Routledge.

Bates, T. (2017). Queer affordances: The human as trans* ecology. *Angelaki Journal of the Theoretical Humanities, 22*(2), 151–154.

Bendiner-Viani, G. (2005). Walking, emotion, and dwelling: Guided tours in Prospect Heights, Brooklyn. *Space and Culture, 8*(4), 459–471.

Benjamin, W. (2002). *The arcades project* (H. Eiland & K. McLaughlin, Trans.). New York, NY: Belknap Press.

Bennett, J. (2010). *Vibrant matter*. Durham, NC: Duke University Press.

Bergson, H. (1988). *Matter and memory* (N. M. Paul & W. S. Palmer, Trans.). New York, NY: Zone.

Bertelsen, L., & Murphie, A. (2010). An ethics of everyday infinities and powers: Felix Guattari on affect and the refrain. In M. Gregg & G. J. Seigworth (Eds.), *The affect theory reader* (pp. 138–157). Durham, NC: Duke University Press.

Beuglet, N. (2016). *Examining equity and sustainability in the Green Line park proposal: The limits of progressive planning in the post-industrial parks movement* (Unpublished master's thesis). York University, Toronto, ON.

Bishop, C. (2004). Antagonism and relational aesthetics. *October, 110*, 51–79.

Bishop, C. (2012). *Artificial hells: Participatory art and the politics of spectatorship*. New York, NY: Verso.

Bissell, D. (2016). Micropolitics of mobility: Public transport commuting and everyday encounters with forces of enablement and constraint. *Annals of the American Association of Geographers, 106*(2), 394–403.

Blackman, L. (2012). *Immaterial bodies: Affect, embodiment, mediation*. London, UK: Sage.

Blackman, L. (2017). "Loving the alien": A post-post-human manifesto. *Subjectivity, 10*(1), 13–25.

Blaise, M., Hamm, C., & Iorio, J. (2017). Modest witness(ing) and lively stories: Paying attention to matters of concern in early childhood. *Pedagogy, Culture, and Society, 25*(1), 31–42.

Braidotti, R. (2006). *Transpositions: on nomadic ethics*. Cambridge, MA: Polity Press.

Braidotti, R. (2013). *The posthuman*. Cambridge, MA: Polity.

Braun, B. (2003). "On the raggedy edge of risk": Articulations of race and nature. In D. Moore, J. Kosek, and A. Pandian (Ed.), *Race, nature, and the politics of difference* (pp. 175–203). Durham, NC: Duke University Press.

Bridger, A. (2009). Psychogeography and feminist methodology. *Feminism & Psychology, 23*(3), 285–298.

Britzman, D. P. (1995). Is there a queer pedagogy? Or, stop reading straight. *Educational Theory, 45*(2), 151–165.

Browne, K., & Nash, C. J. (2010). *Queer methods and methodologies: Intersecting queer theories and social science research.* London, UK: Routledge.

Brussoni, M., Gibbons, R., Gray, C., Ishikawa, T., Sandseter, E. B. H., Bienenstock, A., Chabot, G., Herrington, S., Janssen, I., Pickett, W., Power, M., Stranger, N., Sampson, M., & Tremblay, M. S. (2015). What is the relationship between risky outdoor play and health in children? A systematic review. *International Journal of Environmental Research and Public Health, 12*(6), 6423–6454. DOI: 10.3390/ijerph120606423

Burton, R. D. E. (1994). *The Flâneur and his city. Patterns in daily life in Paris 1815–1851.* Durham, NC: Durham University Press.

Cadogan, G. (2016, July 8). Walking while black. *Literary hub.* Retrieved from http://lithub.com/walking-while-black/

Calderon, D. (2014). Speaking back to Manifest Destinies: A land education-based approach to critical curriculum inquiry. *Environmental Education Research, 20*(1), 24–36.

Cefai, S. (2016, May). *The feeling of a place.* Paper presented at Propositions for Affect 2: Affect, difference, fugitive mobilization, University of New South Wales, Australia.

Chandler, E. (2014). *Disability and the desire for community* (Order No. 3744404). Available from Dissertations & Theses @ University of Toronto; ProQuest Dissertations & Theses Global. (1764221297). Retrieved from http://myaccess.library.utoronto.ca/login?url=https://search-proquest-com.myaccess.library.utoronto.ca/docview/1764221297?accountid=14771

Chen, M. Y. (2012). *Animacies: Biopolitics, racial mattering, and queer affect.* Durham, NC: Duke University Press.

Cheng, Y. E. (2014). Telling stories of the city: Walking ethnography, affective materialities, and mobile encounters. *Space and Culture, 17*(3), 211–223.

Clare, E. (2001). Stolen bodies, reclaimed bodies: Disability and queerness. *Public Culture, 13*(3), 359–365.

Claussen, C. (1993). *Worlds of sense: Exploring the senses in history and across cultures.* New York, NY: Routledge.

Clough, P. (2008). The affective turn: Political economy, biomedia, and bodies. *Theory, Culture, Society, 25*(1), 1–22.

Clough, P. (2010). The future of affect studies. *Body & Society, 16*(1), 222–230.

Clough, P., & Halley, J. (2007). *The affective turn. Theorizing the social.* Durham, NC: Duke University Press.

Coates, J. (2017). Key figure of mobility: the flâneur. *Social Anthropology, 25*(1), 28–41.

Cohen, J. J. (Ed.). (2014). *Inhuman nature.* Washington, DC: Oliphuaunt Books.

Cohen, J. J. (2015). *Stone: An ecology of the in human.* Minneapolis, MN: University of Minnesota Press.

Colebrook, C. (2002). *Gilles Deleuze.* New York, NY: Routledge.

Colebrook, C. (2014). *Death of the posthuman: Essays on extinction.* Ann Arbor, MI: Open Humanities Press at Michigan Publishing.

Colebrook, C. (2015). What is it like to be a human? *TSQ: Transgender Studies Quarterly, 2*(2), 227–243.

Coleman, R. (2017). A sensory sociology of the future: Affect, hope and inventive methodologies. *The Sociological Review, 65*(3), 525–543.

Conroy, B. (2017). www.bekconroy.com

Coole, D., & Frost, S. (Eds.). (2010). *New materialisms: Ontology, agency, and politics.* Durham, NC: Duke University Press.

Corner, J. (1999). The Agency of mapping: Speculation, critique, and invention. In Dennis Cosgrove (Ed.), *Mappings* (pp. 213–252). London, UK: Reaction Books.

Cresswell, T. (2004). *Place: An introduction.* London, UK: Wiley-Blackwell.

Cull, L. (2011). Attention training: Immanence and ontological participation in Kaprow, Deleuze and Bergson. *Performance Research, 16*(4), 80–91.

Cvetkovich, A. (2003). *An archive of feelings: Trauma, sexuality, and lesbian public cultures.* Durham, NC: Duke University Press.

de Certeau, M. (1984). *The practice of everyday life* (S. Rendall, Trans.). Berkeley, CA: University of California Press.

de Freitas, E. (2012). The classroom as rhizome: New strategies for diagramming knotted interactions. *Qualitative Inquiry, 18*(7), 588–601.

de Freitas, E., & Curinga, M. (2015). New materialist approaches to the study of language and identity: Assembling the post-human subject. *Curriculum Inquiry, 49*(3), 249–265.

Debord, G. (1958). *Definitions. Internationale Situationniste #1.* (K. Knabb, Trans). Retrieved from www.bopsecrets.org/

Deleuze, G. (1990). *The logic of sense.* (C. Stivale & M. Lester, Trans). New York, NY: Columbia University Press.

Deleuze, G. (1994). *Difference and repetition.* (P. Patton, Trans). New York, NY: Columbia University Press.

Deleuze, G. (1998). *Foucault.* (D. Smith & M. Greco, Trans). Minneapolis, MN: University of Minnesota Press.

Deleuze, G., & Guattari, F. (1983). *Anti-oedipus: Capitalism and schizophrenia.* (R. Hurley, M. Seem, & H. R. Lane, Trans). Minneapolis, MN: University of Minnesota Press.

Deleuze, G. & Guattari, F. (1986). *Kafka: toward a minor literature.* (D. Polan, Trans). Minneapolis, MN: University of Minnesota Press.

Deleuze, G., & Guattari, F. (1987). *A thousand plateaus: Capitalism and schizophrenia.* (B. Massumi, Trans). Minneapolis, MN: University of Minnesota Press.

Dietrich, R. (2016). The biopolitical logics of settler colonialism and disruptive relationality. *Cultural Studies ↔ Critical Methodologies, 17*(1), 1–11. DOI: 10.1177/1532708616638696

Drobnick, J. (Ed.). (2006). *The smell culture reader.* New York, NY: Berg.

Edelman, E. (2014). Walking while transgender: Necropolitical regulations of trans feminine bodies of colour. In J. Haritaworn, A. Kuntsman, and S. Posocco (Eds.), *Queer necropolitics* (pp. 172–190). New York, NY: Routledge.

Edelman, L. (2004). *No Future: Queer theory and the death drive.* Durham, NC: Duke University Press.

Edensor, T. (2008). Walking through ruins. In T. Ingold and J. Vergunst (Eds.), *Ways of walking: Ethnography and practice on foot* (pp. 123–142). Burlington, VT: Ashgate.

Edensor, T. (2010). Walking in rhythms: Place, regulation, style and the flow of experience. *Visual Studies, 25*(1), 69–79.

Edmonds, P. (2017). Artefact: Landscapes of forgetting. *C Magazine, 134*, 76.

Elliot, P. (2010). *Debates in transgender queer and feminist theory.* New York, NY: Routledge.

Ellsworth, E. (1989). Why doesn't this feel empowering? Working through the repressive myths of critical pedagogy. *Harvard Educational Review, 59*(3), 297–322.

Ellsworth, E., & Kruse, J. (2012). *Making the geologic now.* New York, NY: Punctum Books. Retrieved from www.geologicnow.com/

Engel-Di Mauro, S., & Carroll, K. K. (2014). An African-centred approach to land education. *Environmental Education Research, 20*(1), 70–81.

Erickson, B. (2013). *Canoe Nation: nature, race, and the making of a Canadian Icon.* Vancouver, BC: UBC Press.

Eshun, K. (2003). Further considerations on afrofuturism. *CR: The New Centennial Review, 3*(2), 287–302.

Evans, D. (2013). *The art of walking: A field guide.* London, UK: Black Dog Publishing.

Evans, J. & Jones, P. (2011). The walking interview: Methodology, mobility and place. *Applied Geography, 31*(2), 849–858.

Fisher, M. (2013). The metaphysics of crackle: Afrofuturism and hanutology. *Dancecult: Journal of Electronic Dance Music Culture, 5*(2): 42–55.

Flowers, R., & Swan, E. (Eds). (2015). *Food pedagogies.* New York, NY: Routledge.

Forsyth, J. (2016). The illusion of inclusion. *Public: Art/Culture/Ideas, 53*, 22–34.

Foster, J. (2010). Off track in nature: Constructing ecology on old rail lines in Paris and New York. *Nature and Culture, 5*(3), 316–337.

Freccero, C. (2011). Carnivorous virility, or becoming dog. *Social Text, 106, 29*(1), 177–195.

Freeman, B. M. (2015). The spirit of Haudenosaunee youth: The transformation of identity and well-being through culture-based activism (Unpublished doctoral dissertation). Wilfrid Laurier University, Waterloo, Canada.

Fuller, D., Askins, K., Mowl, G., Jeffries, M., & Lambert, D. (2008). Mywalks: fieldwork and living geographies. *Teaching Geography, 33*(2). 80–83.

Fung, R. (Interviewee) & Smith, D. N. (Interviewer). (2013). *Experience, homonationalism, and equity.* Retrieved from http://blog.ocad.ca/wordpress/site-specific/2013/11/richard-fung/?doing_wp_cron=1500131631.7312328815460205078125

Gagnon, M. K. (2007). Janet Cardiff. *The Senses and Society, 2*(2): 259–265.

Gallagher, M. (2015). Sounding ruins: Reflections on the production of an 'audio drift'. *Cultural Geographies, 22*(3), 467–485.

Gallagher, M. (2016). Sound as affect: Difference, power and spatiality. *Emotion, Space and Society, 20*, 42–48.

Garneau, D. (2016, March). Marginalized by Design. *Border Crossings, 137.* Retrieved from http://bordercrossingsmag.com/article/marginalized-by-design.

Gaztambide-Fernández, R. A. (2012). Decolonization and the pedagogy of solidarity. *Decolonization: Indigeneity, Education & Society, 1*(1), 41–67.

Gendron-Blaise, H., Gil, D., & Mason, J. E. (2016). An Introprocession. *Inflexions, 9*, i–vii. Retrieved from www.inflexions.org/frictions/PDF/introduction.pdf

Giffney, N., & Hird, M. (2008). *Queering the mon/human.* Aldershot, UK: Ashgate.

Gros, F. (2014). *A philosophy of walking.* (J. Howe, Trans.). London, UK: Verso.

Grosz, E. (2004). *Nick of time.* Durham, NC: Duke University Press.

Hagen, T. (2014). *Learning from sonic encounters: Listening emplacement and belonging in Osaka* Retrieved from http://invisibleplaces.org/2014/pdf/ip2014-hagen.pdf

Halberstam, J. (2005). *In a queer time and place: Transgender bodies, subcultural lives.* New York, NY: New York University Press.

Halberstam, J. (2011). *The queer art of failure.* Durham, NC: Duke.

Haraway, D. (2008a). *When species meet.* Minneapolis: University of Minnesota Press.

Haraway, D. (2008b). Companion species, mis-recognition, and queer worlding. In N. Giffney & M. J. Hird (Eds.), *Queering the non/human* (pp. xxiii–xxvi) Burlington: Ashgate.

Haraway, D. (2016). *Staying with the trouble: Making kin in the Chthulucene.* Durham, NC: Duke University Press.

Haritaworn, J. (2015). Decolonizing the non/human. *GLQ: A Journal of Lesbian and Gay Studies, 21*(2), 210–213.

Harney, S. (2013). Hapticality in the undercommons, or from operations management to black ops. *Cumma Papers, 9*, 1–7.

Harney, S., & Moten, F. (2013). *The undercommons: Fugitive planning & black study.* New York, NY: Minor Compositions.

Hartman, S. V. (1997). *Scenes of subjection: Terror, slavery, and self-making in nineteenth-century America.* Oxford, UK: Oxford University Press.

Hayward, E. (2010). Fingeryeyes: Impressions of cup corals. *Cultural Anthropology, 25*(4), 577–599.

Hayward, E. (2015). Tranimacies: An interview with Mel Chen. *TSQ: Transgender Studies Quarterly, 2*(2), 317–323.

Hayward, E. & Gossett, C. (2017). Impossibility of that. *Angelaki Journal of the Theoretical Humanities, 22*(2), 151–24.

Hayward, E., & Weistein, J. (2015). Introduction: Tranimalities in the age of trans* life. *TSQ: Transgender Studies Quarterly, 2*(2), 195–208.

Heddon, D., & Myers, M. (2014). Stories from the walking library. *Cultural Geographies, 21*(4), 639–655.

Heddon, D., & Myers, M. (2017). The walking library: mobilising books, places, readers and reading. *Performance Research, 22*(1), 32–48.

Heddon, D., & Turner, C. (2010). Walking women: Interviews with artists on the move. *Performance Research, 15*(4), 14–22.

Heddon, D., & Turner, C. (2012). Walking women: Shifting the tales and scales of mobility. *Contemporary Theatre Review, 22*(2), 224–236.

Helguera, P. (2011). *Education for socially engaged art.* NY: Jorge Pinto Books.

Henriques, J., Tiainene, M., & Valiaho, P. (2014). Rhythm returns: Movement and cultural theory. *Body & Society, 20*(3–4), 3–29.

Hinton, P., & van der Tuin, I. (2015). *Teaching with feminist materialisms.* Utrecht, The Netherlands: ATGENDER.

Hird, M. (2006). Animal transex. *Australian Feminist Studies, 21*(49), 37–50.

Hochschild, A. R. (2012). *The managed heart: Commercialization of human feeling.* Berkeley, CA: University of California Press.

Howes, B. (2005). *Empire of the senses: The sensual culture reader.* New York, NY: Berg.

Howes, D. (2003). *Sensual relations: Engaging the sense in culture and social theory.* Ann Arbor, MI: University of Michigan Press.

Howes, D. (2013). The expanding field of sensory studies. *Sensory Studies.* Retrieved from www.sensorystudies.org/sensorial-investigations/the-expanding-field-of-sensory-studies/

Hudson, H. (2014). The geographies of blackness and anti-blackness: An interview with Katherine McKittrick. *The CLR James Journal, 20*(1), 233–240.

Hunt, D., & Stevenson, A. A. (2017). Decolonizing geographies of power: indigenous digital counter-mapping practices on Turtle Island. *Settler Colonial Studies, 7*(3), 372–392.

Hunt, S. (2014). Ontologies of indigeneity: The politics of embodying a concept. *Cultural Geographies, 21*(1), 27–32.

Hustak, C., & Myers, N. (2012). Involutionary momentum: Affective ecologies and the sciences of plant/insect encounters. *Differences, 23*(3), 74–118.

Ikoniadou, E. (2014). Affective time and abstract perception in the sonic work of art. *Body & Society, 20*(3–4), 140–161.

Ingold, T. (2000). *The perception of the environment.* London, UK: Routledge.

Ingold, T. (2004). Culture on the ground. *Journal of Material Culture*, *9*(3), 315–340.

Ingold, T. (2007). *Lines: A brief history*. London, UK: Routledge.

Ingold, T. (2011). *Being alive: Essays on movement, knowledge, and description*. London, UK: Routledge.

Instone, L., & Taylor, A. (2015). Thinking About inheritance through the figure of the anthropocene, from the antipodes and in the presence of others. *Environmental Humanities*, *7*, 133–150.

Iscen, O. E. (2014). In-between soundscapes of Vancouver: The newcomer's acoustic experience of a city with a sensory repertoire of another place. *Organised Sound*, *19*(2), 125–135.

Jackson, A. Y., & Mazzei, L. (2013). *Thinking with theory in qualitative research: Viewing data across multiple perspectives*. New York, NY: Routledge.

Jackson, Z. I. (2013). Animal: New directions in the theorization of race and posthumanism. *Feminist Studies*, *39*(3), 669–685.

Jackson, Z. I. (2015). Outer worlds: The persistence of race in movement 'beyond the human'. *Gay and Lesbian Quarterly (GLQ)*, *21*(2–3), 215–218.

Jones, A., & Jenkins, K. (2008). Indigenous discourse and "the material": A post-interpretivist argument. *International Review of Qualitative Research*, *1*(2), 125–144.

Jones, P. & Evans, J. (2012). Rescue geography: Place making, affect and regeneration. *Urban Studies*, *49*(11), 2315–2330.

Kafer, A. (2013). *Feminist, queer, crip*. Bloomington, IN: Indiana University Press.

Kilgore, D. D. (2014.) Afrofuturism. In R. Latham (Ed.), *The Oxford Handbook of Science Fiction* (pp. 561–572). Oxford, UK: Oxford University Press.

Knight, L. M. (2016). Playgrounds as sites of radical encounters: Mapping material, affective, spatial and pedagogical collisions. In N. Snaza, D. Sonu, S. E. Truman & Z. Zaliwska (Eds.), *Pedagogical matters: New materialisms and curriculum studies* (pp. 13–28). New York, NY: Peter Lang.

Kusenbach, M. (2003). Street phenomenology: The go-along as ethnographic research tool. *Ethnography*, *4*(3), 455–485.

Lara, A. Liu, W., Ashley, C. P., Nishida, A., Leibert, R., & Billies, M. (2017). Affect and subjectivity. *Subjectivity*, *10*(1), 30–43.

Lather, P., & St. Pierre, E. A. (2013). Post-qualitative research. *International Journal of Qualitative Studies in Education*, *26*(6), 629–633.

Leahy, D., & Pike, J. (2015). 'Just say no to pies:' Food pedagogies, health education and governmentality. In R. Flowers & E. Swan (Eds.), *Food Pedagogies* (pp. 169–182). Surrey, UK: Ashgate Publishing Limited.

Leander, K., M., Boldt, G. (2013). Rereading "a pedagogy of multiliteracies": Bodies, texts, and emergence. *Journal of Literacy Research*, *45*, 22–46.

Lefebvre, H. (2004). *Rhythmanalysis: Space, time and everyday life*. New York, NY: Continuum.

Leong, D. (2016). The mattering of Black lives: Octavia Butler's hyperempathy and the promise of the new materialisms. *Catalyst: Feminism, Theory, Technoscience*, *2*(2), 1–33.

Livingston, J., & Puar, J. (2011). Interspecies. *Social Text*, *106*, *29*(1), 3–14.

Lorimer, H. (2005). Cultural geography: The busyness of being 'more-than-representational.' *Progress in Human Geography*, *29*(1), 83–94.

Lorimer, H. (2010). New forms and spaces for studies of walking. In T. Cresswell (Ed.), *Geographies of mobilities: Practices, spaces, subjects* (pp. 19–34). Burlington, VT: Ashgate.

Lorimer, H., & Lund, K. (2008). A collectable topography: Walking, remembering and recording mountains. In T. Ingold & J. L. Vergunst (Eds.), *Ways of walking: Ethnography and practice on foot* (pp. 318–345). Aldershot, UK: Ashgate.

Lorimer, H. & Wylie, J. (2010). Loop. *Performance Research, 15*(4): 6–13.

Lorimer, J. (2015). *Wildlife in the anthropocene: Conservation after nature*. Minneapolis, MN: University of Minnesota Press.

Low, K. (2009). *Scents and scent-sibilities: Smell and everyday life experiences*. Newcastle, UK: Cambridge Scholars Publishing.

Luciano, D. & Chen, M. Y. (2015). Introduction: Has the queer ever been human? *GLQ: A Journal of Lesbian and Gay Studies, 21*(2), iv–207.

Lund, K. (2005). Seeing in motion and the touching eye: Walking over Scotland's mountains. *ETNOFOOR, XVIII*(1), 27–42.

Lury, C. (2012). Going live: Towards an amphibious sociology. *The Sociological Review, 60*(S1), 184–197.

MacLure, M. (2013). The wonder of data. *Cultural Studies ⇔ Critical Methodologies, 13*(4), 228–232.

Macpherson, H. (2009). The intercorporeal emergence of landscape: Negotiating sight, blindness and ideas of landscape in the British countryside. *Environment and Planning, 41*(5), 1042–1054.

Malone, K. (2016). Reconsidering children's encounters with nature and place using posthumanism. *Australian Journal of Environmental Education, 32*(1), 42–56.

Manning, E. (2007). *Politics of touch: Sense, movement, sovereignty*. Minneapolis, MN: University of Minnesota Press.

Manning, E. (2012). *Always more than one: Individuation's dance*. Durham, NC: Duke University Press.

Manning, E. (2013). Wondering the world directly – or, how movement outruns the subject. *Body and Society, 20*(3&4), 162–188.

Manning, E. (2016). *The minor gesture*. Durham, NC: Duke University Press.

Manning, E., & Massumi, B. (2014). *Thought in the act: Passages in the ecology of experience*. Minneapolis, MN: University of Minnesota Press.

Marks, L. (2000). *Touch: Sensuous theory and multisensory media*. Minneapolis, MN: University of Minnesota Press.

Massey, D. B. (2005). *For space*. London, UK: Sage.

Massumi, B. (2002). *Parables for the virtual*. Durham, NC: Duke University Press.

Massumi, B. (2014). *What animals teach us about politics*. Durham, NC: Duke University Press.

Massumi, B. (2015). *Politics of affect*. Cambridge, MA: Polity Press.

Massumi, B. (2016). Working principles. In A. Murphie (Ed.), *The go-to how to book of anarchiving* (pp. 6–8). Montreal, QC: SenseLab. Retrieved from http://senselab.ca/wp2/wp-content/uploads/2016/12/Go-To-How-To-Book-of-Anarchiving-landscape-Digital-Distribution.pdf

May, T. (2005). *Gilles Deleuze: An introduction*. Cambridge, UK: Cambridge University Press.

Mazzei, L. A., & Jackson, A. Y. (2016). Voice without a subject. *Cultural Studies ↔ Critical Methodologies, 16*(2), 151–161.

Mbembe, A. (2003). Necropolitics. *Public Culture, 15*(1), 11–40.

McCartney, A. (2004). Soundscape works, listening and the touch of sound. In J. Drobnick (Ed.), *Aural cultures*. Banff and Toronto, CA: Walter Phillips Gallery & YYZ Books.

McCormack, D. (2010). Fieldworking with atmospheric bodies. *Performance Research, 15*(4), 40–48.

McCormack, D. (2014). *Refrains for moving bodies: Experience and experiment in affective spaces*. Durham, NC: Duke University Press.

McCoy, K., Tuck, E., & McKenzie, M. (2016). *Land education: Rethinking pedagogies of place from Indigenous, postcolonial, and decolonizing perspectives*. New York, NY: Routledge.

McKenzie, M., & Bieler, A. (2016). *Critical education and socialmaterial practice: Narration, place, and the social*. New York, NY: Peter Lang.

McKittrick, K. (2007). Freedom is a secret. In K. McKittrick & C. Woods (Eds.), *Black geographies and the politics of place* (pp. 97–114). Cambridge, MA: South End Press.

McKittrick, K. (2011). On plantations, prisons, and a Black sense of place. *Journal of Social and Cultural Geography, 12*(8), 947–963.

McKittrick, K. (2017). Worn out. *Southeastern Geographer, 57*(1), 96–100.

McKittrick, K., & Woods, C. (Eds.). (2007). *Black geographies and the politics of place*. Cambridge, MA: South End Press.

McLean, S. (2013). The whiteness of green: Racialization and environmental education. *The Canadian Geographer/Le Géographie Canadien, 57*(3), 354–362.

Mendoza, M. E. (2017). Racialized landscapes: Marking territory across North America. *C Magazine, 134*, 10–15.

Middleton, J. (2009). 'Stepping in Time': Walking, time and space in the city. *Environment and Planning A, 41*(8): 1943–1961.

Middleton, J. (2010). Sense and the city: Exploring the embodied geographies of urban walking. *Social & Cultural Geography, 11*(6), 575–596.

Middleton, J. (2011). Walking in the city: The geographies of everyday pedestrian practices. *Geography Compass, 5*(2), 90–105.

Miessen, M. (2010). *The nightmare of participation*. Berlin, Germany: Sternberg Press.

Miller, J. (2016). Activism vs antagonism: Socially engaged art from Bourriaud to Bishop and beyond. *Field, 3*, 165–183.

Miner, D. (2012). Radical migrations through Anishinaabewaki: An Indigenous re-mapping of the Great Lakes. In R. Borcila, B. Fortune & S. Ross (Eds.), *Deep routes the midwest in all directions* (pp. 5–243). Texas: White Wire Studio.

Miner, D. (2016). Agamiing, Awasaakwaa – on the shore, across the forest. In S. Mitra & B. Devine (Eds.), *Border cultures* (pp. 56–68). Toronto, ON: Black Dog.

Miner, D. (2017). *To the landless: Visiting with Lucy and Emma*. Author.

Mirzoeff, N. (2016). It's not the anthropocene, It's the white supremacy Scene. Or, the geological color line. In R. Gruisin (Ed.), *After extinction*. Minneapolis, MN: Minnesota Press. Retrieved from www.academia.edu/16131146/Its_Not_the_Anthropocene_Its_the_White_Supremacy_Scene_or_The_Geological_Color_Line

Mishra Tarc, A. (2015). *Literacy of the other renarrating humanity*. Albany, NY: State University of New York Press.

Mortimer-Sandilands, C. (2008). Queering ecocultural studies. *Cultural Studies and Environment, 22*(3–4), 455–476.

Mouffe, C. (2000). *The democratic paradox*. London, UK: Verso.

Mullen, H. R. (2014). *Urban tumbleweed: Notes from a tanka diary*. Minneapolis, MN: Gray Wolf.

Muñoz, L. (2010). Brown, queer, and gendered. In K. Browne & C. J. Nash (Eds.), *Queer methods and methodologies: Intersecting queer theories and social science research* (pp. 55–68). London, UK: Routledge.

Murphie, A. (Ed.). (2016). *The go-to how to book of anarchiving*. Montreal, QC: SenseLab. Retrieved from http://senselab.ca/wp2/wp-content/uploads/2016/12/Go-To-How-To-Book-of-Anarchiving-landscape-Digital-Distribution.pdf

Myers, N. (2016). Becoming sensor in sentient worlds: A more-than-natural history of a black oak savannah. In. G. Bakke & M. Peterson (Eds.), *Anthropology of the arts*. New York, NY: Bloomsbury.

Namaste, V. (2000). *Invisible lives: The erasure of transsexual and transgendered people*. Chicago, IL: University of Chicago Press.

Neimanis, A. (2009). Bodies of water, human rights and the hydrocommons. *Topia, 21*, 161–182.

Neimanis, A. (2012). On collaboration (for Barbara Godard). *NORA-Nordic Journal of Feminist and Gender Research, 20*(3), 215–221.

Neimanis, A. (2017). *Bodies of water: Posthuman feminist phenomenology*. London, UK: Bloomsbury.

Nishida, A. (2017). Relationality through differences: Disability, affective relationality, and the U.S. public healthcare assemblage. *Subjectivities, 10*(1), 89–103.

Nurka, C. (2015). Animal techne: Transing posthumanism. *TSQ: Transgender Studies Quarterly, 2*(2), 209–226.

Nyawalo, M. (2016). Afro-futurism and the aesthetics of hope in Bekolo's Les Saignantes and Kahiu's Pumzi. *Journal of the African Literature Association, 10*(2), 209–221.

Nyong'o, T. (2015). Little monsters: Race, sovereignty, and queer inhumanism in Beasts of the Southern Wild. *GLQ: A Journal of Lesbian and Gay Studies, 21*(2–3), 249–272.

O'Neill, M. (2017). https://walkingborders.com

O'Neill, M., & Hubbard, P. (2010). Walking, sensing, belonging: Ethno-mimesis as performative praxis. *Visual Studies, 25*(1), 46–58.

Oppezzo, M., & Schwartz, D. L. (2014). Give your ideas some legs: The positive effect of walking on creative thinking. *Journal of Experimental Psychology: Learning, Memory, and Cognition*.

O'Rourke, K. (2013). *Walking and mapping: Artists and cartographers*. Cambridge, MA: MIT Press.

Paperson, La. (2014). A ghetto land pedagogy: An antidote for settler environmentalism. *Environmental Educational Research, 20*(1), 115–130.

Paquette, D., & McCartney, A. (2012). Soundwalking and the bodily exploration of places. *Canadian Journal of Communication, 37*(1), 135–145.

Paterson, M. (2009). Haptic geographies: Ethnography, haptic knowledges and sensuous dispositions. *Progress in Human Geography, 33*(6), 766–788.

Phillips, J. (2015). *Scoreography: Compose-with a hole in the heart!* (Unpublished doctoral dissertation). RMIT University, Melbourne, Australia.

Phillips, P. (2004). Doing art and doing cultural geography: The fieldwork/field walking project. *Australian Geographer, 35*(2), 151–159.

Pink, S. (2009/2015). *Doing sensory ethnography*. London, UK: Sage.

Pink, S. (2011). Multimodality, multisensoriality and ethnographic knowing: Social semiotics and the phenomenology of perception. *Qualitative Research, 11*(3), 261–276.

Porteous, J. D. (1990). *Landscapes of the mind: Worlds of sense and Metaphor*. Toronto, Canada: University of Toronto Press.

Povinelli, E. (2016). *Geontologies: A requiem for late capitalism*. Durham, NC: Duke University Press.

Powell, K. (2017). Story Walking: Place-based narratives of identity, history and interculturality in San Jose Japantown, USA. In P. Burnard, V. Ross, E. Mackinlay, K. Powell, T. Dragovic, & H. J. Minors (Eds.), *Building interdisciplinary and intercultural bridges: Where practice meets research and theory* (pp. 142–149). Retrieved from www.bibacc.org.

Puar, J. (2007). *Terrorist assemblages: Homonationalism in queer times*. Durham, NC: Duke University Press.

Puar, J. (2009). Prognosis time: Towards a geopolitics of affect, debility and capacity. *Women & Performance: A Journal of Feminist Theory, 19*(2), 161–172.

Puar, J. (2012). "I would rather be a cyborg than a goddess" Becoming-intersectional in assemblage theory. *PhiloSOPHIA, 2*(1), 49–66.

Puar, J. (2013). Homonationalism as assemblage: Viral travels, affective sexualities. *Jindal Global Law Review, 4*(2), 23–43.

Puar, J. (2015). Bodies with new organs: Becoming trans, becoming disabled. *Social Text, 33*(3), 45–73.

Puar, J. (2017). *The right to maim: Debility, capacity, disability*. Durham, NC: Duke University Press.

Puar, J., & Clough, P. (2012). Editors introduction. *WSQ: Women's Studies Quarterly, 40*(1&2), 13–26.

Reed, P., & Goldenberg, D. (2008). What is a participatory practice? *Fillip, 8*. Retrieved from http://fillip.ca/content/what-is-a-participatory-practice

Rice, C., Chandler, E., Liddiard, K., Rinaldi, J., & Harrison, E. (2016). Pedagogical possibilities for unruly bodies. *Gender and Education*, 1–20.

Rice, C., Chandler, E, Rinaldi, J., Changfoot, N., Liddiard, E., Mykitiuk, R. & Mündel, I. (2017). Imagining Disability Futurities. *Hypatia, 32*(2), 213–239.

Richardson, T. (2014). A schizocartography of the University of Leeds: Cognitively mapping the campus. *Journal of Social Theory, 23*(10), 140–162.

Richardson, T. (2015). *Walking inside out: Contemporary British psychogeography*. London, UK: Rowman & Littlefield.

Rodaway, P. (1994). *Sensuous geographies: Body, sense and place*. London, UK: Routledge.

Rose, M. (2015). Confessions of an Anarcho-Flaneuse of Psychogeography the Mancunian Way. In T. Richardson (Ed.), *Walking inside out: Contemporary British psychogeography* (pp. 147–162). London UK: Rowman Littlefield.

Rotas, N. & Springgay, S. (2014). How do you make a classroom operate like a work of art? Deleuzeguattarian methodologies of research-creation. *International Journal of Qualitative Studies in Education, 28*(5), 552–572.

Sanouillet, M. (1965). *Dada a Paris*. Paris, France: Jean-Jaques Pauvert.

Saunders, A., & Moles, K. (2016). Following or forging a way through the world: Audio walks and the making of place. *Emotion, Space and Society, 20*, 68–74.

Schaub, M. (Ed.). (2005). *The walk book: Janet Cardiff*. Vienna and New York: Thyssen-Bornemisza Art Contemporary and the Public Art Fund.

Sedgwick, E. (2003). *Touching feeling: Affect, pedagogy, performativity*. Durham, NC: Duke University Press.

Seigworth, G. J., & Gregg, M. (2010). An inventory of shimmers. In M. Gregg & G. J. Seigworth (Eds.), *The affect theory reader* (pp. 1–25). Durham, NC: Duke University Press.

Sharpe, C. (2014). In the wake. *Black Studies, 44*(2), 59–69.

Sharpe, C. (2016). *In the wake: On Blackness and being*. Durham, NC: Duke University Press.

Sharrocks, A., & Qualmann, C. (2017). *Walking women: A study room guide on women using walking in their practice*. London, UK: Live Art Development Agency.

Sheller, M. (2014). Vital methodologies: Live methods, mobile art, and research-creation. In P. Vannini (Ed.), *Non-representational methodologies* (pp. 130–145). New York, NY: Routledge.

Shildrick, M. (2015). Why should our bodies end at the skin: Embodiment, boundaries, and somatechnics. *Hypatia, 30*(1), 13–29.

Shomura, C. (2017). Exploring the promise of new materialisms. *Lateral, 6*(1). Retrieved from http://csalateral.org/issue/6-1/forum-alt-humanities-new-materalist-philosophy-promise-new-materialisms-shomura/

Simon, R. (2011). On the human challenges of multiliteracies pedagogy. *Contemporary Issues in Early Childhood, 12*(4), 362–366.

Simpson, A. (2007). On ethnographic refusal: Indigeneity, "voice," and colonial citizenship. *Junctures, 9*, 67–80.

Simpson, A. (2014). *Mohawk interruptus: Political life across the borders of settler states.* London, UK: Duke University Press.

Simpson, L. (2011). *Dancing on our turtle's back: Stories of Nishnaabeg re-creation, resurgence and a new emergence.* Winnipeg: ARP Books.

Simpson, L. (2014). Land as pedagogy: Nishnaabeg intelligence and rebellious transformation. *Decolonization: Indigeneity, Education & Society, 3*(3), 1–25.

Snaza, N., Sonu, D., Truman, S. E., & Zaliwska, Z. (Eds.). (2016). *Pedagogical Matters: New materialism and curriculum studies.* New York, NY: Peter Lang.

Snaza, N., & Weaver, J. (2015). *Posthumanism and educational research.* New York, NY: Routledge.

Solnit, R. (2001). *Wanderlust: A history of walking.* New York, NY: Penguin Books.

Somerville, M. (2013). *Water in a dry land: Place-learning through art and story.* London, England: Routledge.

Somerville, M. (2016). Queering place: The intersection of feminist body theory and Australian Aboriginal collaboration. *Review of Education, Pedagogy, and Cultural Studies, 38*(1), 14–28.

Somerville, M. & Green, M. (2015). *Children, place and sustainability.* London, UK: Palgrave Macmillan.

Sonu, D., & Snaza, N. (2016). The fragility of ecological pedagogy: elementary social studies standards and possibilities of new materialism. *Journal of Curriculum and Pedagogy, 12*(3), 258–277.

Spillers, H. (2003). *Black, white, and in color: Essays on American literature and culture.* Chicago, IL: Chicago University Press.

Springgay, S. (2005). An intimate distance: Youth interrogations of intercorporeal cartography as visual narrative text. *Journal of the Canadian Association of Curriculum Studies, 3*(1). www.csse.ca/CACS/JCACS/index.html.

Springgay, S. (2008). *Body knowledge and curriculum: Pedagogies of touch in youth and visual culture.* New York, NY: Peter Lang.

Springgay, S. (2011a). "The Chinatown Foray" as Sensational Pedagogy. *Curriculum Inquiry, 41*(5), 636–656.

Springgay, S. (2011b). The Ethicoaesthetics of affect and a sensational pedagogy. *Journal of the Canadian Association for Curriculum Studies, 9*(1), 66–82.

Springgay, S. (2013a). How to be an artist by night: Critical public pedagogy and double ontology. In J. Sandlin, M. O'Malley, & J. Burdick (Eds), *Problematizing public pedagogy handbook.* (pp. 133–148). New York, NY: Routledge.

Springgay, S. (2013b). The pedagogical impulse: Aberrant residencies and classroom ecologies. *C magazine for Art and Culture, 119*, 16–23.

Springgay, S. (2014). Approximate-rigorous-abstractions: Propositions of activation for posthumanist research. In N. Snaza & J. Weaver (Eds.), *Posthumanism and educational research* (pp. 76–90). New York, NY: Routledge.

Springgay, S. (2015). *Working with children as pedagogies of refusal.* Toronto, ON: YYZ Books.

Springgay, S. (2016a). Towards a rhythmic account of working together and taking part. *Research in Education, 96*(1), 71–77.

Springgay, S. (2016b). Meditating with bees: Weather bodies and a pedagogy of movement. In N. Snaza, D. Sonu, S. E. Truman, & Z. Zaliwska (Eds.), *Pedagogical matters: New materialism and curriculum studies* (pp. 59–74). New York, NY: Peter Lang.

Springgay, S. (forthcoming). 'How to write as felt?': Touching transmaterialities and more-than- human intimacies. *Educational Philosophy and Theory.*

Springgay, S., & Freedman, D. (2010). Breasted bodies and pedagogies of excess: Towards a materialist theory of becoming mother. In B. Shultz, J. Sandlin & J. Burdick (Eds.), *Public pedagogy: Education and learning beyond schooling* (pp. 351–365). New York: Routledge.

Springgay, S., & Truman, S. E. (2017a). On the need for methods beyond proceduralism: Speculative middles, (in)tensions, and response-ability in research. *Qualitative Inquiry.* DOI: *https://doi.org/10.1177/1077800417704464*

Springgay, S. & Truman, S. E. (2017b). A transmaterial approach to walking methodologies: Embodiment, affect and a sonic art performance. *Body & Society.* DOI: 10.1177/1357034X17732626. Online first.

Springgay, S. & Truman, S. E. (2017c). Stone walks: Inhuman animacies and queer archives of feeling. *Discourse: Studies in the Cultural Politics of Education, 38*(6), 851–863.

Springgay, S. & Zaliwska, Z. (2016): Learning to be affected: Matters of pedagogy in the artists' soup kitchen. *Educational Philosophy and Theory, 49*(3), 273–283.

St. Pierre, E. (2016a). Deleuze and Guattari's language for new empirical inquiry. *Educational Philosophy and Theory.* DOI: 10.1080/00131857.2016.1151761

St. Pierre, E. (2016b). The empirical and the new empiricisms. *Cultural Studies ↔ Critical Methodologies, 16*(2) 111–124.

Steinbock, E., Szczygielska, M., & Wagner, A. (2017). Thinking linking: Editorial introduction. *Angelaki Journal of the Theoretical Humanities, 22*(2), 1–10.

Stengers, I. (2005). The cosmopolitical proposal. In B. Latour & P. Weibell (Eds.), *Making things: Public atmospheres of democracy* (pp. 994–1003). Cambridge, MA: MIT Press.

Stephens, L., Ruddick, S., & McKeever, P. (2015). Disability and Deleuze: An exploration of becoming and embodiment in children's everyday environments. *Body & Society, 21*(2), 194–200.

Stewart, K. (2007). *Ordinary affect.* Durham, NC: Duke University Press.

Stewart, K. (2011). Atmospheric attunements. *Environment and Planning D: Society and Space, 29*(3), 445–453.

Stewart, K. (2013). Regionality. *Geographical Review, 103*(2), 275–284.

Stockton, K. B. (2009). *The queer child, or growing sideways in the twentieth century.* Durham, NC: Duke University Press.

Stoller, P. (1997). *Sensuous scholarship.* Philadelphia, PA: University of Pennsylvania Press.

Stryker, S., Currah, P., and Moore, L. J. (2008). Introduction: Trans-, trans, or transgender? *Women's Studies Quarterly, 36*(3–4), 11–22.

Styres, S., Haig-Brown, C., & Blimkie, M. (2013). Towards a pedagogy of Land: The urban context. *Canadian Journal of Education, 26*(2), 34–67.

Sundberg, J. (2014). Decolonizing posthumanist geographies. *Cultural Geographies, 21*(1), 33–47.

Swan, E. (2016). *Walking as work – Post 2*. [Blog Post]. Retrieved from http://walkinglab. org/walking-as-work-post-2/

Sykes, H. (2016). Olympic homonationalisms. *Public: Art/Culture/Ideas*, *53*, 140–148.

Sykes, H. (2017). *Sexual and gender politics of sport mega-events: Roving colonialism*. London, UK: Routledge.

Tallbear, K. (2012). *An indigenous ontological reading of cryopreservation practices and ethics* (and why I'd rather think about pipestone). Retrieved from www.kimtallbear.com/ homeblog/an-indigenous-ontological-reading-of-cryopreservation-practices-and-ethics-and-why-id-rather-think-about-pipestone

Tan, Q. (2013). Smell in the city: Smoking and olfactory politics. *Urban Studies*, *50*(1), 55–71.

Taylor, S. (2010). *Examined life*. Retrieved from www.youtube.com/watch?v=k0HZaPkF6qE

Thiele, K. (2014). Ethos of diffraction: New paradigms for a (post)humanist ethics. *Parallax*, *20* (3), 202–216.

Thobani, S. (2007). *Exalted subjects: Studies in the making of race and nation in Canada*. Toronto, ON: University of Toronto Press.

Thompson, C. (2011). *Felt: Fluxus, Joseph Beuys, and the Dalai Lama*. Minneapolis, MN: University of Minnesota Press.

Thrift, N. (2007). *Non-representational theory: Space, politics, affect*. New York, NY: Routledge.

Titchkosky, T. (2011). *The question of access: Disability, space, meaning*. Toronto, ON: University of Toronto Press.

Todd, Z. (2014). Fish pluralities: Human-animal relations and sites of engagement in Paulatuuq, Arctic Canada. *Etudes/Inuit/Studies*, *38*(1–2), 217–238.

Todd, Z. (2016). 'An Indigenous feminist's take on the ontological turn: "Ontology" is just another word for colonialism'. *Journal of Historical Sociology*, *29*(1), 4–22.

Truman, S. E. (2013). *Writing affect: Aesthetic space, contemplative practice and the self*. (Unpublished Masters Thesis). University of Toronto, Canada.

Truman, S. E. (2016a). Becoming more than it never (actually) was: Expressive writing as research-creation. *Journal of Curriculum and Pedagogy*, *13*(2), 136–143.

Truman, S. E. (2016b). Intratextual entanglements: Emergent pedagogies and the productive potential of texts. In N. Snaza, D. Sonu, S. E. Truman, & Z. Zaliwska (Eds.), *Pedagogical matters: New materialisms and curriculum studies* (pp. 91–108). New York, NY: Peter Lang.

Truman, S. E. (2017). *Speculative methodologies & emergent literacies: Walking & writing as research-creation* (Unpublished doctoral dissertation). University of Toronto, Canada.

Truman, S. E., & Springgay, S. (2015). The primacy of movement in research-creation: New materialist approaches to art research and pedagogy. In M. Laverty, & T. Lewis (Eds.), *Art's Teachings, Teaching's Art: Philosophical, critical, and educational musings* (pp. 151–164). New York, NY: Springer.

Truman, S. E., & Springgay, S. (2016). Propositions for walking research. In K. Powell, P. Bernard, & L. Mackinley (Eds.), *International handbook for intercultural arts* (pp. 259–267). New York, NY: Routledge.

Tuck, E. (2009). Suspending damage: A letter to communities. *Harvard Educational Review*, *79*(3), 409–427.

Tuck, E. & Gaztambide-Fernández, R. (2013). Curriculum, replacement and settler futurity. *Journal of Curriculum Theorizing*, *29*(1), 72–89.

Tuck, E., & McKenzie, M. (2015). *Place in research*. New York, NY: Routledge.

Tuck, E., McKenzie, M., & McCoy, K. (2014). Land education: Indigenous, post-colonial, and decolonizing perspectives on place and environmental education research. *Environmental Education Research, 20*(1), 1–23.

Tuck, E., Yang, K. W., & Gaztambide-Fernández, R. (2015). Citations Practices Challenge. *Critical Ethnic Studies.* Retrieved from www.criticalethnicstudiesjournal.org/citation-practices/

Uncertain Commons. (2013). *Speculate This!* Durham, NC: Duke University Press.

Vaccaro, J. (2010). Felt matters. *Women & Performance, 20*(3), 253–266.

Vagle, M. D., & Hofsess, B. A. (2016). Entangling a post-reflexivity through post-intentional phenomenology. *Qualitative Inquiry, 22*(5), 334–344.

van Dooren, T., Kirksey, E., & Münster, U. (2016). Multispecies studies: Cultivating arts of attentiveness. *Environmental Humanities, 8*(1), 1–23.

Vannini, P. (2012). In time, out of time rhythmanalyzing ferry mobilities. *Time & Society, 21*(2), 241–269.

Vannini, P. (Ed.). (2015). *Non-representational methodologies: Re-envisioning research.* New York: Routledge.

Vannini, P., & Vannini, A. (2017). Wild walking: A twofold critique of the walk-along method. In C. Bates & A. Rhys-Taylor (Eds.), *Walking through social research* (pp. 178–195). London, UK: Routledge.

Vasseleu, C. (1998). *Textures of light: Vision and touch in Irigaray, Levinas and Merleau-Ponty.* New York NY: Routledge.

Vergunst, J. (2010). Rhythms of walking: History and presence in a city street. *Space and Culture, 13*(4), 376–388.

Vergunst, J. (2011). Technology and technique in a useful ethnography of movement. *Mobilities, 6*(2), 203–219.

Vergunst, J. (2017). Key figure of mobility: the pedestrian. *Social Anthropology, 25*(1), 13–27.

Vergunst, J. L. (2008). Taking a trip and taking care in everyday life. In T. Ingold & J. L. (Eds.), *Ways of walking: Ethnography and practice on foot.* (pp. 105–122). New York, NY: Routledge.

Vora, K. (2017). Labour. In S. Alaimo (Ed.), *Gender matter* (pp. 205–221). Farming Hills, MI: MacMillan.

Waitt, G., Gill, N., & Head, L. (2009). Walking practice and suburban nature-talk. *Social & Cultural Geography, 10*(1), 41–60.

Walcott, R. (1997). *Black like who?: Writing black Canada.* Toronto, ON: Insomniac Press.

Walcott, R. (2016). Questioning citizenship at the Venice Biennale: Responses and interventions. *C Magazine, Winter*, 31–32.

Ware, S. (2017). All power to all people? Black LGBTTI2QQ activism, remembrance, and archiving in Toronto. *TSQ: Transgender Studies Quarterly, 4*(2), 170–180.

Watts, V. (2013). Indigenous place-thought and agency amongst humans and non-humans (First Woman and Sky Woman go on a European tour!). *DIES: Decolonization, Indigeneity, Education and Society, 2*(1), 20–34.

Weaver, J. & Snaza, N. (2016). Against methodocentrism in educational research. *Educational Philosophy and Theory*, DOI: 10.1080/00131857.2016.1140015

Weheliye, A. (2014). *Habeus viscus: Racializing assemblages, biopolitics, and black feminist theories of the human.* Durham, NC: Duke University Press.

Weil, A. (2017). Trans*versal animacies and the mattering of black trans* political life. *Angelaki Journal of the Theoretical Humanities, 22*(2), 191–202.

White, E. (2001). *The Flâneur: A stroll through the paradoxes of Paris*. London, UK: Bloomsbury.

Whitehead, A. (1978). *Process and reality* (corrected ed.). New York, NY: Free Press.

Wolff, J. (1985). The invisible flâneuse: Women and the literature of modernity. *Theory, Culture & Society, 2*(3), 37–46.

Wylie, J. (2002). An essay on ascending Glastonbury Tor. *Geoforum, 33*(4), 441–455.

Wylie, J. (2005). A single day's walking: narrating self and landscape on the South West Coast Path. *Transactions of the Institute of British Geographers, 30*(2), 234–247.

Wynter, S. (2003). Unsettling the coloniality of being/power/truth/freedom: Towards the human, after man, it's overrepresentation – an argument. *CR: The New Centennial Review, 3*(3), 257–337.

Yusoff, K. (2013). Geologic life: Prehistory, climate, futures in the anthropocene. *Environment and Planning D: Society and Space, 31*(1), 779–795.

Yusoff, K. (2015). Geologic subjects: Nonhuman origins, geomorphic aesthetics and the art of becoming in human. *Cultural Geographies, 22*(3), 383–407.

Yusoff, K. (2017a). Epochal aesthetics: Affectual infrastructures of the anthropocene. *E-flux, 83*.

Yusoff, K. (2017b). *Towards a thousand black anthropocenes*. Conference presentation at the New Materialism Conference, Paris, France.

Zaiontz, K. (2016). Inelastic Olympic hopefuls: Rhythmic mis-interpellation in three auditions for the London 2012 Ceremonies. *Public: Art/Culture/Ideas, 53*, 75–89.

Zaliwska, Z., & Springgay, S. (2015). Diagrams and cuts: A materialist approach to research creation. *Cultural Studies ⇔ Critical Methodologies, 15*(2) 136–144.

Zinga, D., Styres, S. (2011). Pedagogy of the Land: Tensions, challenges, and contradictions. *First Nations Perspectives, 4*(1), 59–83.

Index

CPSIA information can be obtained
at www.ICGtesting.com
Printed in the USA
LVHW081317140822
725906LV00004B/162

9 780367 264956